Author's Note

Back in 1992 when *You Count, Calories Don't* was first published, the nondiet message of health and self-acceptance seemed radical. Today, with over 20,000 books sold and thousands of people having gone through the HUGS program, the message is becoming mainstream. We have made an impact in showing people how to break free from dieting and how to get on with the rest of their lives. The common sense approach to life has been embraced and will not get outdated.

Over the years since initial publication, one of the most significant "re-discoveries" we've made concerns the nature of change. When you want change to be sustained, you have to seek out and accept support for your decision. This fact has influenced the way we guide people to stay off the diet roller coaster and grow in their personal nondiet life-style. This age of easy and instant communication via the new technologies the Internet offers has made support more accessible. Visit our website at www.hugs.com to explore our support options.

As midlife sets in many people find that a busy and hurried life-style is the norm for their age range. Juggling 10 or more major issues at a time can seem like "just the way it has to be." Not so! It's important to take time to step back and reassess one's health, life situation and make adjustments to restore balance in one's life. Men and women both experience midlife body change issues that force us to listen — to really listen. Women have the physical impact of menopause changes; but everyone deals with new health issues or risk factors that should make us stop and pay attention to what is going on in our lives.

So when it was time for a reprint of *You Count, Calories Don't*, a new chapter on midlife issues seemed timely. The qualities expressed in the next chapter will guide you on what needs to be done to really begin to focus on your needs. If you are younger than 40, gather preparation ideas for moving through menopause comfortably and painlessly. If you are in your 40s or 50s, draw what you need to reassess and gain the skills to do what it takes to enjoy the process of change that is taking place; the metamorphosis to a new you, one of vitality and vigor and confidence. If you have already gone through menopause and do not possess these qualities, the characteristics alone can help you grab onto this new adulthood that can transport you to new heights. Men and women will be guided : this transition, midlife, a time when many of reassess before we move on.

Ask yourself these midlife questions:

Are you skimming life or experiencing it?

Are you busy or constantly in a hurried state?

Are you cramming too much in a day and don't even have a chance to savor what is there?

Is detail upon detail crowding your brain?

I asked these questions of myself and affirmed that the answers had emerged from the personal support system I had built up around myself. In alphabetical order, they are: Heidi, the qualities of generosity, flexibility, and resourcefulness who has shown me how to really see things wholly, to make everyday moments special and to create memories; Karen, the qualities of patience, systematic planning and resourcefulness, has been an inspiration with her entrepreneurial spirit, family values, practicality, and creativity; Sandra, the qualities of honest analysis, good listening, and resourcefulness shares laughs and tribulations and we serve as mentors to each other. Each month we protect our special time and go out for a nice, long supper and talk things out. We come back rejuvenated, inspired, and grateful for each other's support; Val, the qualities of courage, integrity, and resourcefulness has become my spiritual coach and is helping me on my spiritual journey to connect with and feel God and understand how to grow in this manner. Her wisdom has guided me to appreciate what I do have and enjoy the path I am guided to take; Vicki, the qualities of perseverance, conservation, and resourcefulness has guided me in everyday living and inspired me with demonstrations of how to make something very special from the everyday gifts of nature around us — leaves that can make an attractive arrangement or the tapestry of a blue sky of clouds.

I've shared these stories from my personal journey to illustrate just how key these support systems are to helping you to grow gracefully, make changes and sustain the changes. Do make the time to develop and nurture your own support.

So enjoy the process, take time to prepare yourself for the changes that will inevitably take place, and build in that time for self to reflect, rest, and grow. This time of life can be wonderful if you know what to do and build in the time to do it.

YOU
COUNT,
CALORIES
DON'T

Linda Omichinski
B.Sc., (F.Sc.), R.D.

Illustrated
by
Sandra Storen

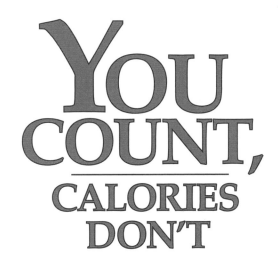

To Barbara,
With compliments,
Enjoy....
For better health,
Linda
Omichinski

HUGS International Inc

*Material used in this book can be used
only with the HUGS program given
by licensed facilitators. It cannot be
used in other unlicensed group
counselling settings.*

Revised edition 1999

ISBN 0-9684716-0-9

Illustrations and cover design by
Sandra Storen
Inside photo by Mitchell Omichinski
Printed and bound by Premier
Printing Ltd.

Printed in Canada

Originally published in Canada in
1992 by Hyperion Press/Tamos
Books Inc.
First published in Great Britain in
1996 by Hodder & Stoughton

**Canadian Cataloguing-in-
Publication Data**
Omichinski, Linda, 1955-
  You count, calories don't
  Includes bibliographical
  references and index.

ISBN 0-9684716-0-9

1. Health behavior. 2. Nutrition.
3. Exercise I. HUGS International
II. Title.

RA776.9.044 1999   613.7
C99-920005-4

Acknowledgments

To my husband Mitchell who gave me the
opportunity to pursue my ideas; to my
mother, who through her insight, provided
me with a healthy attitude towards food and
life; and to my father who allowed me to
mature at my own level, and accepted me for
who I am.

To Valerie Giesbrecht for her
encouragement and insight gained from
being at the other end of the HUGS line; to
Kathleen Harrison for her technical review of
the manuscript and her suggestions, and her
valuable contribution in researching and
writing the new chapter on menopause; to
Sandra Barsy who helped me find my inner
voice for everyday language in initial editing,
guidance, and editing the new chapter on
midlife and menopause and facilitating the
print process; and to Debbie Bride for
preserving the conversational tone of the
book in editing a later version.

To my clients who helped capture the
essence of the HUGS program through the
title of the book and whose suggestions
enhanced the program and will allow the
reader to relate to the examples in the book.

To the following individuals whose
encouragement, ideas, and assistance made
the HUGS program, and hence the book,
possible: Vicki Omichinski, Arlene Draffin
Jones, Maureen Mitchells, Nancy Painter,
Ethel-Mae Greenslade, Susan Ryan, and
many others too numerous to mention.

To Rena Mendelson, M.S., D.Sc. who
inspired me to pursue my ideas and
demonstrated her support by writing the
foreword; Sandra Storen, B.F.A., who
brought the concepts and attitudes to life
through her expressive and humorous
illustrations and for the new cover design;
and to Hyperion Press whose enthusiasm
and expertise has enabled me to build a book
with such longevity.

My deepest thanks.

Contents

Foreword

For the last two decades, in an effort to look good and feel great, North Americans have been caught up in a continuous cycle of weight loss and weight gain. Many people lose weight; however, few maintain their slimmer figures. Almost no one feels great in the up and down weight loss/weight gain process. It seems reasonable to assume that if every weight control product or program on the market could provide the fast, permanent weight loss they promise, the diet industry would have gone out of business years ago. Instead, diet regimens flourish, and countless individuals literally starve themselves for months to lose pounds, only to regain some, all, or more weight as soon as the diet is stopped. The disappointment and loss of self-worth have taken an emotional toll on the victims of these unrealistic promises. To make matters worse, the focus on "diet" and "thin" seems to have spawned an epidemic of such eating disorders as anorexia nervosa and bulimia which often began as a simple effort to lose a few pounds. Clearly, the programs and products that are designed to promote rapid weight loss do not offer permanent help and because of this, those people who follow these diets can neither look good nor feel great in the long term.

Perhaps we are placing the emphasis on the wrong aspect. All of our scientific evidence suggests that ideal weights are individual and that maintaining the weight that is right for you contributes to better looks and better health. This approach is founded on two important concepts. First, we must recognize that we cannot all expect to look like the thin models we see in magazines and movies. Secondly, each of us can be individually attractive and vibrant through a healthy life-style which includes a balance of regular, enjoyable exercise and healthy tasty food choices. This is the best way to look good and feel great!

In the following pages, Linda Omichinski tells us how to achieve this goal. She has utilized all the most up-to-date scientific theories on energy metabolism and food behavior and put into practise a set of activities designed to enhance physical and emotional health. In a clear and practical way, she helps each reader to recognize that inside every body shape there is a person of worth who can achieve pleasure and satisfaction from his or her own abilities. Ms Omichinski's advice enables each reader to be freed from the trap of inflated promises and unfulfilled desires and allows him or her to embrace the positive day-to-day changes that promote healthful living and a sense of well-being.

The advice is excellent. The pages in this book should be read over and over again until the principles have been gradually integrated into a life-style change for a better healthier you.

Rena A. Mendelson, M.S., D.Sc.
Director
Professor Of Nutrition
School of Nutrition, Consumer
and Family Studies
Ryerson Polytechnical Institute
Toronto, Ontario

Preface

The HUGS™ Program is for Everyone

North Americans are obsessed with being slim. It is a cultural fad that totally ignores the importance of healthy living. Unfortunately, this preoccupation with diet can be transmitted to others. A recent study indicated that 2 out of 3 mothers who thought they weighed too much (even when they didn't), passed this anxiety on to their daughters who became chronically unhappy with their weight.[1]

1700's

Although diets seem to have increased people's consciousness about weight and food, they have not made people healthier. Research proves that diet and exercise regimens that focus on weight loss as the goal are seldom successful long term, which leaves the person feeling discouraged and less in control of his or her own body.[2,3] Increasingly, people are becoming fed up with dieting and are seeking an alternative that will work with their bodies, not against them.[4]

1800's

As a consulting dietitian in hospitals and with private clients, I am continually concerned about my clients' food and weight problems. Initially, I used the traditional approach of designing individualized diets for clients whom I saw for weight control, diabetes, risk factors for heart disease, and other health reasons.

1960's

Of course in the short term, diets did work. Weight loss and modified eating habits were always evident. Following my prescribed diet for them, clients returned to report their successes and this led me to believe that this approach was valid.

1990's

TIMELY
TORSOS

Yet on follow-up a few years later the results were disappointing. In many cases, clients were worse off in terms of health than when they first came to see me. Unfortunately, health professionals tend to blame the client for the failure. Diets after all do work, if you follow the strict regimen.

As I continued to observe this weight loss/weight gain cycle, however, I began to question the traditional approach. Following the medical model I had learned seemed to work only for the short term. I searched through the scientific literature to find answers, but found them instead by questioning my clients. It was through studying the needs of my clients and listening to their concerns, that the life-style program emphasizing a nondieting approach to healthy living called HUGS™ came into existence.

This book is based on the HUGS™ program that I established and tested in the community over the past five years. It has provided high client satisfaction. The process is satisfying and fun to do, and it works! It can help you to be the best that you can be.

In this book, *You Count, Calories Don't*, you will become acquainted with the HUGS™ philosophy as you read through each chapter. HUGS™ works and it has helped many people.

"The HUGS™ program was very informative and enjoyable. It helped me to realize that we have the power to change our way of thinking and eating and our attitude about ourselves through other methods than dieting."

"I really enjoyed the HUGS™ program. It was very enlightening to learn that a lot of my eating behaviors were part of the 'dieters' thinking and not as a result of 'psychosis' on my part. I'm more positive about myself and believe in a one-step-at-a-time life-style change!"

"I have an increased understanding of the role of carbohydrates in diet, in fact, a great change in viewpoint! HUGS™ has increased my awareness of factors affecting my eating behavior, and given me a new guilt-free acceptance of myself."

You Count, Calories Don't focuses on the importance of building a sense of mastery or control over your life which helps build self-esteem. Empowerment to do this is skill-based and is accomplished in a step-

9

by-step manner. As one skill is mastered, the next skill is introduced while still reinforcing the skill already learned.

This skill-building process involves changing your thinking and gradually fine-tuning your life-style in order to enjoy healthy living. The focus is on the process, not a quick end result. The journey is designed to be fun so that it can be continued and the results can be permanent.

To achieve this, *You Count, Calories Don't* addresses the underlying causes of many health problems. These are poor self-esteem and life-style habits, and lack of confidence. By realizing that *you count*, and by feeling better about yourself, you will want to take time to nurture yourself through healthy enjoyable eating and active enjoyable living. *You Count, Calories Don't* provides a health promotion model that allows the individual the freedom to take responsibility for his or her own health.

Anyone who has ever dieted, whether for a particular health reason or for weight loss, will benefit from this book. This alternative concept focuses on health and wellness and shows how to put food and activity into a healthy perspective that is comfortable to continue for life.

The life-style you choose is important. Unhealthy life-styles can cause such life-threatening conditions as heart disease, cancer, and stroke. Yet 80 percent of life-style diseases can be prevented. By recognizing and reducing health risks, a person can start making wellness the preferred life-style.

This book emphasizes celebrating and enjoying food, not depriving yourself. Everyone can do this by acquiring a taste for less sweet, less fattening foods which will lead to choosing different foods as tastes change.

This approach is for everyone and it does work. Even for individuals with diabetes you ask? The answer is yes. I remember instructing clients on a diabetic diet and then when they got complications (i.e. high-cholesterol levels), instructing them on a low-

10

cholesterol diet. The clients became confused and frustrated and I thought there must be a simpler way that would provide a unified approach. The HUGS™ program was my answer.

The first chapter in *You Count, Calories Don't* shows how this program coincides with the principles and recommendations of the Diabetes Association, Heart Foundation, Dietetic Association, and Cancer Foundation, as well as addresses the issue of obesity. All of these programs emphasize eating more high-fibre foods (carbohydrates) for immediate energy, some protein for sustained energy, and gradually decreasing fat intake.

The difference in the program is the approach. Most special diets are based on "do's" and "don'ts." Eat only 30 percent of your calories from fat. Watch your weight. Increase your activity. These are necessary, but they miss the point by focusing on giving instructions to follow rather than empowering the individual to want to make healthier choices. This book shows you how to enjoy adjusting your life-style and it can be used effectively in conjunction with any of the cookbooks put out by the above associations. *You Count, Calories Don't* shows you a simple and effective way to healthy living!

The concepts presented in this book are in sync with the direction now being taken by Health Services and Promotion Branch, Health and Welfare Canada, and Fitness Canada, Fitness and Amateur Sport who have recently initiated a program called "Vitality." It integrates 3 positive life choices: enjoyable, healthy eating; enjoyable, physical activity; and positive self-image and body image. *You Count, Calories Don't* shows you how to integrate these components of well-being and quality of life into your everyday life-style so that you too can feel better about yourself.

Exercise is the number one predictor of long-term success in a weight-loss program, yet many clients are hesitant about exercise because of negative perceptions about activity. This book shows you how to be aware of your body's needs in order to eat and exercise for energy and fun! It shows you how to

11

restore balance in your life in order to be better prepared for stressful situations. In fact, you will see how you can make stress work for you.

This refreshing approach is welcomed enthusiastically by health professionals. Yet many counselors are hesitant to try the method since it is new and unfamiliar and different from professional training. My recommendation to health professionals is to introduce the method gradually. With this step-by-step process as a guide, you can begin to focus on health indicators rather than numbers on the scale as the new measure of success.

If people focus on wellness and learn to help themselves to achieve their potential for spiritual, mental, social, and physical well-being, they will get on the road to healthy living.

Introduction

Better Living Through
HUGS™

Is something wrong in your daily eating routine but you don't know what it is? Are you famished, tired, listless, lacking drive and energy? Do you identify with one of the following scenarios? If you do, the HUGS™ program presented in this book can help you develop a better and healthier life-style. HUGS™ came into existence as an alternative to dieting. It allows people to regain control of their weight, food, and life. It presents a positive approach to healthy living by helping you to feel better about yourself.

WHY HUGS™ WORKS

HUGS™ works on the premise that diets set you up for failure. Deprogramming a person from the diet mentality is the key to regaining control. HUGS™ focuses on health and wellness rather than on weight and slimness. It allows each person to adjust to his or her natural weight according to what the body is genetically predestined to be.

Rush! Rush! No breakfast. Quick lunch. Dragging by 4 o'clock. Raiding the fridge before dinner and lunching and munching after dinner until bedtime. Your eating is out of control.

You're preoccupied with food and weight. Your life is centered around the "do's" and "don'ts" of eating, leading to a round of indulging, guilt, and denial. If you eat a piece of cake today you'll have to diet tomorrow. You feel you are chained to a diet. You would like to be "free" from the chains of dieting and get on with the rest of your life.

HUGS™ counters the pervasive cult of slimness in our society. It helps you recognize that the desirability of a perfectly proportioned, ultra slim body is an unnatural goal that has been forced on all of us by multimedia advertising. We are conditioned to believe that we must conform and that the illusionary perfection of slimness can be ours if we follow the perfect diet, eat the right way, and allow the pursuit of this false ideal to overtake and control our daily lives.[1] The HUGS™ program helps people realize that individual differences are important. HUGS™ will show you how to be the best that you can be, physically and emotionally.

The HUGS™ program is a unique approach to self. It was developed to make you aware of your natural strengths and free you from dependencies. HUGS™ is a process of self-discovery. As you learn alternate ways to look at yourself you will acquire the skills,

You plan to starve during the week to compensate for the anticipated binge at Uncle Joe's wedding next Saturday. But your willpower runs out and suddenly the cookie jar is empty. Your nagging hunger gets the better of you.

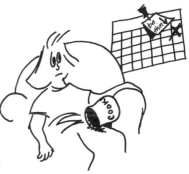

You're on a diet, but overeating on holidays is socially acceptable. Your guilt feelings lead to the next diet. This on-again off-again dieting leads to the weight-loss/weight-gain cycle.

You're a nibbler. You eat food simply because it's there. You feel tired and draggy. Now you're interested in learning how you can live a healthier life-style.

15

techniques, attitudes, and ways of thinking that will allow you to take charge of your life. You will be the master. You will like yourself. This is what the HUGS™ program is all about.

THE HUGS™ PHILOSOPHY

A positive attitude and self-esteem form the basis of the HUGS™ philosophy. Once you have acquired these you will move forward more quickly and you will be successful. The inner strength that comes from a feeling of self-worth creates a desire to nurture yourself by taking care of your body and mind. By creating a nucleus of positive thinking, you suddenly find the energy and desire to fine-tune your eating habits and to be more active. This sense of accomplishment and satisfaction from increased levels of activity and improved eating kick off the cycle: positive thinking, healthy enjoyable eating, and active enjoyable living. You will become a vibrant, attractive person at the weight that is right for your body, and you will maintain this new you through the balanced cycle you have established.

BALANCE IN LIFE: Healthy Living

self-acceptance

healthy enjoyable eating

active enjoyable living

WHAT TO EXPECT

The HUGS™ program expressed in *You Count, Calories Don't* will help you achieve a balance in life. Sometimes overeating or a preoccupation with food is a sign of low self-worth.

You will learn how to face reality in a positive way, how to empower yourself to have the power of choice, and how to have a normal response to foods, that is, one of celebration rather than denial. Best of all you will rediscover the pleasure of good food and healthy living.

16

Introduction

This book will help you become a healthy person and show you how to learn from past experiences. During the period of self-discovery and inner growth you will be motivated from within and you will live in the present and focus on the moment at hand and savor it.

Growth does not mean trying to be someone else or comparing yourself to other people or accepting imposed standards of diet and fitness. It means striving to be the best that you can be with what you have been given genetically![2]

This book will kick your mind into gear. You will be freed from the traditional quick fix of instant weight loss and the disappointment when the weight returns. With HUGS™, you will find an internal quick fix; that is, you will find out what works for you and you will be able to maintain the new healthy life-style. You will be set up to win!

And what about *fun*? The struggle to maintain or reach an unrealistic ideal weight goal puts people to work against their bodies. There is a proper weight for each individual called the set point, and this comfortable level should be the weight focus for healthy living. It's unfortunate that society tells us in a hundred subtle ways how we should look and behave. It takes courage and determination to decide to listen to your own body for the right weight and accept yourself as you are. When you do this there is no stress and maintaining the new you is actually fun. One of HUGS™ top priorities is enjoyment, not struggle.

Since formulas and diets are not the answer, you need something that works. *You Count, Calories Don't* will show you a simple approach that can be used by many people. It's for the new nonsmoker, the large man or woman or compulsive dieter, the individual with high cholesterol, the person with diabetes, the person with premenstrual syndrome, and for the children of people with diet and health problems. Once you have achieved your new healthy life-style you'll find it's suitable for the whole family.

This book will help you
- **end dieting forever,**
- **be in charge of food and life,**
- **stimulate new ideas and ways of thinking,**
- **improve your health, both physically and emotionally, and**
- **show you how to be the best that you can be.**

17

HOW TO USE THIS BOOK

To derive the most benefit from the book, read it slowly one chapter at a time, taking time to digest the information and put the suggestions into action. Tune into the excitement of the ideas presented and look at the examples. This will help make the information real for you. As you proceed step-by-step, try out each suggestion and enjoy the journey to healthy living. Repetition and practical examples that create momentum to get you going are what make this approach work. These serve as building blocks to internalize and assimilate the information. Reading the book over again will always reveal new ideas that will help you discover the real you and help you fine-tune your life-style to become a happier, healthier person.

You Count, Calories Don't has evolved as a written guide to the HUGS™ program but it can be used by itself or in conjunction with the affirmation tapes and fitness video (see order form at end of book). The book was written with you the client in mind. Use it to put the fun back into healthy living!

Before you continue, take a moment to fill out this life-style quiz. As you move through the book, you will notice that your attitudes will change. This is part of the internal quick fix that will set you up to win! As you proceed the process will become easier. Discovering the new inner you gradually changes the outer you. This will be observed and these changes will be permanent. The life-style quiz will help to rate your progress in achieving a healthy life-style and obtaining a healthier outlook towards life. Your life out of balance will become your life in balance. You will learn how to revitalize yourself by seeing your life as a series of challenges, not as a series of problems.

HOW TO GET THE MOST OUT OF THE BOOK

The first step in seeing your life as a series of challenges is to feel in charge. In order to feel in charge you have to make your own choices. Try changing the way you speak and the phrases you use. Think enthusiastically.

LIFE-STYLE QUIZ

1 Always
2 Very often
3 Often
4 Sometimes
5 Rarely
6 Never

☐ I am unhappy with myself the way I am.

☐ I am preoccupied with a desire to be thinner.

☐ I weigh myself several times a week.

☐ I am more concerned with the number on the scale than my overall sense of well-being.

☐ I think about burning up calories when I exercise.

☐ I am out of tune with my body for natural signals of hunger and fullness.

☐ I eat for other reasons than physical hunger.

☐ I eat too quickly, not taking time to focus on my meal and taste, savor, and enjoy my food.

☐ I fail to take time for activities for myself.

☐ I fluctuate between periods of sensible, nutritious eating and out-of-control eating.

☐ I give too much time and thought to food.

☐ I tend to skip meals, especially early in the day, so I can "save up" my food for one big feast.

☐ I engage in all-or-nothing thinking. I tend to feel that if I can't do it all, or do it well, what's the point?

☐ I try to be all things to all people.

☐ I strive for perfection in my life.

☐ I criticize myself for not achieving my goals.

☐ Total   Add 4 to the score to determine your percentage.
(Note: Compare this score with same quiz at end of book.)

Use sentences in your subconscious such as
"I like and respect myself."
"I am worthy of the respect of others."
"No matter what anyone says or does, I am a worthwhile person."

Replace "have to"
with phrases such as
• "I want to,"
• "I like to,"
• "I choose to,"
• "I love to,"
• "I believe I can."

When you approach a task, put your heart in it, go with the flow and experience the power within you that will allow you to develop your inner strengths. Allow the experience of learning about your inner resources to develop, and picture yourself being effective in stressful situations.

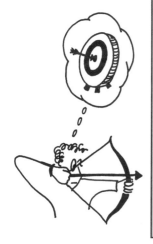

• SET YOUR GOAL. Make it realistic. Focus on the attitude and life-style change. Be specific.
For example, say to yourself "I will eat regularly, starting with a balanced breakfast."

• VISUALIZE THE GOAL. Picture yourself in your mind eating regularly as part of your daily routine.

• AFFIRM THE GOAL. Repeat it in your mind and practise it so that it becomes second nature at the subconscious level.

• LOCK ONTO THE GOAL. Develop a sense of momentum that will move you forward, creating the inner excitement of "mini-successes" that keep you progressing. Focus! Focus! Focus and take action.

If you feel good about yourself, you don't need to use food as a crutch to make yourself feel better. If you use affirmations to feel better about yourself, you no longer need to turn to food as a temporary comforter. Use the following affirmation to help you put this way of thinking into action.

"I like myself. Therefore I will take care of myself and nurture myself with healthy eating and enjoyable activity. If I feel good about myself, I don't need to turn to food to comfort me."

LIFE-STYLE ADJUSTMENT

"I don't want to make a life-style change—I want to follow a diet." This is what most people say when confronted with this new way of thinking. It's easier to just follow a prescribed regimen than take control

20

yourself. But life-style change is exciting. Once you've started you won't want to stop. Let's begin by understanding what it means.

Change is always difficult at first, but once you believe that you have the ability to find the right balance of food, activity, and life attitudes, you can break free from diet sheets and meal plans forever. Once you understand the HUGS™ method, you can put it to work for yourself, leaving room for flexibility. My experience has shown me that HUGS™ works even for people with diabetes, and it will work for you.

I think most of us agree that diets don't work. You gain back the weight you lost because you go back to your former way of eating and living. When you realize this you no longer blame yourself for the failure of the diet. A change of life-style and change of attitude towards food and yourself are what is needed. You need to acquire skills that can be used in every aspect of life. This will result in a healthier you.

Changing your way of life and thinking is a step-by-step process. It's gradual but it's fun. Once the goal of natural weight and healthy life-style is achieved, it is for a lifetime! With life-style change you keep on learning and improving.

Dieting produces results too. But the weight loss achieved after following a rigid diet is usually temporary. The new diet is often too drastic to be maintained, and as soon as you stop following the diet you gain weight again. Because it is an artificial and unpleasant way of eating, a diet is stressful, both physically and emotionally. The diet controls you. You live by the diet sheet. You lose the weight but have you really learned anything about eating or about yourself? Can you realistically eat this way for the rest of your life, depriving yourself, always thinking of food? Is your goal of weight loss realistic and can you possibly reach the goal expected of you? Can you endure until the end of the diet without going off it?

So many of my clients have told me that when they

were in weight-loss programs they would starve themselves before weighing in so they could mark the weight loss in their little book and appear to be successful. When I asked them about activities after a weight-loss meeting, they replied, "We reward ourselves at the donut shop. We were starving!"

Did you ever notice how few people stay for the lecture at many of these weight-loss meetings? All that is important to clients is the number on the scale. This is a negative approach to weight control. It involves cycles of starvation and binging. No new skills are learned and the problem of weight control is never solved.

Actually, the scale, as your measure of success, gives you a false sense of security. A scale focuses solely on results, and causes you to work against your body to achieve this end. Diets follow an external cue. They try to impose change on your behavior and your way of doing things. This external motivation or "hype" that occurs at each meeting keeps you going for a while. Eventually you come to rely on this support and can't do without it. There is no motivation from within.

When the weight is lost you feel good because of all the acceptance and compliments you receive. When the compliments stop and the attention is gone, the weight goes back on. You cannot maintain the rigid diet, but you feel ashamed that you lack the willpower. Your sense of self-worth diminishes and you begin to equate slimness with self-confidence. You lose sight of who you are. That poses a critical question. Are you losing weight for society's approval or for yourself?

Then you diet again to punish yourself for not looking the way society dictates that you should look. Then you binge to rebel against dieting and society's refusal to accept different body

22

shapes. Up and down you go, along with your sense of self-worth and self-esteem.

In contrast to this, life-style changes are gradual because they are a learning process. Step-by-step adjustments allow your body to embrace the newness. This does not mean going from fried potatoes to brown rice all in one swoop. Your body would likely rebel by craving sugar, because the change was too sudden to allow your body to adjust. A more acceptable approach would be to gradually introduce white rice, possibly once a week, then with time, mix white rice with brown rice, and only a year later would you have brown rice more frequently.

Life-style changes are positive and enjoyable. As your body adjusts it doesn't rebel. You can live with it and you feel a sense of accomplishment. Stress also diminishes when you are not competing against others, but rather looking within yourself to find your own level of progress. The focus is on the process, the facts, the skills, and the techniques. These are the "how-to's" of living a healthy life-style. You are not controlled by your diet. Rather you are empowered to effect change and take back control.

With the HUGS™ program the motivation for change comes from within as you proceed towards a new you. You make changes simply because it makes you feel good and gives you more energy. Once you have mastered this you are permanently successful. HUGS™ is a hug for you. It allows you to accept yourself as you are, the first step in increasing control and improving your self-esteem. You choose to change your life-style for yourself, not for anyone else. And with more confidence you are not dependent on compliments from others to continue to practise your new life-style.

Working with life-style change can breathe new excitement into your life. It is a totally positive experience that allows you to eat again, taste, savor, and enjoy food without starving and binging. It puts carbohydrates back into your meals, leaving you satisfied, happy, clear-headed, and in charge.

You count, calories don't. By focusing on yourself and your needs, learning to tune into and be aware of your body, you will feel better about yourself and your energy level will improve. If you feel better about yourself you will gain confidence in your ability to focus on mini changes as measures of success.

You will learn skills and ways of thinking to take the focus off calories, scales, and weight which will allow you to rediscover yourself and become a happier, healthier individual. This process occurs naturally without counting calories and being obsessed with food and weight. Rather than complaining or exhibiting the "poor me" attitude, taking responsibility creates a positive and energetic momentum.

You don't need to count calories. You need to change your attitude. You don't need self-control for denial, you just need to think normally. You will learn to look at your eating as part of your life. You will be given the tools to deal with the problems as they arise.

This renewed confidence in your ability shows you how to think positively and makes you realize that if you believe you can do it, YOU CAN.

1
HUGS™
A Unified Approach for Everyone

If you want to be a winner choose the HUGS program

Refer to the section that describes your situation or area of interest. It will provide you with a focus to make the book work best for your needs.

THE PROBLEM	WHAT HUGS™ CAN DO FOR YOU

New nonsmoker Reduce sugar and fat cravings and the urge to smoke by making a life-style change and eating in a way to reduce blood sugar swings.

Weight concerns Adopt regular eating habits lower in fat content, increase physical activity, adopt a healthier attitude towards food and activity.

High cholesterol Adopt regular eating habits lower in fat content, increase physical activity to help reduce the chance of heart disease.

People with diabetes Balance carbohydrate and protein to stabilize blood sugar, address concerns of weight, acquire a taste for less sweetening foods.

Premenstrual syndrome (PMS) Reduce blood sugar swings that bring on symptoms of PMS. Achieve a balance in eating, physical activity, and decrease caffeine intake to relieve PMS symptoms.

Next generation Principles that apply to adults can be transferred to children. Getting them away from the diet mentality and helping them accept themselves nurtures an environment conducive to improved self-esteem and a healthier life-style.

HUGS™ FOR THE NEW NONSMOKER

"I'm afraid to stop smoking because I'll get fat."
"Smoking helps me keep slim."
"I need cigarettes to curb my appetite."
"I'll quit smoking when I've lost 30 pounds."

Do any of the above statements sound familiar to you? *Do you "jump-start" your body with caffeine and cigarettes, the chemical dynamite that gets you up and running every morning?* Can your body survive this torture?

Myths of Smoking and Weight Gain

At first glance Brent looked like a healthy individual. He appeared to be of ideal body weight and was bright and alert. A few weeks later when I walked into his office, the first thing I noticed was the smell of smoke. He related to me how he was trying to stop smoking and how he was compelled to have a cigarette. He had been trying to go "cold turkey" but the withdrawal symptoms were unbearable! Yet he was tired of cigarettes having a hold on his life.

Since Brent was also a heavy coffee drinker, understanding the effect that nicotine and caffeine had on blood sugar levels helped him understand why increased hunger was one of the withdrawal symptoms he was experiencing. Caffeine, like nicotine, can temporarily mask hunger feelings by stimulating the body to release more glucose from its stores in the bloodstream. After our discussion, he decided to gradually wean himself off cigarettes to minimize withdrawal symptoms. At the same time, he would start eating more regularly to combat the increased hunger cravings, and use the appropriate balance of foods to sustain his energy level.

Was that cigarette really necessary after the meal or was it purely habit to be used as a reward? Could the renewed taste in the food itself be satisfying on its own as he learned to taste and savor his meal? These were some of the questions that he was answering in his own mind.

Smoking is widely used as a technique to control weight. Female smokers are more apt to use smoking to avoid weight gain. Women will also return to smoking to curb weight gain and increased appetite. In contrast, men return to smoking because of excessive stress and a craving for cigarettes.[1]

Brent's life-style had been unhealthy. He didn't eat breakfast and was proud of it. He had erratic eating habits, and he smoked one pack of cigarettes and drank 10 cups of coffee a day. This excessive stimulation made him on edge. His smoking was really more harmful than excess weight. Because of his life-style Brent at 130 pounds had the same health risk as a nonsmoker weighing 210 to 230 pounds.

To use smoking as a method of weight control is clearly an inappropriate choice. If he continued smoking Brent's chance of dying before age 70 was almost twice as great as that of a large individual who was a nonsmoker.[2] See chart p28.

Nicotine increases metabolism (the number of

27

calories you burn at rest) by about 10 percent for heavy smokers, but it is not a recommended way to burn up calories to keep weight down.

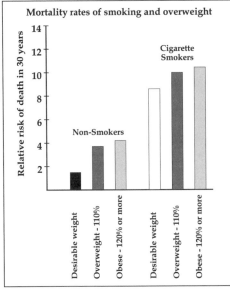

Mortality rates of smoking and overweight

Relative risk of death in 30 years

Cigarette Smokers

Non-Smokers

Desirable weight — Overweight - 110% — Obese - 120% or more — Desirable weight — Overweight - 110% — Obese - 120% or more

If you use smoking for weight control, remember that not everyone gains weight once they stop smoking. If you make a life-style change, this can decrease the incidence of gaining weight. The decrease in metabolic rate that occurs can be offset by an increase in physical activity. Exercise for enjoyment in order to make it permanent. Experience the "high" that comes from activity.

You should know that even if you smoke this won't keep you from becoming obese. Although smokers weigh an average of only about 7 pounds less than nonsmokers they can gain weight and often put it on in places that seriously affect their health. Smokers tend to accumulate fat around the waist rather than the hips, and this is associated with a greater risk of heart disease, diabetes, and early death.[3] Once you have stopped smoking, diet for weight control is not the answer. Dieting has a negative effect on the metabolic rate bringing it down by 15 to 30 percent within a 24 to 48 hour period.[4] On the other hand, the immediate health benefits of life-style change will decrease your desire to smoke.

The secret of successfully stopping smoking and not gaining weight depends on life-style change. If you, as Tom does, order salad for lunch but spread 2 packets of salad dressing over it you may as well eat the hamburger your friends are eating. Tom remains hungry, and he is unhappy that he didn't have a hamburger. All he ever talks about is food. His metabolism is being slowed down by a poor way of eating. Since he had used cigarettes to dampen his appetite he was out of tune with his natural hunger signals. Now he is using false impressions about healthy eating and denying himself some of the real pleasures of food. Substitution of lower calorie foods

(salads) don't satisfy unless the person truly enjoys the replacement. Life-style change will show Tom how to rev up his metabolism using food and activity.

When you stop smoking, don't diet. Eat sensibly balanced meals that consist of more substance than simply water, vitamins, minerals, and fiber.

Another point to remember is that as a new nonsmoker you will get hungry more often because your stomach empties more quickly. Smoking keeps food in your stomach longer so that you can go without food and not feel hungry. When you stop smoking, do not turn to water and diet drinks to help fill you up. You may feel bloated and temporarily full, but this will not keep you going. You need to learn how to eat in a way that keeps you satisfied longer by naturally allowing you to keep food in your stomach longer. Soluble fiber and the right balance in your eating can achieve this end.

Some scientists believe that nicotine affects the level of blood sugar (glucose) in the body, so that nicotine withdrawal triggers an increased craving for sweet foods. This may be the result of the lower blood sugar levels that occur when you stop smoking. When your blood sugar levels are low, you feel hungry, especially for something sweet. A balanced life-style will show you how to stabilize your blood sugar levels so that those "highs" and "lows" level out.

The secretion of insulin pushes glucose (all food is eventually broken down to this simple sugar) into cells for energy thus lowering the blood sugar level, and causing hunger. Smoking inhibits insulin secretion causing blood sugar levels to remain higher. This suppresses appetite. Many smokers reach for a cigarette when they are actually physically hungry. Life-style change will help you get back in tune with your body. You will learn to eat when you are physically hungry and stop when you are full.

Another disadvantage of smoking is that it cues the end of a meal. At that time you often crave the oral

29

gratification of something sweet. Smokers often turn to a cup of coffee. You will learn the effect that caffeine has on your blood sugar. Cutting back on coffee will stabilize your blood sugar and you will begin to rely on food for energy and a state of alertness rather than on caffeine and cigarettes. You can learn how to break the habit of a cigarette and coffee to end your meal and replace these with healthier options that you will enjoy.

ASK YOURSELF THESE QUESTIONS

Do you really want that cigarette or sweet at the end of a meal or is it merely psychologically satisfying? Can it be a habit? If so, you will not feel deprived if you delay smoking the cigarette and confront the urge. Tell yourself that you can have that cigarette later if you still want it.

Breaking the familiar associations and patterns will not give you any anxiety since the real reason you thought you wanted the cigarette is habit, not desire. This is an effective technique for gradually weaning yourself off cigarettes when using them is just part of a routine. Ask yourself if there is enough variety in your meals so that you can turn to food for psychological contentment. Of course you will not want to allow food to replace cigarettes which would result in overeating. You can learn to explore these issues and deal with them.

Smokers often use cigarettes when under stress. When Allison feels pressured, the first thing she does is reach for a cigarette. She says it helps her think. Is it because of that initial high that occurs when nicotine from the first few puffs hits the brain? You can learn how to think clearly without relying on cigarettes. Learning how to be in control of your life, how to adopt a new perspective towards stressful situations, reduces the need to smoke. Changing your thinking and attitude towards the situation can allow you to reduce the number of times you need to turn to smoking or eating to relieve stress. You can learn how to relax naturally. If you opt for life-style change it will give you skills for a lifetime and allow you to get the full enjoyment out of life.

There are extra benefits for becoming a nonsmoker. A

30

recent study showed that by quitting smoking, even long-term smokers can reduce their risk of stroke to the same level as nonsmokers within 5 years.[5] Within 2 years of quitting smoking, much of the tobacco-related risk of heart disease will also have disappeared.

HUGS™ FOR WEIGHT CONCERNS

If you are concerned about weight and find that food is the center of your attention, you would probably like to find a way to deal with this. You need new skills and a different mind-set to help you take charge. HUGS™ can help you find out why diet sheets have prevented you from taking responsibility for your own health.

"I can't lose weight without a diet. The diet sheet tells me what to do."

"I'm losing control. Every time I see food, I want it."

"I seem to be able to keep the weight off only if I stay on the diet. I can't imagine being on a diet for the rest of my life."

Learning to eat regularly according to your hunger signals will allow you to stabilize your blood sugar level and reduce your craving for sweets. Acquiring a taste for less sweetening and fattening foods will help you to make healthier choices because you no longer crave fats and sugars. HUGS™ will guide you to allow this to happen naturally.

HUGS™ FOR CHOLESTEROL CONCERNS

Each year 40,000 Canadians die from heart attacks. One of the major risk factors for heart disease is high blood cholesterol levels. As the artery openings become narrower, blood cannot pass through to carry oxygen and nutrients to the brain or heart (depending which artery is affected) and a stroke or heart attack will result.

Of the 3 major risk factors—smoking, high blood

31

"HUGS™ meets my needs completely. I'm really beginning to feel like a thin person, and it is becoming more natural to me. I can't believe how little I actually knew about nutrition. I thought of food items only as 'legal' and 'illegal' until HUGS™. The HUGS™ program is truly the best thing to happen to me in a long time. I love it."

"HUGS™ got me to change my attitude. I didn't need self-control, I just needed to think normally. This program has given me the ability to look at my eating as part of my life, not as an all-consuming hobby. I still have lots to work on, but I now have the tools to deal with the problems as they arise."

"What a great learning experience! The program helped me to motivate myse' without pushing a diet and exercise o me. I now enjoy exercise and meals ar do not dread them. HUGS™ helped n tune into my body. Now I know when a why I'm hungry. I eat a healthy breakfast and lunch which means I'm not as hungr later in the day."

pressure, and high-cholesterol levels, the former two put the individual at a greater risk for heart disease. High level of cholesterol is a risk factor for heart disease for only 2 percent of Canadians. Since a risk factor is not a disease, is cholesterol becoming another word for paranoia?

According to Dr. Corday, President of the American College of Cardiology and Clinical Professor of Medicine at the University of California Los Angeles,

FRAMINGHAM HEART STUDY - CHD RISK PREDICTION WORKSHEET

1. FIND POINTS FOR EACH RISK FACTOR.

Age (if female)						Age (if male)						HDL Cholesterol - mmol/L				
Age	Pts	Age	Pts	Age	Pts	Age	Pts	Age	Pts	Age	Pts	HDL-C	Pts	HDL-C	Pts	HDL-C
30	-12	37	-2	46-47	5	30	-2	42-43	6	59-60	14	0.60-0.62	8	1.01-1.06	2	1.71-1.84
31	-10	38	-1	48	6	31	-1	44	7	61-63	15	0.65-0.67	7	1.09-1.16	1	1.87-2.02
32	-9	39	0	49-51	7	32-33	0	45-46	8	64-66	16	0.70-0.75	6	1.19-1.27	0	2.05-2.20
33	-7	40-41	1	52-53	8	34	1	47-49	9	67-69	17	0.78-0.83	5	1.29-1.40	-1	2.23-2.41
34	-6	42	2	54-57	9	35-36	2	50-51	10	70-72	18	0.85-0.90	4	1.42-1.53	-2	2.44-2.56
35	-5	43	3	58-61	10	37	3	52-53	11	73-74	19	0.93-0.98	3	1.55-1.68	-3	
36	-4	44-45	4	61-74	11	38-39	4	54-55	12							
						40-41	5	56-58	13							

Total Cholesterol - mmol/L				Systolic Blood Pressure					
Total-C	Pts	Total-C	Pts	SBP	Pts	SBP	Pts	Other	Pts
3.37-3.63	-4	5.67-6.19	2	95-97	-4	140-149	2	Cigarettes	4
3.65-3.96	-3	6.22-6.76	3	98-104	-3	150-159	3	Diabetic-male	3
3.99-4.33	-2	6.79-7.38	4	105-112	-2	160-171	4	Diabetic-female	6
4.35-4.72	-1	7.41-8.08	5	113-120	-1	172-184	5	ECG:LVH	9
4.74-5.16	0	8.11-8.81	6	121-129	0	185-190	6		
5.18-5.65	1			130-139	1			*0 pt for each NO*	

2. SUM POINTS FOR ALL RISK FACTORS.

_____	+	_____	+	_____	+	_____	+	_____	+	_____	+	_____	=	_____
Age		HDL-C		Total-C		SBP		Smoker		Diabetes		ECG:LVH		Point tota

Note: *Minus points subtract from total.*

KEY: HDL-C = HDL Cholesterol; Total-C = Total Cholesterol; SBP = Systolic blood pressure (top number)

"Every time that I eat something I shouldn't, I get an argument from my spouse. This low-cholesterol diet is sure stressful. Isn't there a better way?"

"My cholesterol level is high. I'm not supposed to eat butter but I love it."

billions of dollars have been spent on studies investigating the link between cholesterol levels and heart disease. Billions more have been spent on campaigns encouraging people to reduce their cholesterol and now people are frightened to eat anything with cholesterol. Dr. Corday states that the issue has made people neurotic about life and he expresses a caution about the effects of restricting the cholesterol intake of children.

Cholesterol is especially important in the development of the nervous system during infancy and childhood. It is required to produce healthy cells in the body and brain, which is why it is particularly important for growing children. Feeding a low-fat milk to children can be harmful for this reason.

There is no evidence that reducing cholesterol will extend life. On the other hand, adopting a healthier

3. LOOK UP RISK CORRESPONDING TO POINT TOTAL											
	Probability			Probability			Probability			Probability	
ts	5 yr	10 yr	Pts	5 yr	10 yr	Pts	5 yr	10 yr	Pts	5 yr	10 yr
1	<1%	< 2%	9	2%	5%	17	6%	13%	25	14%	27%
2	1%	2%	10	2%	6%	18	7%	15%	26	15%	29%
3	1%	2%	11	3%	7%	19	8%	16%	27	17%	31%
4	1%	2%	12	3%	7%	20	8%	18%	28	18%	33%
5	1%	3%	13	4%	8%	21	9%	19%	29	20%	35%
6	1%	3%	14	4%	9%	22	10%	21%	30	21%	37%
7	1%	4%	15	5%	11%	23	12%	23%	31	23%	39%
8	2%	4%	16	5%	12%	24	13%	25%	32	25%	42%

4. COMPARE TO AVERAGE 10 YEAR RISK								
	Probability			Probability			Probability	
ge	Women	Men	Age	Women	Men	Age	Women	Men
0-34	1%	3%	45-49	5%	10%	60-64	13%	21%
5-39	1%	5%	50-54	8%	14%	65-69	9%	30%
0-44	2%	6%	55-59	12%	16%	70-74	12%	24%

Keavin Anderson, Ph.D., Framingham Study; Dr. W. B. Kannel, Boston University of Medicine[6]

NAME:_____ PT. TOTAL:_____ DATE:_____

life-style can improve the quality of life. To help put the issue of cholesterol in perspective, several clients were plotted on the chart on the previous page to determine their overall risk for heart disease.

Wayne had a high cholesterol level of 8.58 where 5.2 mmol/L or less is desirable. This 51-year-old man was physically fit with good blood pressure (108/78) and he was a nonsmoker. He also had a healthy waist/hip ratio (more about this in Chapter 2).

Robert, a large, 46-year-old man had an unhealthy waist/hip ratio, and a cholesterol level of 6.34. He did no exercise and smoked cigars. His blood pressure was 125/90 because his heart had to work harder due to his extra weight and poor fitness level. It takes an extra mile of blood vessels to nourish an extra pound of fat.

Allen's only form of activity fit his Type A personality. His day was rush rush, got to get it done. His total cholesterol was 6.7, he had a healthy waist/hip ratio, and he was at a healthy weight for his height. His blood pressure was good at 106/70, but he smoked 1/2 to 1 package of cigarettes a day.

You will notice that Wayne who was more fit than the other two had the highest HDL (a cholesterol carrier that acts as your body's drain cleaner; different from LDL the lazy cholesterol) level of 1.47 which protected him against heart disease and lowered his overall risk. Allen's HDL value was 1.23 with Robert's trailing behind at 1.15.

	Age	Cholesterol	HDL	LDL	Triglycerides	BP	Smoker
Wayne	51	8.58	1.47	6.04	2.37	108/78	no
Robert	46	6.34	1.15	4.23	2.13	125/90	yes
Allen	49	6.70	1.23	4.60	1.92	106/70	yes

Following the above chart and working through Wayne's sum points for all risk factors as per chart based on the well established Framingham Study referred to in more detail later in the book, it would look like this:

$$10 + (-2) + 6 + (-2) + 0 + 0 + 0 = 12$$

This means that even though the average risk for

heart disease for a man Wayne's age within the next 10 years is 14 percent, the probability of his getting heart disease in that time frame is 7 percent. His healthy blood pressure and high HDL value and the fact that he is a nonsmoker make his high-cholesterol level insignificant.

On the other hand Robert's probability of getting heart disease within the next 10 years is 12 percent, 2 points higher than the average of 10 percent. Even though his cholesterol level is lower, his high blood pressure, minimal activity which would reflect on a lower HDL value, as well as the fact that he is a smoker are higher risk factors for heart disease.

Allen is also a smoker, one of the major risk factors for heart disease. His risk of heart disease within the next 10 years is about average at 9 percent while the average for his age is 10 percent.

Focus on overall health rather than one contributing factor, such as cholesterol.

These case studies show that it is better to focus on overall health rather than on one contributing factor, such as cholesterol. Yet too much misleading inform-ation on this subject has become a great concern for many people. You might like to consider the following facts.

• Blood cholesterol is a wax-like material produced in the liver and is used to make hormones, bile acids, and cell walls. HDL known as the "good" cholesterol and LDL known as the "bad" cholesterol are among the different types of cholesterol that are produced to make up the total cholesterol.

• Dietary cholesterol is found in all foods from animal sources, such as meat, eggs, and dairy products. However, *dietary cholesterol has a very small effect on blood cholesterol levels.*[7,8,9]

• "I use 100 percent whole wheat bread with no cholesterol and no fat and add butter to it." In this case the client's wise choice of bread is negated by the fact that he loads the bread with butter, the real culprit in raising cholesterol levels. Saturated fat is a key factor in raising blood cholesterol levels. Saturated fat can be defined as any fat that is hard at room temperature such as butter and lard. Other examples of hidden saturated fat could be processed meats such as sausages, luncheon meats, hot dogs, and dairy products such as cream, whole milk, cheese, and ice cream.

• Processing foods (e.g., peanut butter) can change a healthy kind of fat into one that will raise blood cholesterol levels. Convenience foods often contain palm and coconut oils, which are saturated fats that improve the shelf-life of the product but also raise blood cholesterol levels. Peanut butter naturally contains the monounsaturated fat peanut oil which will not affect blood cholesterol levels. These types of fats are now being shown to possibly lower cholesterol levels.[10,11]

> **NO ONE FAT IS BETTER THAN ANOTHER.**
>
> ---
>
> A fat
> • low in saturated fat,
> • high in trans fatty acids, and
> • containing hydrogenated vegetable oil,
>
> is the same as a fat that is
>
> • high in saturated fat,
> • having no trans fatty acids, and
> • containing no hydrogenated vegetable oil.

As a guide to your buying you could read the label! As soon as hydrogen is incorporated into the product to maintain shelf-life (that is, keep it on the shelf without going rancid), it becomes hard at room temperature and is saturated. Therefore, hydrogenated peanut butter will raise your cholesterol level. *Note* Buy the natural peanut butter, stir it around, and keep it in the fridge. Some of my clients prefer to get rid of the fat on the surface altogether and add a little jam to it for moisture.

• Oils do not contain cholesterol. Cholesterol is made by the liver of an animal and since vegetable oils do not have livers, they cannot have any cholesterol! "No cholesterol" could be featured on the label of all vegetable oils.

• Oat bran has some effect in lowering blood cholesterol levels. The exact mechanism by which the reduction occurs is uncertain. Recent studies suggest that incorporating oat bran or oatmeal into one's meal plan reduces the overall saturated fat content of meals.[12]

• Polyunsaturated fats (corn oil, sunflower oil, and safflower oil) and monounsaturated fats (olive oil, peanut oil, canola) help to lower blood cholesterol levels. More recently, there has been a shift to the monounsaturated fats (olive, peanut, and canola or rapeseed oils) due to their affect on lowering LDL ("bad" cholesterol) without affecting the HDL ("good" cholesterol) that protects you from heart disease.[13]

36

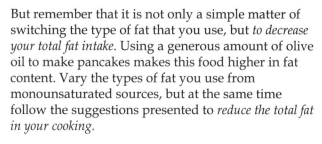

But remember that it is not only a simple matter of switching the type of fat that you use, but *to decrease your total fat intake.* Using a generous amount of olive oil to make pancakes makes this food higher in fat content. Vary the types of fat you use from monounsaturated sources, but at the same time follow the suggestions presented to *reduce the total fat in your cooking.*

Eating a balance of more carbohydrates and less protein while including more sources of soluble fiber such as legumes (peas, beans, and lentils), fruits, and vegetables will help to lower cholesterol levels.

If you make a gradual change in your eating habits this will allow you to lower your blood cholesterol levels. Strict avoidance of certain foods only leads to cravings for those "forbidden" items. In fact, the increased stress may offset any lowering of cholesterol levels that you are trying to effect by avoiding certain foods. You can lower your cholesterol level naturally by learning how to acquire a taste for less fattening foods so that you can choose lower fat foods because you like them. Adding physical activity that you enjoy will help to increase the type of cholesterol (HDL) that will actually protect you from heart disease.

You can learn how to modify recipes during food preparation and baking to lower fat content without removing the "punch" in the meals. For example, gravy is great for adding flavor, moisture, and color to your meal but is the fat really necessary?

You can learn how to read labels. If you know the real meaning of the word "light" you can purchase products that are actually "lighter" or lower in fat content rather than simply lighter in color, taste, or texture. Read the label for the M.F. (milk fat) or B.F. (butter fat) content and gradually acquire a taste for those foods with a lower fat content. "Gradual" is the key in order to make a lower fat way of eating permanent.

Increasing aerobic activity increases HDL[14] which carries cholesterol out of the arteries to the liver

37

where it is excreted from the body. This protects you against heart disease. On the other hand, life-style habits such as smoking can increase LDL (the lazy, sticky cholesterol carrier) which has the effect of plugging up your system by depositing cholesterol in the arteries. This adds to the risk of heart disease.

Your positive outlook on life in combination with a healthier life-style can improve your health status and lower your risk for heart disease.

HUGS™ FOR PEOPLE WITH DIABETES

A person with diabetes maintains blood sugar control through the way of eating. Fortunately, the prescribed diabetic way of living is a healthy life-style. You can make the routine more "normal" and flexible by making gradual life-style changes so you can begin to think like a nondieter.

"It's supper time and I have to count out my exchanges to have the right balance according to my meal plan or diet sheet. I have to do this, not because I want to but because it's something that's controlling me. But some days I'm hungrier and some days I'm not. There's no flexibility."

If you're on a diet, you may still want sweets but you try to say "no" and you feel deprived. By learning to acquire a taste for less sweetening foods, the power of choice rather than the diet sheet is the controlling mechanism. The blood sugar control will be achieved.

I have observed in the diabetic clinic over the past 5 years that those who adopt a more positive attitude are more relaxed with diabetes. They handle stress more positively and stabilize their blood sugar better than those who are worried and preoccupied with food and weight, portion control, and the "magic" diet that they believe is the perfect way of eating.

Life-style changes are less stressful and more positive than diets. They are for life!

Even the person with diabetes who is on insulin can

38

benefit from a healthier way of thinking, can normalize eating and activity habits, and can work on skills to improve overall well-being. Consistency of carbohydrate intake and scheduled meals and snacks will be required to account for the action of insulin, but empowering yourself to focus on health instead of diet details will make the process easier. You can make healthy living a choice that you desire!

> **Fluctuations in body weight are less healthy than if you stabilize at a higher weight.[15] Yo-yo dieting where weight is lost and then regained seems to be associated with more fat being distributed around the stomach area.[16] Increased risk of obesity-related diabetes has been associated with fat in the stomach area rather than fat in the hips and thighs.[17]**

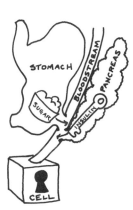

As many as 80 percent of all people who have diabetes and are not on insulin are significantly overweight. By losing even a modest amount of weight, these patients may lower their insulin resistance to the point where the insulin their pancreases produce is sufficient to keep blood sugars down. A modest goal of a 5 or 10 pound weight loss will often provide good results.[18,19]

Encouraging research indicates that physical training, even without weight loss, seems to increase the body's sensitivity to insulin, making the available insulin work better. Aerobic exercise may improve the fit between insulin (key) and the cell receptor site (lock) allowing better control of blood sugar levels.

Improvement can be noted in as little as one month after beginning a regular exercise program. Within one year of doing this activity, aerobic exercise may even increase the number of receptor sites. Adjustment of diet also improves the insulin action within several days of initiation even if body weight or body fat have decreased only slightly.[20]

Despite the benefits of an improved diet and exercise program, estimates suggest that one third to one half of the people with diabetes have difficulty following these programs for any length of time. Once blood sugar levels have been brought under control, old

eating and exercise habits often return, along with the former life-style. Diet and exercise programs treat diabetes but make little attempt to address the emotional response people have to food. Difficulties faced by people with diabetes are similar to those faced by other people who diet to try to lose weight:

- frequent feelings of hunger,
- feelings of restriction and deprivation due to elimination of some favorite foods,
- feelings of awkwardness at mealtimes because of eating differently from friends and family or because of having forced sudden changes in eating habits on the family,
- feelings of guilt when "cheating," which inevitably occurs and often leads to going off the diet, and
- a feeling of total dependence on the diet sheet resulting in a total preoccupation with food.

Dieting for anyone is usually viewed as a stressful sacrifice. For people with diabetes, dieting is more stressful because of the consequences if they go off the diet. If persons with diabetes add exercise that may be at too high a level resulting in pain, discomfort, and stiffness, they may give up and return to a former life-style. It's very important to find the balance that allows proper eating and appropriate activity for each individual.

For diabetics on insulin, this approach can be used together with the individual's diabetic meal plan. Check with your registered dietitian.

For those people who have a genetic predisposition to diabetes, the disease will develop into Type II diabetes only if an abnormal weight gain occurs. People with diabetes who lead healthy life-styles with regard to eating and exercise habits not only make their diabetes less severe and reduce the probability of complications, but also set an example of prevention for their children. For a person with diabetes, a minimal weight loss, especially early in the course of Type II diabetes, can cause diabetes to be reversed. A weight loss of 5 to 10 kg (11 to 22 lbs) is sufficient for diabetic control to be restored.[21]

One of the ingredients of quality of life is to be in control of your life. The ability to direct the course of events in your life and being able to do what you want to do is challenged by having diabetes.

*"The week before my
period, I am absolutely
driven to eat sweets and
junk food. I don't
understand it because I
usually have a lot of self-
control."*

HUGS™ life-style approach to diabetes, leading to
permanent adjustments in life-style through
progressive gradual change, now offers the person
with diabetes hope for less stressful and more lasting
control of diabetes. It provides the individual with
confidence to adopt a new life-style rather than
continue with the perception that food controls you.

HUGS™ FOR PREMENSTRUAL SYNDROME

PMS is brought on by high progesterone levels in the
body during the second half of the menstrual cycle.
High progesterone levels can cause the body's cells to
be resistant to insulin. This means that even though
there are normal to high levels of glucose in the blood
the glucose is not able to enter the body's cells. This
causes cravings for sweets and increased appetite—
a roller coaster effect.

• Well-balanced eating helps to avoid premenstrual
binging. You may be hungry more frequently during
this time because the hormone progesterone reduces
the amount of glucose your body's cells receive.
Binging can produce higher levels of insulin which
may increase the cell's resistance to insulin. Then a
roller coaster effect may occur where binging can
result in increased hunger.

• Eat more carbohydrates that are complex or lower
on the glycemic index (see Ch 4). Eating sweets or refined sugars may give symptoms of low blood sugar.

• You can stabilize blood sugar swings and reduce
symptoms of irritability by a balanced way of eating.

• If you experience premenstrual abdominal
bloating choose less salty foods.

• If you experience symptoms of anxiety or
irritability, choose foods and beverages lower in
caffeine content.

• Stay physically active and partake in regular
aerobic activity to increase your sense of well-being,
decrease fluid retention, and help relieve depression.
This lessening of symptoms may be linked to the rise
in endorphins during physical activity which have a
relaxing effect.

• Be aware that alcohol, a mood-altering drug, can
cause depression and feelings of hopelessness.

41

If these suggestions don't work you may have a relative deficiency of vitamin B$_6$. This is common among oral contraceptive users. Vitamin B$_6$ is involved in the production of serotonin, a brain chemical related to mood. A relative deficiency of B$_6$ results in reduced synthesis of serotonin and a resulting depression.

Note The literature on B$_6$ is controversial at this time. Many articles state that 100 mg of B$_6$ (pyridoxine) taken daily one week prior to the onset of your period is beneficial. However, a recent study indicates that women who take B$_6$ supplements for long periods of time can develop neurological symptoms even with dosages previously thought safe. The minimum dosage that can cause trouble is unknown but is less than the amount commonly prescribed for premenstrual tension.[22] The women in this study had taken vitamin B$_6$ in quantities from less than 50 mg to over 200 mg daily for a period of anywhere from 6 months to over 5 years. If you are using this supplement, do not use it on a daily basis but only one week prior to the onset of your menstrual period.

Cuing into the enjoyment of exercise is a natural and healthy way to relieve symptoms of depression. Satisfied HUGS™ clients have related that symptoms of PMS have decreased when they follow the HUGS™ philosophy.

HUGS™ FOR THE NEXT GENERATION
A mother's constant dieting and discontent with her body often sends messages to the child that he or she is not okay and needs to go on a diet. Our society's preoccupation

"Mommy, will I have to be on diets all the time when I grow up?"

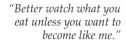

"Better watch what you eat unless you want to become like me."

with perfection whether it's the "perfect body," or being the best in school or in sports, can lead a child into a constant struggle of trying to keep up.

Studies indicate that an important factor in adolescent depression and low self-esteem is poor body image. Up to two-thirds of young women between the ages of 12 to 23 are unhappy with their weight. The astonishing fact is that most of those who wanted to lose weight were not even overweight. Both boys and girls desire flat abdomens and hard bodies more than they desire health. This fuels the diet industry and produces bestsellers and gimmicks. Ironically, the nation continues to gain weight.[23]

Childhood and adolescence are critical stages in the development of behaviors and attitudes that foster wellness for daily living. Nutrition and exercise habits established prior to adulthood are most likely to persist as an integral part of life-style! A sedentary child becomes a sedentary adult. Yet even though parents generally recognize the importance of establishing healthy life-style habits, a positive role model can set a good example. As well, optimal growth, fitness, and feeling good need to be emphasized as goals in order to translate into improved life-style for the adults of the 21st century.[24]

Preschool is the time when influences by parents have the greatest impact. If parents foster the attitude that activity is an important part of everyday life and focus on physical movement rather than sedentary games and television watching they can encourage children toward a healthy life-style.

Because of working parents, today's children are more responsible for household duties including meal preparation and grocery shopping. They tend to fend for themselves, and eat convenience foods more frequently. Yet, sufficient nutrients are particularly important for the child's health and well-being in the growth process. For the adolescent who has limited experience, supervised involvement in food preparation and the purchasing of food can help make the learning more meaningful. The focus could be on the immediate benefits of healthy living such as

43

energy to keep the child increasing his or her desire for health and wellness.

As parents go through the process of self-discovery by tuning into their bodies for signals of hunger, appropriate levels of activity, time for themselves, and basic needs for happiness, they will notice how these positive attitudes transfer to their children.

Some Suggestions to Consider
• Think twice before asking your child to clean his or her plate before having dessert or in order to be considered a good child.

• Avoid using food as a reward for good behavior or to comfort a child when he or she is not feeling well.

• Try not to establish erratic eating habits where everyone fends for himself instead of cultivating a special family mealtime.

• Avoid taking the enjoyment out of eating by controlling the child's food intake rather than allowing the child to tune into his or her internal hunger signals for a feeling of fullness.

• Accept the child as he or she is. Don't instill a feeling of not being good enough.

• Think twice before introducing diets as a form of control rather than adopting positive life-style habits that become a way of life for the family.

• Avoid centering the focus of holiday occasions on food alone rather than the occasion itself and its meaning, including friendship and conversation, as well as the activities of the event.

• Try not to make the child rely on diet products (i.e. diet drinks) that do not allow him or her to acquire a taste for less sweetening foods.

The bonus gained in living a healthy life-style is that there is a sense of inner satisfaction when you take responsibility for your own health. It can help to create a better balance in family life.

2

Resetting the Stage

*Throw the scales away and
focus on rebuilding your health.*

THE ALMIGHTY SCALE

For many of us, the scale rules our lives. It has the power to dictate what we eat, how we feel, and how we act. We weigh in and according to the needle indicator we feel happy or depressed. Weight up, weight down. Our moods swing with the needle.

Eighty percent of the women in Canada believe they are overweight, yet data from the Canada Fitness Survey indicate that only 20 percent of women over 20 years of age experience a health risk due to excess body weight. This same survey showed that 33 percent of Canadian men are at a health risk because of excess body weight.

Men are at a higher health risk because of obesity, yet women are more preoccupied with food and the number on the scale.

In fact, many women allow the number on the scale to put their life on hold until they reach their weight goal. This obsession with weight prevents them from getting on with their lives. They rationalize: "I'll be happy only when I've lost 10 pounds. I'll start exercising once I've lost the weight. I don't look good in a sweat suit now." Unfortunately this kind of weight loss is usually temporary. Your moments of happiness are gone when you gain back what you lost and the cycle begins again. Your problem with weight is not solved and your self-esteem gets lower and lower.

When did this preoccupation with weight begin? Probably in the late 50s when the new Metropolitan height/weight tables came out followed by Twiggy's shape in the 60s. Women discovered that according to the tables they were 10 pounds overweight and the image that was projected in the media reinforced an ever slimmer figure.

Dieting began as women tried to obtain the ideal figure. The intense pressure that society's cultural values place on women to conform to specific body shapes creates an obsession with external appearance at the expense of basic body needs. Focusing on the scales ties your self-worth and self-esteem to an external artificial cue and doesn't allow you to

46

discover yourself and pay attention to your body's needs. It prevents inner growth.

Because you admire society's ideal shape and want to lose weight to obtain it, you are temporarily motivated to pursue a diet and lose the pounds. But you haven't dealt with why you overate in the first place so when you stop the diet and the weight returns you are devastated. Focusing on a life-style change that will deal with the basics of your problem is the only way that you can prevent this up-and-down cycle and the depression that accompanies it.

In order to use life-style change as a measure of success, let go of the control the scale has over you.

Deanna, 18, came to see me for weight loss. She had been in a weight-loss program and her mother was attending one of the popular weight-loss programs and was constantly on and off a diet. Deanna and her mother both attended the first session with me. Her mother remarked that I was trying to deprogram them from the diet mentality. That was true. No diets and no scales were involved in what I had to say.

The Yo-Yo Syndrome

total fat (increases)
yo-yo weight
total muscle (decreases)

gain lose gain lose

A few months later, Deanna said that her clothes felt looser and she and her mother were curious to know if she had lost weight. Deanna was down 2 sizes, yet she had lost only 5 pounds. She had a noticeable improvement in her waist/hip ratio (from .80 to .73) which means that she was healthier. Her menstrual period resumed, and she was no longer cranky or grouchy. She was eating only until she was satisfied, not stuffed. She was more energetic.

It was obvious that scales had not told the true story. The composition of weight for each pound lost during the first 3 days on a 1500 calorie reducing diet is 70 percent water, 5 percent protein, and 25 percent fat.[1] Over the long term, without exercise, only 50 percent of the weight is lost as fat, the rest is muscle tissue and water. The big weight loss the scales indicate is water loss. This deceives the dieter into believing that progress is being made —

47

until the weight comes back.

Since muscles burn more calories at rest, they are more metabolically active than fat is. The trouble is that when we lose weight, we lose some of that tissue, and when it is gained back, we gain back more fat (see graph p47). The result may be less on the scale, but we have traded valuable muscle tissue for fat.[2]

> As the saying goes, "If you don't use it, you'll lose it." What counts is not how much you weigh, but how much of that weight is fat.

Muscle weighs more than fat since it needs to be stored with water. So if we gain more muscle, we may not lose as much on the scale or may actually gain some weight. Exercise preserves muscle mass.

Women are often concerned about large hips. Yet nature intended it that way. This extra fat around the hip area is to protect women in childbearing so they will have enough energy stores to call on. Fat around the stomach area is a higher health risk, and is lost more easily than fat situated lower on the body.

Take a moment to determine your present waist/hip ratio, a measure that will be used to check your indicator of health risk. You can throw out the scales. From now on use the waist/hip ratio to replace it.

With a tape measure, measure your girth at the waist, at your navel, and around your hips at their widest point. Be consistent each time you measure. Be careful not to measure more frequently than once every few months. Otherwise, the obsession with the scale may be inappropriately replaced by a new

Measure of Health (Annual Health Log)

	BEGIN	3 MONTHS	6 MONTHS	9 MONTHS	12 MONTHS
WAIST					
HIP					
WAIST/HIP RATIO					

* The risk increases sharply when the ratio of waist to hip circumference exceeds 1.0 in men and 0.8 in women.

48

crutch, the waist/hip ratio. The purpose of this measurement is simply to provide a periodic indication for those individuals who wear loose-fitting clothes and are therefore unable to measure change by the way their clothes fit. Normal values are 0.8 for women and 1.0 for men.

This example is for a full-figured woman and demonstrates that a larger body size does not necessarily determine one's health status.

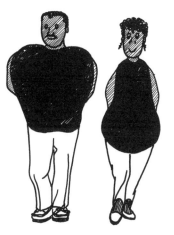

Female   waist 40 inches
hips 50 inches
waist/hip ratio 40/50 = 0.8

This means that this woman's waist is 80 percent of her hip measurement, or putting it another way her waist is 20 percent less than her hips. This ratio gives her a slight curvature. Since fat around the waist determines the risk for heart disease, high blood pressure, and diabetes, this woman whose fat is more concentrated around her hips, is at a lower risk for these diseases.

Male   waist 50 inches
hips 40 inches
waist/hip ratio 50/40 = 1.25.

This signifies that this man has a pot belly. The weight concentrated around the waist is a higher health risk for disease. He is more apple-shaped, in contrast to the woman who is more pear-shaped.

Don't despair! Fat comes off easiest from the waist, the area which lowers your waist/hip ratio and improves your health status.[3]

Now plot your own waist/hip ratio on the chart on the opposite page and note your progress on a quarterly basis by retaking measurements.

REALITIES OF DIETING
Most people go on diets to lose weight quickly. If quick weight loss does not occur they become bored and are not motivated to stay on the diet. According to some scientists, quick weight loss is barbaric

because these individuals are being set up to gain that weight back very quickly.

Individuals focusing on achieving quick weight loss usually do well for a few months. Then, with a loss of interest or as they plateau, weight gain inevitably occurs. These individuals are not in tune with their body's needs which is why they put weight on in the first place. The half pound per week weight loss recommended to minimize a drop in metabolic rate[4] is exceeded on quick weight-loss programs which focus only on weight and not life-style. These people need to look a certain way in

Losing weight quickly causes the weight to return 3 times as quickly. Dr. Wayne Callaway, Associate Clinical Professor of Medicine at George Washington University stated that with rare exceptions, none of the popular commercially available programs for treating obesity are based on current scientific knowledge. They could no longer promise rapid weight loss if they were.[5] Yet women fall prey to these quick weight-loss schemes to shed unwanted pounds for some important occasion or social event that they believe requires them to be slimmer. Some actually achieve their goal, only to regain the weight once the crash diet is stopped.[6]

order to feel good about themselves, instead of making the best of what they already have. Rather than focusing on one event and living for the moment, they could take a broader focus and enjoy the process of life-style change.

Laxatives won't help dieting or weight control. Approximately 5 to 15 percent of the U.S. population are laxative abusers. These are people who use these drugs at least weekly for several months. They include not only many elderly patients but also individuals with eating disorders and others who are preoccupied with weight. However, studies have shown that a maximum of only 12 percent of calories are unabsorbed as a result of laxatives.[7] Laxatives are not a quick fix.

If you take regular exercise and enjoy healthy eating by putting food in its proper perspective, your body will do the work for you to get you to the size right for you. According to Dr. David Williamson, an epidemiologist at the Center for Disease Control in Atlanta, it may be better for a woman in the long term to maintain a given weight, and focus efforts on counseling to accept herself and how she views herself at her current weight, unless the weight is actually causing some medical problems.

It is not how much you weigh that counts, but rather where the fat is distributed. [11] Stabilizing at a higher weight is actually healthier than yo-yo dieting.[12] This shift of weight down and then up results in a higher percentage of upper body fat distribution, in other words, more fat in the stomach area.[13] This tendency to carry fat in the upper body is associated with higher risk for diabetes, high blood pressure, and heart disease.[14,15] Rather than concentrating on weight loss, focus on health and wellness.

Enjoying the process of self-discovery associated with life-style change lasts a lifetime. During the course of the HUGS™ program, the involvement and enthusiasm of participants are high, and this results in steady progress in life-style changes. However, in Jill's case, her progress led her to believe that she could tackle the internalization of life-style changes on her own. Her success was short-lived. She was intimidated by projected media images of slim, svelte, perfect bodies and this destroyed her progress towards her personal goal. She joined yet another diet program. Success was once again measured by the number on the scale. She was creating a stressful situation for herself and the physical and psychological shortcomings of dieting resulted in eventual weight gain. It is interesting how many times we have to reach the wall in order to realize that **diets do not work**.

Another example may also be convincing. Kerry

When someone has heart disease, diabetes, high blood pressure, or any ailment, they are told to lose weight. Yet in a study of a community with a high incidence of overweight but in which obesity was socially acceptable, levels of heart disease and diabetes were found to be below the average for slender Americans.[8] It is losing the weight and gaining it back known as weight cycling that makes one more susceptible to disease.[9] The obsession to be thin causes more people to be on a diet than off a diet at any given time.[10]

participated in the HUGS™ program in its developmental stages when it was still focused on diet, exercise, and behavior modification. Kerry lost weight and, in fact, a year later when I saw her she was even slimmer, almost too slim.

I spoke to her about how the HUGS™ program had evolved to a nondieting approach to healthy living. She was not very receptive because she was doing well on her diet. Her focus was to eat and exercise in the right way for weight loss. Finally, however, the constant deprivation years caused cravings for food that resulted in binging on chips, cheesecake, and all those "forbidden" foods that were now unbearably enticing.

Once Kerry began to regain weight she was interested in hearing the HUGS™ message. Her body was going through a normal reaction as she was rebelling against dieting. Binging does not occur without periods of restriction (dieting). Kerry realized that it was only by changing her thinking that she would be able to prevent more weight gain.

It is true that stressful situations may cause you to go off the diet; but a healthy life-style helps you to take control and work through the situation.

Life-style changes help you to deal with stressful situations more positively, allowing you to learn from your mistakes and accept life's hills and valleys as challenges. Diets which cause body stress are difficult to maintain when the stressful situations occur. Since life is filled with everyday stresses, you need the tools to handle stress positively.

As you have seen diets and scales are not the answer to weight problems. I hope by now you have been convinced to put the scale in the cupboard. If you are unable to let go, your preoccupation with your weight can prevent you from focusing on life-style changes. If you think you can do both, think again. By worrying about your weight and feeling unhappy about the way you look, this unhealthy attitude will lead to an energy drain and you will lose your motivation to correct your life-style and lose weight permanently.

52

The message in this book focuses on life-style skills that you can use for a lifetime. The results will be feeling better about yourself, improvement in overall health, and increased energy. You will accept yourself the way you are and use newly learned skills to focus on your strengths and improve your weaknesses.

Accepting yourself the way you are is one of the most difficult skills to master. Most of us have been conditioned to believe that we should aim for size 10 or even size 6. Unfortunately only 10 percent of the population can naturally fall into this category.

Understanding and accepting who you are will help you progress with the HUGS™ philosophy. Once you are happy to be you the HUGS™ techniques will help you to make some positive changes in life-style.

Instead of having to be thin to feel good about yourself, reverse the process. You have to accept yourself and feel good about yourself first in order to want to nurture yourself and take care of your body and mind. Accepting yourself as you are does not mean that you are absolutely okay and you will do nothing to improve yourself. Rather, it implies that you have the energy to feel good about yourself, and because you do care about yourself, you want to do what is best for your body and mind so that you can be the best that you can be!

"I like myself."

To help put this into practice, say the phrases to the left to yourself first thing in the morning and last thing at night.

"I am a worthwhile person."

Gradually this will become part of your subconscious mind and set up your day on a positive note. This is a very important step. If you are having problems saying it with conviction, keep saying it until you believe it. Give yourself time to gain confidence. It will happen if you believe it can and take the steps to increase the chances.

"I am going to have a great day!"

Being unhappy with the way you look provides only temporary external motivation which usually results in a diet and eventually weight gain. When you focus

53

on the positive, you will eventually start saying the phrases with conviction, allowing them to move you forward on your road to better health.

You will gradually learn to tune into your body and when you understand your body you will learn to fuel your body according to its needs. Accepting yourself allows you to understand these needs and listen to your body more attentively. Your body will naturally adjust to what it is meant to be. This will help you to stabilize your weight. No more up and down weight and no more diets!

Let's go a step farther. In order to focus on life-style changes, you need to accept that diets don't work. Remember that a lot of the weight lost when dieting is your state of dehydration (water loss). Even some popular "balanced" diets are relatively low on carbohydrates. So when you start depleting or getting rid of your carbohydrate stores (glycogen), out goes the water with it. No wonder you are always running to the washroom, since every pound of glycogen is stored with 3 to 4 pounds of water. Also restricting carbohydrate foods such as potatoes, bread, cereals, pasta, and rice leads to an energy drain along with your dehydrated state. No wonder this produces a cranky, irritable you.

The diet fad of the 80s was low carbohydrates resulting in energy drain. The calorie-obsessed, protein-is-in, starches-are-out habits of this generation of adults are in part responsible for high rates of cancer and heart disease. After all, low carbohydrate automatically implies higher protein content at meals and that is more hidden fat.

Now a new round of diets is evolving based on an obsession with fat and cholesterol. Instead of counting grams of carbohydrate, we are told to count grams of fat. A new set of health problems will emerge from this.

DIETS AREN'T THE ANSWER[16]
John had an iron deficiency. For 8 months he had been on a low-fat diet that he considered to be healthy. After all, he was eating more fruits and

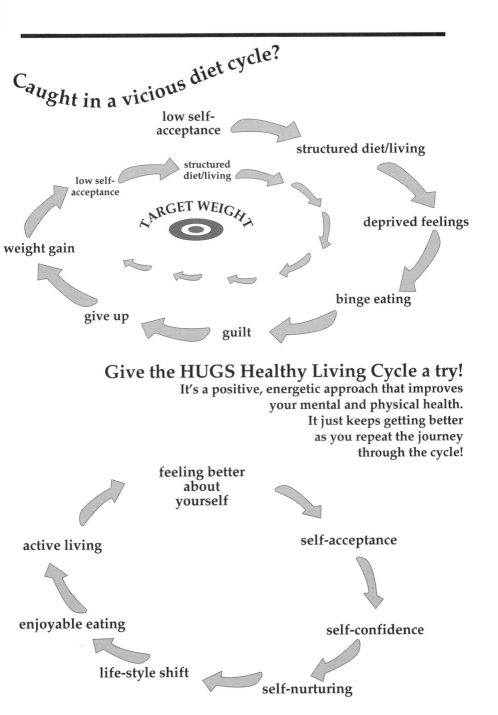

Caught in a vicious diet cycle?

low self-acceptance

structured diet/living

low self-acceptance

structured diet/living

TARGET WEIGHT

deprived feelings

weight gain

binge eating

give up

guilt

Give the HUGS Healthy Living Cycle a try!

It's a positive, energetic approach that improves
your mental and physical health.
It just keeps getting better
as you repeat the journey
through the cycle!

feeling better about yourself

self-acceptance

active living

self-confidence

enjoyable eating

self-nurturing

life-style shift

vegetables, very little fat, and chicken and fish were his only protein sources. He was not eating any foods rich in iron such as red meat and any iron he ingested from vegetable sources was not effectively absorbed because of his consumption of coffee with his meals (see Chapter 11 for more detail).

John ate very little breads and cereals which are rich in vitamin B and his low-fat diet probably impaired the absorption of some fat-soluble vitamins such as A, D, E, and K.

His reason for going on the diet in the first place was to lose weight. He lost 15 pounds in the first 2 months. Then he began to go on and off the diet. After 8 months his constant weight fluctuation had provided a weight loss of only 5 pounds below his starting weight. John loved fatty foods and whenever he went off the diet he binged on some of these fat-laden foods.

His unhealthy attitude towards food and his temporary drastic change in eating because of his diet caused a starve/binge cycle and consequent up-and-down weight which provided a greater health risk for heart disease. It took some convincing to make him realize that he was doing harm to his body by his eating habits. Since he realized he could not diet for the rest of his life he decided to opt for life-style change.

What about those diets that reduce calorie intake and are nutritionally sound? They don't work either. After all, if you normally consume 2000 calories a day, you would have a hard time staying healthy on 1200 calories, or even staying on such a diet for a long time without becoming physically incapacitated.[17]

We've all tried to diet. Did you ever notice that after a few weeks of losing weight you plateau and you don't lose weight anymore. Think about why this happens and it will help you to understand why diets don't work.

The plateau occurs because of a drop in metabolic rate, the number of calories that the body burns at rest in order for your heart to pump, your blood to flow, and your lungs to work. When you begin a calorie-reduced diet your metabolic rate may drop slightly.[18] When you diet, your body slows itself down and packs on a bit more fat so that it has something to call on when you put it in a starvation situation again. It is your body's natural reaction in order to defend you from the sudden drop in calories that you are experiencing.

Eventually, when you deprive yourself of food to reduce your caloric intake, especially if it's the kind of food you like or the quantities you are used to consuming, you won't be able to maintain the diet. For some people, even the thought of going on a diet conjures up a desire for those forbidden foods, and the cravings for those calorie-laden foods are too strong to resist.

Once there were 2 dogs named Sable and Chelsea. Sable, the more dominant one, controlled the approach to the food and the amount eaten, thus keeping Chelsea's eating controlled. When Sable aged and died, Chelsea constantly binged on food. In a short time the dog was quite obese and died of a heart attack. Because Chelsea had felt constantly deprived of food she binged when the other dog died and her overeating was responsible for her death.

One small bite for man, one giant leap for Sandra.

It's easy to cheat but it's always accompanied by feelings of guilt. In this way we are not extracting the full enjoyment from food and need more food to derive psychological satisfaction. If diets worked, there would not be a new one on the market all the time. People would not have to go back to the same program over and over again for the rest of their lives. Yet it's not their fault. Dieting failed them.

**You didn't fail.
Diets failed you.**

Unfortunately, during the loss-and-gain cycle of a weight-loss diet you lose the same 20 pounds over and over again. Each time the weight comes back it's more difficult to lose and easier to put back on.

In fact, *diets make you fatter*. What about the traditional safe weight loss of 1 to 2 pounds per week you ask? This may be safe but even these diets cause

dieters to experience a drop in their metabolic rate. Most dieters (95 percent) who lose weight regain the weight within a 5-year period and many gain back even more than they lost.[19] It's nature's way of protecting you for the next onslaught of deprivation.[20]

Some movie stars, for example Delta Burke from *DesigningWomen,* are leading the way into new ways of thinking about their own bodies and dieting. In an interview with *National Enquirer* she states "You can make the most of your shape with good nutrition and exercise for fitness, but you can't make yourself tall and willowy if your body type is squat and muscular." She goes on to say that the only answer is to accept the body type you were born with, and learn to feel comfortable in your own skin. People weren't meant to be stamped out with cookie cutters, and wouldn't it be boring if we all were?

Take the first step. Start right now by accepting your body and stop separating your wardrobe into thin clothes and fat clothes. Stop concentrating on the hope of being thin again and make the most of what you have right now. You're you and proud of it. The next time you go shopping treat yourself to a new outfit that looks good on you right now. Learn to accent your best features. It's amazing the lift in energy this will give you, and it will help to channel that energy so you will take care of the rest of your body. Accepting the way you are is a lot easier if you help it along with something nice that will make you feel better immediately. Stop punishing yourself and start pampering yourself. You are worth the effort!

Calories don't count. It is not how much you eat, but the type of food you eat that counts.[21] It takes about 4 times the calories to convert carbohydrates into fat than it does to convert the fat you eat into fat tissue.[22] Switching to eating more carbohydrates *without guilt* allows you to shift the type of calories you eat without significantly changing the total quantity of calories. This minimizes the drop in metabolic rate.[23]

58

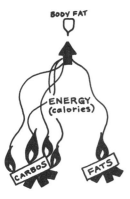

BODY FAT

ENERGY
(calories)

CARBOS

FATS

This may be a difficult concept to grasp since it is the direct reverse of what many dieters are used to hearing. "How can I expect to eat properly and in a healthy manner and expect to lose weight," you ask? My reply is a question also. "Do you have to subject your body to some type of torture, denial, and restriction in order to feel that you are accomplishing something? When you exercise do you expect to feel pain in order to feel that you have had a good workout?"

The secret is to fully enjoy the food while you are eating. If you do not allow yourself the enjoyment of tasting and savoring the food *without guilt*, you will be hungry later on. You will need more food to satisfy you psychologically since you were not focusing on your food while you were eating. Remember, eating bread (carbohydrates) does not mean eating the whole loaf. You need to understand your body's needs and change your thinking about food so you can take charge of your eating.

An increase in calories, especially carbohydrates, is necessary to increase your metabolic rate. Most diets are low in carbohydrates which initiate immediate weight loss. It is the depletion of carbohydrate stores which results in water loss that makes the scale register weight loss. Eventually the incomplete breakdown of fat produces ketone bodies. This is a very unhealthy way of losing weight.[24] It is also very temporary, since rehydration occurs once carbohydrates are eaten again. An example of this would be to lose weight to get into that special dress for the wedding only to regain the weight (rehydrate) by eating some cake at the wedding. "I only have to look at cake and I gain weight," you say. In order to minimize the feelings of deprivation and to make healthy eating a life-style change it must be done gradually so there is no shock to your body.

HOW DIETS RULE YOU
• Diets decrease metabolism, slowing your motor down to a halt as you eat less and less to prevent weight gain.

• Diets foster poor eating habits which lead to periods of starving and binging.

59

• Diets decrease your self-esteem because the weight comes back and you feel that you are a failure. In this way your self-worth is tied to the number on the scale.

HEALTHY LIFE-STYLE PUTS YOU IN CHARGE

• **Stop dieting and get your metabolism moving again. Food of the proper types will get your system revved up again.**

• **Eating regularly and not starving yourself prevents overeating. If you know you can have it, the desire for it is less.**

• **Don't equate self-worth with the number on the scale. Focus on health rather than weight. Kick that scale into the garbage and take control of your health.**

DOES SLIMNESS EQUAL HEALTH?

According to Ellen Parham[25] a new set of goals and benefits for health can be defined.
• Relieve a health problem.
• Increase fitness and flexibility through exercise.
• Achieve a sense of control over your eating.
• Increase your self-esteem.
• Improve nutritive adequacy.
• Develop a family life-style that will reduce the risk of obesity for children and others.

Think about these alternatives. They will help you to be successful.

I think you will agree that slimness does not necessarily mean healthy. Many slim people compromise their health to retain their ideal figure. How do they do it?
• Are they starving and binging?
• Are they more preoccupied with food and weight?
• Is their life focused around food?
• Are they over-exercising?
• Are they happy with their lives and their bodies?
• Are they using cigarettes to control their weight?
• Do they get more colds; are they sick more frequently?

Dieting exacts its price. Protein breakdown results in breakdown of the immune system which makes you more susceptible to disease. The physical and mental stress of dieting add another stress to weaken the immune system. According to scientific studies, deficiencies of protein and some amino acids, the building blocks of protein, as well as vitamins A, E, B6, folate, zinc, iron, and copper are associated with reduced functioning of the immune system which wards off disease.[26]

Some research indicates that even mild upsets causing swings in daily mood can disturb the immune system. Since the immune system is the central link that controls disorders such as heart disease and cancer, upsetting this balance is not good for the body.

Many movie stars and models undereat and overexercise to maintain their figures. Since their careers are built on ideal shapes, they can't afford to lose them.

Cher exercises 2 hours or longer every day. She eats very little, but if she overeats or will be appearing in public, she increases her exercise up to 4 hours a day.

Kenny Rogers who has tried every diet without success had fat surgically removed from his stomach and chin. Dolly Parton, Jane Fonda, and Karen Carpenter suffered from anorexia nervosa. In fact, Karen Carpenter died in 1983 from a heart attack brought on by complications of this eating disorder.

Fluctuation in body weight due to yo-yo dieting is more harmful to your health than stabilizing at a higher weight.[27] It causes an increased risk for heart disease, gall stones, and high blood pressure. In the Framingham Heart Study, which monitored more than 5,000 people for 40 years the following was reported:

- people who lost 10 percent of their body weight had a 20 percent reduction in risk of heart disease.

- people who gained back 10 percent of body weight increased risk of heart disease to 30 percent.[28]

In other words, stabilizing at a higher weight is healthier (i.e. 20 percent increase in heart disease) than losing and then regaining weight (i.e. 30 percent

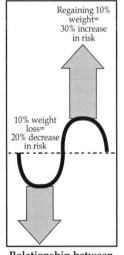

Regaining 10% weight= 30% increase in risk

10% weight loss= 20% decrease in risk

Relationship between weight loss/gain and the risk of heart disease increase in heart disease).[29] Genetically, if both parents are large, children have an 80 percent chance of being large. If one parent is large, children have a 50 percent chance of being large.

We are not all meant to be model size even though slim females and lean muscular models are paraded before us as ideals. In reality, there is no perfectly shaped person without the help of plastic surgery.

Three Main Body Types

Endomorph heavy build, rounded on all sides, shoulders often narrower than hips, higher percentage of body fat, often carried on the hips, waist, thighs, and buttocks; stocky individual with round body features, prominent abdominal viscera, large trunk and thighs, and tapering extremities.

Mesomorph broad shoulders and some narrowness in the rib cage, waist, and hips; weight concentrated in the upper body, giving them extra power and strength, more muscular than other body types, relatively predominant bony and muscular framework, strong physique.

Ectomorph tall, slim body, small-framed with narrow shoulders, often hips narrower than shoulders, low levels of body fat, low muscularity.

If you understand and appreciate your body you will be able to work with it, not against it. You cannot become another type. No matter how you starve yourself, your basic body shape will remain.

The HUGS™ program will allow you to work with your body and develop your full potential. It will show you a new way of thinking about yourself. Acknowledging 2 basic premises is crucial to allowing you to move forward in this program. You must accept yourself as you are and develop your potential and you must be convinced that diets don't work. Now you can forget past failures and move into a positive future. You're doing very well. Now, check the following chart to make sure you are ready to proceed.

Discuss with your family the philosophy of HUGS™

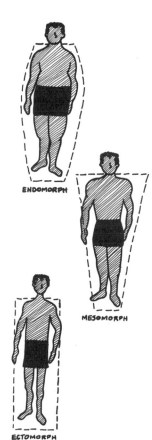

ENDOMORPH

MESOMORPH

ECTOMORPH

In order to make life-style changes you need to
- accept yourself as you are
- believe that diets do not work
- give up the past failures and move on to the present
- give up judging your self-worth by the number on the scale
- trust your ability to let go and relax and allow changes to happen naturally rather than forcing them; by letting go, you are better able to experience who you really are and to give yourself permission to develop and actualize who you might become
- care about yourself enough to listen to your internal hunger signals and your physical and psychological needs to guide you
- listen to your body with regard to food intake, physical activity and its intensity and benefits, as well as psychological needs to schedule special time for yourself
- begin to observe how dieters and nondieters handle situations differently, especially with regard to food.

so they do not sabotage your efforts. Otherwise if they think you are on a diet and do not understand the HUGS™ philosophy and catch you eating a piece of cake or some cookies they may try to make you feel guilty. This can lead you to eat more, since you are being robbed of the satisfaction from the piece that you ate. This can once again lead to "secret eating" which puts you right back into the diet mentality.

LIFE EXPECTANCY VERSUS HEALTH EXPECTANCY

My dentist does not practice HUGS™. He told me that he heard a renowned speaker say that losing weight to ideal body weight improves how long you live by only a few years. So what's the point of giving up those foods you like. "I want to live and I want to die happy," was my dentist's conclusion.

What he said is true up to a point. Achieving ideal weight for large persons, as a group, would gain an average of only 0.7 to 1.7 years for men, and 0.5 to 1.1 years for women. Further evidence suggests that lowering the risk factors of high blood pressure and high serum cholesterol to recommended levels would add 1.1 to 5.3 and 0.5 to 4.2 years, respectively, for men; 0.9 to 5.7 and 0.4 to 6.3 for women. Further evidence shows that male smokers, as a whole, would gain 2.3 years from quitting smoking; female smokers 2.8 years.[30] These projected gains from weight loss are minimal. So if this is the case, why are we as a society focusing on weight to begin with? Is doing the bare minimum in order to live longer the answer? What about quality of life?

Some studies indicate that 20 million Americans will be over the age of 85 by the year 2000. This may indicate their life expectancy but what about their health expectancy, which is a measure of their quality of life?

Health expectancy indicates how long you are likely to be healthy and active, rather than how many years you may live. Let's compare the health expectancies of two individuals who live to the same age. Person A smokes, is overweight, and has high cholesterol. This person develops heart disease at age 50, emphysema by age 60, and lung cancer at 75. The later years are filled with pain, mental depression, financial problems, and emotional isolation.

Person B does not smoke or have high cholesterol and is at a healthy weight. Because of hereditary factors, Person B develops heart disease diagnosed at 75. The later years for Person B are vital and fulfilling up until death.

Annual Restricted Activity Days

Chronic Disease vs Aging

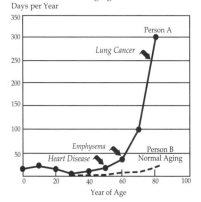

(from The National Centre for Health Statistics)

Giving up the foods you like is not where we're heading. My dentist was partly correct when he said "I eat what I want and enjoy it." HUGS™ wants you to do this. The difference is to retrain your taste buds so that you acquire a taste for less fattening foods. The roller coaster effect of eating perfectly and cutting out all fats even though you may enjoy these foods is not the answer. Such a drastic denial only leads to feelings of deprivation and cannot be maintained. Take it slowly and gradually for lasting effects.

"I can't wait till the fat substitute gets into more products. Fat is the culprit in obesity, but I like the taste of high fat foods."

Fat substitutes that my dentist thinks will be the answer to the fat problem, won't help him to acquire a taste for less fattening foods. Just as sugar substitutes don't make a person lose the taste for sweets. My dentist's theory is that sugar substitutes caused everyone to indulge in more fats. Was it that the sugar substitutes were not satisfying enough? The incidence of obesity has not decreased.

Since fat-substitute products will have few calories we probably will eat more of them. But are we solving the basic problem or are we fooling ourselves into believing that we are actually improving our health?

It's human nature to want instant gratification, instant success. Why bother trying to modify eating habits when a fat substitute will do the trick? The answer is healthy living. It's the long term that's important.

Being healthy is the key. The proper weight for each individual which is called the setpoint, should be the weight focus for health. *Listen to your body.* It will guide you to the right weight for you. Accept yourself as you are. It's fun to be you. You don't have to try to remake yourself according to someone else's fantasy.

Let's start anew by having an open mind and trying to fine-tune our present life-style and grab onto a healthier one. Make mini-changes one day at a time. The "internal quick fix" of healthy living is one that will "kick your mind into gear" about the exciting possibilities of the healthy living life-style.

> **When preparing for the later years, investing in your health now may be as important as investing your money for retirement.**

3
Physical Activity for Fun

Exercise regularly at your own level with an activity you enjoy.

The entire principle of HUGS™ is focused on life-style change that you allow to happen naturally. In order to make your activity level a life-style change, it must be increased gradually. It's important to find an activity that you truly enjoy so you feel you are doing it for yourself, not because you have to do it. For this to happen, it is necessary to understand the principles of fitness in relation to HUGS™.

Part of the balance sought in life-style change is that daily physical activity is included. This refers to the normal day-to-day movement of a moderately active person going about the business of living. Called "active living," it involves such activities as getting up, getting dressed, working, lifting things, putting them down, walking around, doing housework, going out in the evening, etc. Active living burns 25 percent of your total calories if you are moderately active. However, most people are not moderately active and when they do not reach their calorie burning potential they retain the calories and accumulate fat.

New from the exercise industry.

Buy now, lose later.

In the past, exercise was viewed as a form of punishment rather than reward. Push-ups or running around the block were activities forced on you if you were bad. Aerobics was also hard work. Each evening you went to the fitness studio, and put up with the hour of pain. No gain without pain, you thought. You continued out of perseverance or after a few months gave it up, feeling that exercise was not for you.

My own experience attending regular aerobic classes was that I felt exhausted. I was often dizzy and in pain, but I thought this was a normal reaction and I wanted to be in shape. But when the soreness and stiffness persisted I decided to give up on aerobics.

A few years later, with new knowledge and a new attitude, I tackled other types of physical activity. It's now 3 years later and I enjoy exercising, mainly walking, cross-country skiing, and cycling. Now I teach HUGS™ aerobic classes at a lower intensity that emphasize fun.

The HUGS™ concept is back-to-basics active living which is a self-paced, integrated activity. It refers to working out in more natural surroundings, such as your garden, a playground, or skating rink. It involves natural movements used in everyday living. Sustained, strenuous exercise is now thought to be unnecessary according to Canadian fitness experts. *You need only take the equivalent of a few brisk walks weekly to increase your odds of living a long and healthy life.*

> **Active living refers to enjoying physical activity and learning how to integrate it into your daily life.**

Living actively rewards you twice: immediately, in the pleasure of doing the activity, and over time, through improved health, well-being, and quality of life. Moving the way you like to move is good for you. It's the moving that counts.

Active living refers to enjoying physical activity and learning how to integrate it into your daily life. This refining process indicates that longevity is enhanced through any kind of activity and that people can be fit by doing ordinary, useful activities whether it is shingling your roof, cleaning your bathroom, or working in the yard.

You can pursue this active living at work as well. Take the stairs instead of the elevator; put a pair of walking shoes in your car and take a walk if you're early for an appointment; walk around the mall after lunch before returning to work; park your car a distance away from your workplace so that you can enjoy a short walk before the day's activities. All of these life-style moves do not even take extra time; rather they give you time. These changes get you moving and keep you moving. This leads to more energy and a healthier and longer lifespan.

Dependence on fitness classes or other structured group experiences for physical activity to get fit results in the activity of the participation decreasing or stopping once you move out of the activity structure. It's the same kind of dependence that people place on a diet. They follow the diet as long as they are involved in a group situation to reinforce and encourage. They go off the diet as soon as they stop attending classes. When the reason for doing exercise is weight loss and not fun, people find excuses not to go to classes. The focus of exercise should be to encourage the development of the individuals so that they find active living the answer to exercise needs.

Active living is an entirely different way to view activity. It promotes enjoyment of life and the awareness of what is going on around you. The main focus is to make choices for yourself, based on what you want and enjoy. Then you will find new excitement in activity and it will become a pleasurable part of your life.

If you listen to your body and tune into your body's needs you will know what intensity of activity you should follow.

MYTHS OF EXERCISING
Myth 1: No pain, no gain

Painful, intense exercising will not lead to life-style change. Continued discomfort will discourage you from continuing the exercise. In fact, painful exercise can damage your body.

New fitness information emphasizes *train but not strain*. The old pain-for-gain thinking destroys the sense of fun and enjoyment and does not fit into your new active life-style.

Forget the old way, "I went for a walk to the donut shop where I can have one as my reward," or "I ate a piece of cake, so I'll have to go for a walk to wear it off." Activity is for pleasure which in itself is the reward. The old "calories taken in versus calories used up" attitude traps you in the diet mentality of counting calories.

Calories Taken In		Exercise needed to use up calories		
		WALKING	BICYCLING	RUNNING
Average cake donut	150 calories	29 min.	18 min.	8 min.
1 slice cheesecake	260 calories	50 min.	32 min.	13 min.
1/6 of 2-crust fruit pie	410 calories	79 min.	50 min.	21 min.

69

Finally, you ask yourself whether exercise is really worth the effort. You walk a half hour to the donut shop so that you have used up enough calories to reward yourself with a small cake donut. The sense of discouragement that develops further extracts your energy because of the poor attitude towards exercise that results.

Normal glycogen (carbohydrates) stores provide fuel for about 2 hours of moderate-intensity exercise.[1] Intense exercise, in which you work at over 75 percent of your maximum aerobic capacity, can deplete the working muscles' glycogen reserves in as little as an hour or two, depending on how fit you are and on your prior glycogen reserves.[2]

The body also burns fat for energy, but not as efficiently. As muscle glycogen is depleted, the liver contributes some of its reserves, but if you continue to exercise intensely, the liver may be unable to keep pace, and you may feel the effects of a sharp drop in blood sugar. If this happens, your muscles simply "give out" and you experience extreme exhaustion. At the same time the glucose deprivation in your brain and nervous system may make you confused or disoriented.[3] The result of a high-intensity workout may leave you feeling exhausted and famished. It is common in such a situation to overeat to replenish glucose stores.

For example, if you put the resistance up on an exercise bicycle to get a better workout this can result in increased stress not only on the knee joints but also on the soles of the feet. Pedaling hard with few revolutions per minute can make it difficult for oxygen to reach the muscles, especially if you are not a conditioned cyclist. In addition, increased metabolic demands may promote a build-up of lactic acid, a factor in muscle pain and fatigue. Draining your energy will not help you establish a better life-style.

Activity could be part of your life-style change and not just the means to losing weight. Increasing the physical activity until you lose the weight is parallel to going on a diet until you lose the weight. If a life-style change isn't in place and the enjoyment isn't

70

there, you will stop exercising and go off the diet. The result is short-term success and a sense of failure when the weight returns.

Myth 2: Exercising only until you lose weight
"I'm going to the fitness class 6 times a week and I'm losing inches. I can't wait till I reach my goal weight so that I can stop exercising." Unfortunately this person found exercising stressful and didn't know that there is evidence that if you start and stop exercise, you can increase body weight. In fact, animal studies have shown that cessation of exercise can lead to increased body fat later. So if you treat exercise only as a method to lose weight you are actually making your body fatter.

Studies have shown that making activity part of your life-style change is more effective for permanent weight loss in the long run. Gradual increase in activity that becomes ingrained as part of your routine is the way to go. Lower intensity, longer duration types of activity make the activities more likely to become part of your life-style. The activities will eventually become habit, but it will take time. *Enjoying the process eliminates the desire to stop.*

Incorporating activity into your life-style means adding it into your daily routine whenever possible. For example, if you have a half hour to spare between appointments why not go for a walk in the area? Be prepared for these opportunities by carrying some comfortable shoes in your car.

In order to allow yourself to "get hooked" on exercise, be aware of how you feel and how your body reacts before and after exercising. After exercising regularly (i.e. every second day) for a few weeks, try skipping a week and find out if you miss it. The feeling of energy, vitality, and exhilaration that you get from activity may make you want to continue. The endorphins, a chemical released while exercising, serve as a natural tranquilizer that soothes both the body and mind. Once you experience the internal benefits of activity, it is difficult to do without it.

71

Myth 3: Exercising vigorously burns more fat

Higher intensity activity burns more carbohydrates rather than fat.[4] In the first 12 to 30 minutes of activity, you use up mainly carbohydrates as your fuel source.[5,6] This means that your body will be drawing from the carbohydrate stores in your liver (glycogen stores). Engaging in higher intensity activity such as jogging or running is hard on the knees and does not build up endurance if you continue the jogging for only a short period of time. With vigorous exercise you are not giving your body a chance to switch over to using more fat as the fuel source. This occurs only after about 30 minutes of activity.

As you become more fit, the training effect will allow you to increase the use of fat as a fuel source.[7] Running may wear off the calories more quickly and for this reason burn more total fat. However, working at this higher intensity level may reduce the duration of the activity. In this way, the benefits of sustained activity are lost.[8]

People who do aerobics at a higher intensity level are often starved after a workout. They may have burned more total calories which used up some of their carbohydrate stores and caused some burning of fat as their fuel source. But because of their hunger and eating after the workout they replenished their glycogen stores and minimized the burning of fat.

> **The lesson here is that you can**
> - work at a level that is comfortable for you where you can sustain the activity for a longer period of time rather than engage in short bursts of activity;
> - increase your intensity gradually as you become more fit;
> - use an activity that you enjoy that leaves you feeling energized not exhausted, and tune into how you feel before and after your activity with regard to energy level and appetite control; and
> - work at a level that controls your appetite rather than leaves you feeling famished. (Even if you do eat a little more due to activity, there will still be a net loss of energy expended. Remember to replenish your fluids first to rehydrate any fluid lost. You may actually be thirsty and not hungry.)

Karen, her mother, and her sister went for a walk. The mother walked with her arms flinging, racing to get to her destination. "It doesn't do any good unless you walk briskly," she said, as she huffed and puffed to keep her pace. "I want to lose 5 pounds by next week." At the end she was exhausted and had not enjoyed the walk or the scenery. Her focus was the destination, not the journey.

Karen walked at a rate comfortable to her, and was still able to talk to her sister. Her heart rate was going up, but not racing, so she felt both physically and psychologically refreshed at the end of the walk. In fact, she enjoyed it so much that she made this a habit. Each time she walked, it became easier to walk slightly more quickly and still feel comfortable. She was gradually becoming more fit and she reveled in the experience.

Like many people coming into the HUGS™ program, Janice was jogging regularly to lose weight. She felt tired because jogging was hard on her body. She was thrilled to hear that walking was more effective for weight loss due to its lower intensity and she enjoyed the activity much more. She noted the difference in the effectiveness of walking in helping her to stabilize her weight.

Another client commented, "I tried to fit jogging in. What a relief to find I can enjoy walking at lunch with a friend and it's okay!"

> **Comparison of impact forces being generated and delivered to the lower body**
> WALKING – one times your body weight
> RUNNING – 3 times your body weight
> JUMPING – up to 10 times your body weight

Walking at a comfortable speed may increase the heart rate 40 to 50 percent above the normal heart rate. This is more than enough to stimulate the lungs and heart and increase oxygen uptake and delivery to all body tissues. According to experts in the field of exercise physiology, 2-1/2 miles (4 km) of walking will produce the same aerobic benefits as 5 miles (8 km) of bicycling, 1/4 mile (.4 km) of swimming, or 1 mile (1.6 km) of running.

It is interesting to note that it is often Type A personalities—the hard-working, aggressive, competitive individuals — who choose jogging or competitive sports because they think that aggressive activities will lessen their chance of heart disease. However, instead of running off their aggression and tension, they actually run into it and increase their chances of developing heart disease above the 25 percent chance they already have due to their personality type.

Myth 4: Activity burns only calories

Regular activity provides more benefits to your health than simply burning calories. It revs up your system from 4 to 6 hours after the completion of the activity.[9] It gives you the energy to meet everyday and emergency requirements, and to effectively use and enjoy leisure time. It is not how many calories you use up during the activity but how much you increase your metabolic rate and keep it going at a faster rate even when the activity is completed. This is why regular activity as part of your life-style is important.

For example, if you exercise from 8:00 to 8:30 in the morning, your body will continue to burn calories at a faster rate than if you had not participated in the exercise program. The increase in metabolic rate is caused by the demand for energy for muscle building and repair resulting from exercise, providing that the exercise is of an appropriate intensity and duration. If you work at the level that is comfortable for you it will allow activity to control rather than increase your appetite.

Regular activity gives you sustained energy

Gradually increase your activity so that you can participate in the activity at least every second day in order to derive the benefit of the training effect. Start more slowly if you wish. As the activity becomes a life-style change, you will eventually choose to do it more frequently. *Let it happen naturally.*

THE PERKS OF PHYSICAL ACTIVITY
Exercise and obesity

According to experts, exercise may carry important benefits for the large person even in the absence of weight loss. In sufficient amounts, physical activity

> If you think it is difficult to take time for an activity in terms of a half hour off from your daily routine, keep in mind that you will get back that time and more in terms of your increased efficiency and energy level which will allow you to accomplish more in less time.

74

can improve nearly every ill consequence of obesity.[10,11]

Improved self-concept

Being fat in a weight-conscious society can undermine self-esteem. Yet some studies have shown that large men and women in physical training programs exhibit marked improvement in self-satisfaction, self-acceptance, and a sense of personal worth. A Harris poll in 1979 found that physically active people reported more self-confidence, a better self-image, and greater psychological well-being than inactive people.

Control over one's life — the ability to make choices — is vital for a positive self-image and a feeling of personal power. A renewed sense of control is expressed after a period of regular activity, which facilitates the ability to resolve problems of personal dissatisfaction and poor body image.

The body adapts to the demands of physical exertion by increasing muscular strength and endurance, whereas long periods of food restriction produce diminishing returns, and increase both physical and psychological stress. During periods of increased stress, feelings of lethargy often result with the release of adrenalin and cortisol, both stress-related hormones. These hormones are metabolized by exercise, which decreases their undesired effect. As well long-term activities result in the secretion of endorphins by the brain. These small, morphine-like substances can produce a feeling of exhilaration, which reduces stress and, through a complex process, may even reduce fat storage.

The improved self-concept and sense of accomplishment resulting from exercise may be instrumental in the development of long-term life-style changes that lead to permanent weight control and a healthier life. For health, walk tall with shoulders back, pelvis forward and bum tucked in. *For health, walk like a tiger with confidence.*

Depresses mood swings

During physical activity, the release of endorphins acts as a pain killer and tranquilizer making you feel more relaxed. Eating and laughter can also release

> Tune into how you feel before and after physical activity.

75

this chemical. Changing your attitude and your life-style by adopting a more light-hearted approach can make you happier and healthier. The same temporary "high" that you get from eating can be transferred to a more sustained "high" from activity.

Make that special time for yourself
Physical activity can serve as a release valve for stress and give you the time to think things through.

Improve body image and self-esteem
Roz went tobogganing with her sister, niece, and nephew. She had to run after the toboggan. While she was running her niece and nephew called out, "Come on Auntie, you can do it, you're a HUGS™ lady." She found that she was able to run after the toboggan without being "pooped" or totally out of breath. What an accomplishment! With HUGS™ life-style change you will notice health benefits within a few months and feel a sense of accomplishment. The outward energy through activity can help you to channel that energy inward to deal with the inner problems.

Physical activity regulates appetite
Sedentary people who do little activity may overeat because their appetite control mechanism is not functioning properly. The stomach is not sending the signal to the brain that they are full when they are full. Exercise at a proper intensity puts this back in balance.

"New attitude" in fitness — focus on the process of enjoyment, not the end result.

Deanna was tuned into her body with regard to food and ate till she was satisfied; she felt that she was not overeating. If her eyes were bigger than her stomach and she overloaded her plate, she would eat till full, and then leave the rest on her plate. This was quite an accomplishment for her. She had lost weight and it had stabilized. But even though she was following her internal hunger signals, she seemed to be gaining back some weight.

In this case, she was no longer active and tended to be in a constant "rush" with her new job. Some of this rushed feeling transferred to her eating and she was able to eat more before her stomach signaled her

76

brain that she was full. Without activity, her appetite control mechanism was not working properly and so she may have been taking in more quantities of food before she was signaled to be satisfied. Keep in mind that activity, done at an intensity appropriate for you, can regulate your appetite.

Physical activity keeps you fit
Activity improves joint problems and decreases muscle cramps. Drinking sufficient water also helps to lessen muscle cramps.

Physical activity lowers blood pressure
Blood pressure is the force of blood pushing against the walls of the arteries as it flows through them. Physical activity lowers blood pressure in 3 ways. First, it aids in the loss of body fat. For every extra pound of body fat you need an extra mile of blood vessels to nourish it. Second, it tones the blood vessels to make them more elastic. Third, exercise reduces the deposition of fat on the artery walls, preventing the opening from becoming smaller. A larger opening requires less pressure against the artery walls.

The bonus is that as you become more fit, your heart becomes stronger. With each contraction, it pushes more blood to the rest of the body.

Physical activity lowers blood sugar level
With exercise the immediate rise in blood sugar after a meal is less pronounced, and sugar is released in smaller doses. This is accomplished by increased sensitivity to the receptors of the cells permitting the insulin to allow blood sugar to enter cells more readily. The curve is flatter (not as steep) and therefore the blood sugar is released into the bloodstream at a slower, more gradual rate, providing a more steady supply of energy.

Eating properly as HUGS™ defines it, coupled with activity, allows you to feel more energetic. This is partly due to blood sugar control. Even if you do not have diabetes, poor eating habits may lead to erratic blood sugar control. For example, 24-year-old Brenda was not overweight but had poor, erratic eating

77

habits. She was always tired and lived on cake and little food. Blood tests indicated that Brenda had hypoglycemia (low blood sugar level).

When Brenda established a regular eating pattern balancing both carbohydrate and protein sources, she had the energy to become more active, which in turn, gave her more energy. She became more efficient and productive. It's a matter of balance!

Physical activity improves circulation
Physcial activity adds to an increased energy level as oxygen and nutrients are carried throughout the body more efficiently.

Physical activity improves digestion
You will find that constipation decreases as the natural movement of the intestine is improved.

Myth 5: The same exercise every day is necessary
Some people think that doing the same type of exercise activity every day is necessary. Rather, cross-training for a more balanced body is preferable. Alternating the type of activities done on a daily basis gives specific muscles a chance to relax. For example, walking on one day and rowing another day uses different muscles. However, activities such as cross-country skiing use the entire body. Cross-training allows you to exercise more muscle groups than a single activity would do. For instance, cycling builds your lower body, and rowing works your upper body, so alternating them can help give you the benefits of both while you build aerobic endurance. It also minimizes the stress felt from always using the same muscles and joints.

Allowing your muscles to rest and using other muscles reduces the risk of injury. Better muscle balance is also achieved. For example, walking or running strengthens the hamstring muscles (located at the rear of the thigh) more than it does the quadriceps at the front of the thigh. This muscle imbalance may lead to injury. By adding cycling on alternate days (which strengthens the quadriceps) you can work complementary muscle groups in your legs and thus achieve better muscle balance.[12]

78

Vary the types of exercise you do. People in long-term aerobic programs strengthen their hearts, and typically build up their leg muscles, but may lose muscle mass in their upper body. To balance your exercise program, use your own body weight as resistance in push-ups, sit-ups, and pull-ups. There's no set amount of weight you should lift and no standard against which you should measure yourself: *the goal is to work out according to your capabilities.*[13]

Myth 6: Eat little, exercise a lot for weight loss

The type of the activity rather than the amount of activity is what counts. Restrictive eating (dieting) combined with frequent physical activity will cause you to drain your protein or muscle tissue if insufficient carbohydrates are consumed.

If your calorie consumption is too low to supply your energy needs, your body then breaks down valuable protein tissue to use for energy. With the breakdown of protein, your metabolic rate is further decreased.

Many diets are low in carbohydrates and if you remember that regardless of the intensity of the activity, in the first 30 minutes, carbohydrates are the main fuel source, you will need them for fuel. Carbohydrates break down into glucose, which is your energy source for the first half hour of activity. If insufficient breads, cereals, potatoes, rice, and pasta are consumed muscle protein will be broken down into glucose.[14] *Exercise preserves lean muscle tissue only if sufficient calories are consumed, including carbohydrates.*[15]

Between the ages of 30 and 70 the average person loses 30 to 40 percent of the body's muscle mass. Exercise can retard these changes by as long as 20 years.[16]

Myth 7: Exercise increases appetite

Exercising at a higher intensity depletes your glycogen stores faster, leaving you with a lower blood sugar level. The result is that instead of activity controlling your appetite, it may actually increase it. Lower intensity activity will draw less from your

79

glycogen stores and allow you to sustain the activity for a longer period of time. *Tune into your body and decide on the level that is right for you.* You could increase your heart rate and still be able to carry on a conversation with a friend. Putting an extra strain on your body with stressful activity gives no added benefit. You can feel energized, not exhausted after exercise, and not feel famished.

> **Exercise for energy, not exhaustion.**

Myth 8: Exercise is boring

Taking on an exercise program and giving it up just as quickly produces the same short-term gain as a quick weight loss diet. The extra physical strain that comes from exercising above your capacity or eating below your basic needs leaves you in a weakened condition.

Having fun with activity will ensure that you are doing what your body can endure. Choose something you enjoy and learn to work at your own level. If you do not like aerobics, find a program or activity that interests you. Don't participate only because your best friend is doing it.

Exercise is a skill. Once developed it is difficult to do without it. It becomes part of you and when it's fun it's something that you look forward to. As June stated, "I discovered swimming and it's great. I feel so invigorated."

A positive attitude is also necessary. Once out for a Sunday cross-country ski trip, I had to go down a small hill. I froze. I couldn't face this challenge. In my mind, I felt that I could not do it, and so the self-fulfilling prophecy came true as I went down the hill on my bum. I didn't even give myself a chance to fall down or fail. I got it over with, not allowing myself to experience the exhilaration of trying.

Contemplating this and becoming more comfortable with skiing, I tried to implant a positive "I-can-do-it" attitude. I did it gradually, stopping partway to decrease my fear of speed. I fell from time to time but I also made more hills with my skis in place. Best of all I allowed myself to enjoy the whole experience.

Focusing on the fun and the improvement of self

80

rather than on the competition can keep you going. So many of us fail because we feel we aren't good enough to compete, so we don't exercise at all. If you have a positive attitude and find an activity that you enjoy, you will keep coming back.

Kevin was anxious every time he had to play baseball. His father always concentrated on winning. Eventually Kevin found excuses to stop playing and began watching more television. At least this was non-threatening. On the other hand, Tim's father's attitude towards fitness emphasized fun. He practised with his son so that he would feel more confident with the ball. The sport became an enjoyable event that kept him active, and Tim continued to include activity as part of his everyday activity as he got older.

Myth 9: Exercise plus dieting increases metabolic rate

Physical activity increases the metabolic rate about 10 percent which may offset some of the 15 to 30 percent decrease in metabolic rate when dieting. However, the net decrease in metabolic rate is still 5 to 20 percent.[17,18] The answer of course is to stop dieting. Rather, focus on "eating healthier" by gradually changing the type of foods you are consuming. There may not be a great difference in the total number of calories eaten but the type of calories will change, and this is important. By avoiding a marked drop in caloric intake your body will have a chance to adjust to the gradual change. Gradual is the key. Then the body won't be fooled into dropping the metabolic rate to protect you from starvation since you are not drastically cutting calories but maintaining them at close to the original level.

Initially when teaching the HUGS™ program, I noticed that clients dropped the fat content of their meals quickly when they realized that it was these calories that contributed to weight gain (more about this in Chapters 4 and 5). Many lost weight more quickly but did not give their systems a chance to adjust either physically (with regard to metabolic rate) or psychologically (change in taste) to the sudden change. If you do this the result is quicker

> Remember, it is not the quantity but the types of foods consumed that contribute to weight gain.

"I can't go out for a walk today because I didn't bring my walking shoes and I only have 20 minutes to walk instead of the usual 45 minutes. Can't get my heart rate up, so it's not worth it."

It is not what you weigh that counts, but how much of the weight is fat.

weight loss which inevitably results in quicker weight gain.

Escape from the all-or-nothing mentality.

Myth 10: Exercise causes you to lose weight on the scale

Without activity, only 50 percent of weight lost is fat. Muscle cannot be stored in a dry form; it is stored with water. This makes muscle weigh more than fat.

Therefore, an increase in muscle mass may mean inches lost, but not necessarily weight lost. This is another indication of why the scales do not count.

An increase in muscle mass results in an increase in metabolic rate. Muscle tissue burns more calories at rest than fat does. Men, whose body composition consists of more muscle mass, burn more calories at rest. Frequent dieting can result in weight loss, including muscle mass. Unfortunately, once the weight is regained, it is mostly fat. Exercise provides an opportunity to rebuild muscle tissue that is vital to your health and well-being.

Myth 11: Sit-ups get rid of fat in the stomach area

Spot reducing tones, but it does not get rid of fat in the area you are working on. Results from new products that claim to do this are only temporary. The gut buster, toning clinics, and new gadgets to rid you of that paunch are not the answer.

These fads in the exercise field are comparable to fad diets. They work temporarily, and some may shed inches, but often at the expense of health. Poor techniques may result in back problems. Fat loss does not occur. These methods merely tone by making muscles more taut and helping with body alignment. They certainly do not improve your health or make you fitter.

Body builders work out with weights. They want to display muscle tone but since abdominal muscles, for example, are beneath fat they must get rid of the fat. The body builder or weight trainer may look fit but his endurance may be poor. In order for the weight trainer to lift weights, he needs the stamina that comes from improving heart-lung functions of the cardiovascular system. The weight lifter may be strong, but does he exude inner health?

Doing sit-ups helps with alignment and toning only by making muscles tighter. While strong abdominal muscles provide better support for the back, in order to get rid of the fat, some form of aerobic activity is necessary. Lifting weights can help to increase muscle mass which indirectly will increase metabolic rate due to the change in body composition. However, for sustained energy and fat loss to occur, aerobic activity is the answer. Aim for the balance in different types of activity to achieve the right combination for you!

Myth 12: Exercise takes time
If you make physical activity important enough in your life to give it priority, the regular activity will give you the added benefit of increased energy level and improved efficiency. By accomplishing tasks in less time, exercise actually gives you time back, rather than taking time away from your daily routine.

HOW TO MAKE AN EXERCISE PROGRAM WORK FOR YOU
If you exercise consistently and regularly at a lower intensity level you will develop a training effect. The result is an increased capacity to work with less effort due to the glycogen sparing effect of using more fat as the fuel source. If you do this you will not get tired as quickly because you preserve carbohydrate stores that supply you with continued energy.

However, it is important to keep up the exercise. *This adaptation or training effect will be lost within 3 or more days of inactivity.*[19]

Exercising at too high a level for your body to feel comfortable can result in heavier breathing or feeling out of breath. This indicates that you are no longer using oxygen, and are switching over to anaerobic activity. This leads to a build-up of lactic acid causing muscle fatigue. There is absolutely no advantage to pushing yourself to work at this high level.

> When doing sit-ups or any other type of mat exercise, breathe out as you are doing the work. With sit-ups, that means breathing out as you are coming up.

" IT'S BEAUTIFUL!
I DIDN'T NEED
RUNNERS AFTER ALL!"

Work on changing those past negative experiences that you may have had with exercising into positive activities that are enjoyable, interesting, safe, and meaningful to you. To keep the activity you choose safe, it is important to work in a warm-up, aerobic, and cool-down routine, even for walking.

Exercise for energy, not exhaustion. If you are tired after exercising and sore, you are exercising at too high a level.	Pay attention to your body. Do you feel your heart rate increasing, yet you can still carry on a conversation? This is the level that is right for you.

**Component
WARM-UP**

Warming up your body can be compared to warming up the engine of your car. If you turn on the ignition and don't take time to warm it up

Purpose
• **to stretch, loosen up,** and relax muscles
• **to prevent injury**
• **to stimulate circulation**
• **to prepare you physically and psychologically for the workout**

*Duration
5 - 10 min.*

on a cold day, you may do some harm to the engine. Usually the car tells you to take a little longer to warm it up by stalling as you start to drive. If you do not take the time to warm up your body, you may harm it as well. Walking slowly, doing some stretches to prepare our muscles, or partaking in the activity of your choice at a slower pace warms up our body.

I like the game of tennis. I used to go on the court and start to play vigorously almost right away, not having the patience to take the time to warm up. I ended up running for the ball a lot and was not systematic in my approach. These days, I warm up my muscles first by doing a few shoulder rolls, stretching out my calves, bouncing the ball against my racket, then rallying slowly at first. I am taking it slowly, gradually, and building up to a level that is comfortable for me.

Physical
Activity
or Fun

Warm-up ⟶ **Aerobic Exercises** ⟶ **Cool-Down**

Keep intensity up for
20 minutes of activity!

Gradually
speed-up
activity

Gradually
slow down
activity

Before Each Activitiy:
1. Walk, cycle, or march on a spot at a pace comfortable to you for about 5-10 minutes.
2. To prepare yourself and help protect yourself from injury, do the

EASY WARM-UP EXERCISES.

After Each Activity:
1. To prevent the possibility of sore muscles later on, repeat the warm-up activity and exercises and add the

COOL-OFF STRETCHES.

• Hold each exercise /stretch for 15-20 seconds.	• Do each exercise /stretch 2 times for warm-up & 2 times for cool-off.	• Keep stretching movements slow and even, do not bounce	• To keep strain off back muscles, press hips forward in all excercises.	• The greatest gains in flexibility are possible during cool-down.

━━━━━ **WARM -UP** ━━━━━

• Hip Flex	• Reach Up	• Lunge	• Calf Stretch	• Achilles Stretch
tilt pelvis/hips forward, slightly drop by bending knee of back leg.	knees slightly bent, reach up and slightly over.	lean hands on knee, leg bent 90 degrees, toes, heel, and knee of bent leg lined up.	lean against wall or steady object: back leg extended, in line with body.	same as Calf Stretch except back leg slightly bent.

• Hamstrings	OR place leg on	• Thigh/Quads	OR sit on edge of	• BREATHE DEEP
toes up, hands and weight on bent knee, lean forward slightly,	steady support with knee sligthtly bent, lean forward and reach from hips.	hold onto steady object, hold ankle of opposite leg back and up, sligthly bend other leg,	chair, lower knee towards floor, and press it back.	AND FEEL GOOD

━━━━━ **COOL-OFF** ━━━━━

• Reverse Hurdle	• Reach Down	• Hug	and swing arms	• Relax
rest sole of foot on thigh, other leg straight, bend from hips and reach forward.	reach down back, gently press elbow down with other hand.	hug yourself	comfortably back.	gently pull knee towards chest.

used with permission of the Manitoba Fitness Directorate

My tennis game has improved because my body is more focused on what I am doing. Instead of rushing to get the ball and stopping cold, and in many cases missing it, I pace myself better and have more rhythm to my steps. I also focus on the ball and what I am doing which helps improve my game. I can now take this more methodical approach because I have the energy to think clearly. I am no longer trying to wear myself out in the first few minutes. Best of all, I enjoy tennis more as well as the process of gradually improving.

Component
AEROBIC PORTION

An aerobic activity is any exercise that increases the body's intake and use of oxygen. The exercise does this by increasing the heartbeat, within

Purpose	Duration
• improve heart-lung function (cardiovascular benefits)	maintain intensity for 20 min. of activity

prudent limits, and improving the heart-lung action. The adequacy of your oxygen supply depends on how much you take in by breathing, and how efficiently the blood distributes it throughout the body. To be aerobic, exercise must be active and sustained, enough to cause you to breathe more deeply and more often. This will increase your heart rate, causing more efficient blood circulation.

In the target heart rate zone this is presented as the 65 to 70 percent range where maximum heart rate is calculated by using the following formula: 220 minus person's age.

For example, for a 45-year-old woman, the maximum heart rate is equal to 220 - 45 = 175. 65% of 175 = 114 beats/min. (.65 x 175) = 19 beats/10 sec. This gives the range of 65 percent of maximum heart rate at which this woman needs to be working when in the aerobic zone. This range will allow enjoyment of the activity while participating in it, and will allow the activity to be sustained in order to derive the benefits from it.

If you aim, with your aerobic exercise program, to be slightly to moderately out of breath, the benefits are that you will burn more fat as a fuel source, you will have the ability to carry on the activity for a longer period of time, and your cardiovascular system will work better to make you more fit as well.

Your heart is a muscle. When you work it you strengthen it. With a strengthened heart, each contraction pumps more blood throughout the body thus making it more efficient. With efficiency, your heart does not have to work as hard to achieve the same effect. Compare the effort it takes to walk up 2 or 3 flights before and after 3 months of training. As you become more fit, your heart rate at rest in the morning will be lower because your heart will not have to work as hard to achieve the same effect.

AGE	Target Heart Rate Zone
20	22 - 23 beats/10 sec.
30	20 - 22 beats/10 sec.
40	19 - 21 beats/10 sec.
50	18 - 20 beats/10 sec.
60	17 - 19 beats/10 sec.
70	16 - 18 beats/10 sec.

The purpose of including target heart rate zones here is merely to familiarize you with them. You will see them in fitness clubs; however, *the HUGS™ program is related to fitness and life-style rather than to a number on the chart.* Learn to tune into working at the level where you feel your heart rate coming up, but are still able to carry on a conversation. This is the intensity for you. Aim for feeling energized rather than exhausted at the end of your fitness break. Including warm-ups and cool-downs, listening to your body, and participating in an activity that you enjoy will help you to achieve this goal.

BEFORE

AFTER

Component
COOL-DOWN

Once again compare your body to a car. When you are driving quickly at 60 miles (100 km) per hour and you are coming to a traffic light, you slow down

Purpose	Duration
• to allow heart rate to gradually return to normal • to stretch and relax all body muscles • to reduce the chance of pain or injury to muscles • to prevent the possibility of sore muscles later on	5 –10 min.

gradually rather than slam on the brake. The same applies to your body. You don't want to get going at full speed and then come to an abrupt stop.

The result will be fatigue and sore muscles the next

day. After exercise your muscles are warm. It's a perfect time to stretch them out and increase your flexibility. Cooling down may involve working the same large muscle groups as you did for the warm-up, walking slowly, or partaking in the activity slowly. Going full speed to come home and flop in the chair is not enforcing a life-style change. If you make it fun and enjoyable, you will derive more energy from the activity. *Listen to your body!*

Any of these different activities will help you make fitness into a life-style change that you can enjoy for a lifetime.

CYCLING Work up a faster cycling rate and heart rate without the tension on the bike. Using the tension will work your leg muscles but you won't derive the aerobic benefit. Increasing the tension on the bicycle will also tire your legs more quickly so that you may not be able to sustain the activity over the required period of time.

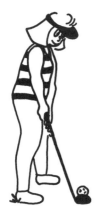

GOLF Walking around the course rather than using the motorized cart is beneficial. Formerly, it was thought that this type of activity was "stop and go" and would not allow your heart rate to stay in the target heart rate zone for the required period of time to derive the cardiovascular benefit. But the aim of a more active life-style is achieved with this activity. It also creates a good balance in life-style.

ROWING This activity uses the arm muscles and is a good complement to walking. Be gradual and consistent rather than racing and then doing nothing. Pace yourself.

TENNIS The aerobic benefit can be derived from this activity if you pace yourself rather than undergoing the more fanatic "stop and go" method of playing tennis.

AEROBICS For maximum benefit find a fitness routine that incorporates life-style moves and fun. Be sure to include warm-up, aerobic, and cool-down in the routine. Many routines also include a mat portion that helps you with strength and flexibility. Ensure that the atmosphere allows you to work at the level at which you feel comfortable and that you do not come away feeling sore or stiff.

Safe techniques are crucial so that you do not injure your body. HUGS™ has a fitness video specifically geared to persons who are not used to regular activity and aimed at fun. These life-style moves can help you with your everyday life. The safe techniques are designed to reduce the chance of injury. For more help in this area, see the order form at the end of this book.

CROSS-COUNTRY SKIING This is an all-round activity. Warm up by doing a few stretches. Start slowly, then gradually work up to a faster pace that you can continue for a period of time. Gradually slow down during the last 5 to 10 minutes of skiing.

WALKING The best and safest exercise for people of any age is walking. It is
• safe and efficient,
• can be followed throughout life,
• strengthens bones and organs including the heart,
• improves many body functions especially blood circulation, digestion, and elimination (stimulates contractions of the intestine, helping to push food through),
• lubricates the joints, reducing the pain of arthritis,
• lowers high blood pressure and reduces risk of heart attack and stroke by improving cardiovascular function,
• helps to relieve pain from varicose veins,
• is the least likely activity to cause any muscle, joint, or bone injury, and
• has these other benefits of regular activity (sleep better, reduces tension and related headaches, relieves depression, improves emotional health, sharpens the senses, increases mental alertness, helps maintain a youthful outlook).

As a life-style change, walking does not mean just going out for a walk every day or second day. It could also include taking every opportunity to walk during the day as well.

HELPFUL HINTS

Use the stairs instead of an elevator or escalator where appropriate. At airports, hotels, shopping centers use the stairs or walk up or down the escalator. An interesting study found that merely climbing 5 flights of stairs or walking more than 5 city blocks daily reduced the incidence of heart attack by 25 percent.[20]

Park your car a little farther and walk the rest of the way. This will also save you from the congestion in the parking lot at quitting time.

When friends come over try going for a walk instead of engaging in conversation while sitting and eating. There is nothing like scenery to stimulate exciting conversation.

Plan vacations to include your new life-style of increased activity. A more active life-style becomes a way of life; it is not simply something that you turn on and off. It may take some time to internalize it and make it part of your inner being, but eventually it will be as routine as brushing your teeth. You won't feel right if you don't get a walk in during the day.

Walking a mile burns 10 to 20 percent fewer calories than jogging a mile, though obviously it takes longer. If you walk briskly, you can obtain nearly the same aerobic benefits provided by running.

Physical activity allows you to think more clearly, be more efficient, have a happier disposition, and renew energy to allow you to accomplish more in less time. The result is that you have more free time to do the things you really want to do.

Remember to replace fluids lost through exercise.
Physical exercise without fluid replacement enhances
crystallization of both calcium oxalate and uric acid,
largely as a result of reduced urine output and acid in
the urine. If you do not drink enough fluids, your
body protects you from becoming dehydrated by
reducing the amount of fluid you excrete in the form
of urine. The more concentrated urine, noticeable by
its darker color, increases the chance of formation of
kidney stones. Increase fluid intake during physical
activity to compensate for sweat loss.[21]

If you lose a few pounds of weight after exercising,
this is water loss in the form of sweat. Replenish your
fluid intake to bring you back to your original weight
prior to exercise. Another indication of rehydration is
the lighter color of your urine. Keep in mind that
taking vitamin pills may color your urine darker so
that you may mistake it for a state of dehydration.

GETTING HOOKED ON ACTIVITY
Computers and modern technology make your life
easier and you are less likely to have an active life-
style. Children are growing up using less and less of
their muscle capacity. Playing ball or running around
are being replaced by sitting comfortably on a tire
and being pulled by a speedboat, playing computer
games, or working radio-controlled machines or
airplanes.

If you continue to do this you will lose your energy
and vitality. How can you break this cycle and
increase your leisure time physical activity? You
could plan more active holidays and get involved in
more sports.

Many of us live a fast-paced life-style. We work out
because it's good for us, not because we enjoy it.
Since we work intensely we tend to work out
intensely. It's difficult to enjoy physical activity with
this approach. On the other hand, many people
become addicted to exercise and suffer from
withdrawal pains when they are deprived. They
exhibit the same dependence on exercise as dieters
are dependent on diets. These individuals exercise as
an end unto itself rather than a means to physical

91

fitness. Some of them cannot stop exercising, even when their muscles and joints have become seriously injured. The symptoms of exercise addicts are as follows:

- needing to run or exercise daily to maintain a basic level of functioning,

- expressing minor withdrawal symptoms, such as irritability, guilt, or anxiety, when unable to exercise for a day or two; experiencing major withdrawal symptoms, such as depression, loss of self-esteem, or lack of interest in other activities when unable to exercise for longer periods of time,

- exercising even against medical advice,

- risking physical injury,

- organizing life around exercise,

- putting exercise above everything else, including job or relationships, and

- striving for greater achievement.

Intense commitment to exercise as a means in itself cannot have long-term benefit. You cannot hurry to be fit or stop when you reach your goal. Exercising for the wrong reason won't help you to adopt exercise permanently into your life-style.

The good news is that recent studies show that even mild physical activity is helpful in counteracting the effects of an unhealthy way of eating or in lowering cholesterol and high blood pressure. So if you have been laughing at your neighbors as they garden or rake leaves (life-style moves) while you are riding your stationary bike that goes nowhere, take a second look at who is getting hooked on an active life-style. Observe the enjoyment they get from living a more active life-style.

In the past 20 years the fitness movement has been focusing too much on performance that stresses the importance of doing more. When you change your focus to overall fitness and well-being and redefine success, you will realize that you can improve your health by doing those simple chores around the house or even taking a leisurely stroll.

Regular physical activity protects you against heart disease. Even if you are not working out to a point that brings your heart rate up to the target heart rate, you will still benefit.

Ellen's speed-walking leaves her husband Ron tired when he tries to keep up, causing him to lose interest in exercising. At the next outing, Ron, who weighs 330 pounds, was determined to work at his own level. Now he feels good after walking instead of ending up "pooped" and with sore legs. "This is for life," he says to Ellen, "and it will take time for me to comfortably work up to your level, so go on ahead of me."

Remember that exercising above your comfort level in an effort to get fit too quickly will make you feel exhausted and will make it difficult for you to transfer from an inactive to active state. Develop a positive rather than a negative association with activity and the rest will follow.

Regularity is the key for exercise and if you don't enjoy the type or intensity level of the activity then the activity may be short-lived. Your memory of the activity could be one of enjoyment.

When you stop exercising, you lose the beneficial effects of exercise. This process is known as detraining. How quickly this occurs depends on how fit you are and how long you have been exercising or how long you have been sedentary.

Find an activity that you enjoy. Work at your own level. Increase the amount of activity time gradually. Stick with it.

In a study done at Washington University School of Medicine in St. Louis, runners, cyclists, and swimmers who had worked out regularly and vigorously for years abstained from exercise. After 12 weeks they lost more than half their gains in aerobic conditioning compared to a sedentary control group who hadn't exercised regularly for at least 8 years.

In another study, sedentary people undertook an 8-week cycling regimen and then stopped for 8 weeks. The result was that all their aerobic gains were lost. They returned to their pretraining fitness levels. Cutting back on exercise is less devastating than stopping exercise. Studies show that these people are often able to avoid or postpone the effects of detraining.[22]

93

Life-style activities (walking or climbing stairs) that are done regularly can help you become fit while enjoying it.

A recent report in the *Journal of the American Medical Association* studied more than 13,000 people for an average of 8 years to analyze the effects of fitness on longevity. Five groups of people were divided according to fitness levels. The least-fit group who were also the most sedentary had the highest mortality rates by far. The big surprise was that the death rate dropped most sharply in the second least-fit group, by 60 percent for men and 48 percent for women.[23]

So why not take opportunities to use the stairs or go for a walk? Build up the strength of your heart and enhance your level of active living.

Researchers estimated that a person need only walk briskly for 30 to 60 minutes everyday to be in this group. The 3 most fit groups including people who jogged up to 40 miles a week, derived relatively small additional benefits from their exercise. Why kill yourself to maintain a grueling schedule when in fact you don't have to be a marathoner to greatly reduce your risks of heart or other disease. Modest increases in lower intensity activities such as brisk walking will probably add years to your life.

As you gradually make modest improvements in aerobic fitness, the energy expended will increase the high density lipoprotein (HDL) that will protect you against heart disease. Here is an example of daily leisure time activities that can provide you with the satisfaction of getting your work done, add enjoyment to your life, and keep you energized and in good health.

MONDAY	Walk	40 minutes
	Stairs at work	10 minutes
TUESDAY	Stairs at work	10 minutes
WEDNESDAY	Walk	30 minutes
	Rake lawn	40 minutes
	Stairs at work	5 minutes
THURSDAY	Stairs at work	10 minutes
FRIDAY	Walk	60 minutes
	Stairs at work	10 minutes
SATURDAY	Mow yard	60 minutes
	Dancing	60 minutes
SUNDAY	Walk with family	60 minutes

The good news is that all that is needed to significantly prolong life is a moderate level of activity.This fact applies regardless of the presence of other risk factors such as cholesterol levels, blood pressure, body composition, cigarette smoking, or family medical history. According to Dr. Steven Blair, one of the physicians conducting the study, the men were better off to have high cholesterol and be fit, than to have low cholesterol and be in a low fitness category.

Another study of 17,000 Harvard alumni found that exercise levels to use 2000 calories a week through day-to-day activities such as walking, stair climbing, and light sports such as golf, afforded significant protec-tion from heart disease.[24] This maximum protective effect of a 64 percent reduction in risk of heart disease was reached by including leisure time physical activities as seen in the table (p94). It is interesting to note that if you exceed 2000 calories per week in leisure time physical activities you gain little further benefit; in fact, you increase the risk of orthopedic injury.

Boredom can make you feel lazy and tricks you into thinking you're physically tired. It catches all of us if we don't watch out, so fight back by finding an activity you really enjoy and stick with it.

If you ever tried an activity and you didn't care for it, try it again with your new attitude towards activity. When I was first introduced to golf, I went to the driving range, took a few lessons, and tried my hand at the golf course. But I just couldn't get interested in trying to shoot this small ball into the hole. So I gave up and never considered trying again.

One day, a friend took me for lunch overlooking a beautiful golf course. It was lovely, but I never considered trying golf again until she presented me with a new perspective. "Golf is an excuse to walk in a really nice park," she said. "We don't even keep score, Linda."

We often feel that we have to be good at an activity in order to enjoy it. Yet the very act of participating in an

95

invigorating, natural, and stimulating environment can be enjoyable in itself.

One weekend my husband, Mitchell and I packed up the canoe to go on a spontaneous adventure to a lake. We arrived, went canoeing for a couple of hours, and then Mitchell decided to move on. "Why don't we stay here?" I asked. "After all, isn't one lake similar to the next?"

"Linda," he said, "we are not in a cowboy movie where the same scenes are repeated over and over again. Look around you and observe." So I did, and he was right.

We went canoeing to 3 different lakes that weekend and had 3 totally different experiences. We felt revitalized when we returned home. What a process of self-discovery!

So you see, you may regress from time to time in order to grow. Tune into your surroundings and allow yourself to relax. Observe those around you who are tuned into nature and its wonders and who enjoy the internal benefits of active living.

The next time you go to a social event where there is dancing, try staying on the dance floor at least 20 minutes and just keep dancing. Feel the music and enjoy yourself!

Remember to stop every half hour or so to drink water, whether you feel thirsty or not. Proper hydration keeps you going but too much alcohol will dehydrate you and make you feel sleepy.

Enjoyable occasions such as these will allow you to build in some special time for yourself while being more active in a creative way. It puts the fun into activity and puts you in charge. Find more precious moments to "kick up your heels" and enjoy yourself while gradually increasing your level of activity.

4

Healthy Eating the HUGS™ Way

Balance your meals to fill your needs for fullness and energy. Eat regularly starting with a balanced breakfast.

Part of the balance in the quality of life includes healthy eating. Most of us eat out for one third of our meals. Even the meals eaten at home are not the tasty home-cooked kind but are the quick-to-prepare kind because of our busy life-styles.

Yet healthy eating is important and it is the next step in giving you more energy to focus on your road to health. Don't worry, that doesn't mean eating salads and fruits alone. That would only set you up to binge. After all, it's human nature to want something that you can't have.

If you've been dieting, that will put you out of tune with your body and its signals of hunger and fullness. You must begin by eating regularly, starting with a breakfast in order to tune back in. One of my clients felt that when she started to eat breakfast, it made her more hungry by lunch time and she began to eat more frequently; whereas formerly she did not eat all day until supper. It takes 3 to 4 hours to digest a balanced breakfast, so you will be hungry by lunch. If you eat these meals and stop eating when you are full you will ultimately eat less at supper time and throughout the evening. Once you get "hooked" on eating breakfast, your body will find it difficult to do without it.

"I was in a hurry today, dashed out the door without breakfast and by noon I was starved. I really missed eating breakfast and noticed the difference in how I felt," Diane remarked. When you starve during the day or your body gets attuned to not eating until evening, you are usually famished by supper time and gobble your food down as fast as can. Your plate is empty but do you really feel satisfied?

People who skip meals actually lower their metabolism which is the energy required to keep your heart pumping, brain active, organs functioning, lungs breathing, and eyelids blinking. It's the level of energy needed to sustain your body's vital functions.

According to Dr. Wayne Callaway's research on overweight individuals, those who were breakfast-skippers had metabolic rates 4 to 5 percent below

98

normal. The meal-skipper had a mild form of starvation the same as you see in bingers. Under-eating early in the day inevitably leads to overeating later on. People who snack in the evening tend to cut back the next day to make up for it. They're not hungry until they start to eat, then their appetite goes up. If they eat breakfast, they are hungry at lunch because this is part of the normal body function that has been ignored due to dieting.

BREAKFAST BREAKTHROUGH

Regular eating, starting with breakfast, enhances the thermic effect of food. This can be defined as the energy expended above the resting metabolic rate for several hours after a meal. This makes you burn up more calories during and after the meal. On the other hand, extreme hunger and other factors can cause overeating in obese individuals who eat infrequently, and this may also reduce the number of calories burned because of diet-induced thermogenesis (the way individuals store and burn calories). With comparable total calories, people who eat just one meal a day have increased skinfold thicknesses (more fat), compared with those who eat more than 2 meals a day.[1]

Studies by Dr. George Bray[2] and others have produced evidence that eating infrequent, large meals favors the storage of fat known as lipogenesis.[3] In other words, if the same number of total calories are consumed in one large meal at supper time and there is also nibbling throughout the evening, more calories will be stored as fat. Eating frequently according to your actual hunger will rev up your system. In this way you will burn more calories because of the effect of increasing the metabolic rate.

Eating regularly increases your metabolic rate. You need to eat more, not less, in order to get your body working and your system revved up.

One of my clients felt famished only at the evening meal. Her system, accustomed to being without food until 6:00 o'clock was adjusted to that time frame. When I introduced her to eating at regular times of the day, she was amazed after a period of a few weeks that she actually felt hungry in a regular time frame. Her system adjusted to more frequent eating. The amount she consumed at the evening meal was much less.

HERE ARE SOME GUIDELINES TO HELP YOU INTRODUCE BREAKFAST

• Try cutting back on your evening snack. Your body stores carbohydrates as glycogen, primarily in the liver. Glycogen is converted in the liver to glucose, your energy source, and released into the bloodstream as needed. These energy stores in the liver run out after about 12 hours of rest[1] (faster if you are more active, since a heavy workout can deplete your energy stores). By morning, your body will have gone about 8 to 12 hours without food, and you will be ready to break the fast and refuel your energy supply.

• Traditionally, breakfast-skippers are higher on calories but shorter on nutrients, especially vitamin C which you often get from fruit or juice in the morning.

• The brain needs a steady source of glucose, the breakdown product of carbohydrates, to function. Breakfast helps to replenish this source of energy. A recent study proved that children participating in the national school breakfast program improved more in achievement test scores than those who didn't participate. By eating breakfast you no longer need the caffeine boost to keep alert.

• Missing breakfast and starving all day, you are so hungry by dinner that you don't focus on your food or taste it, so you don't feel satisfied and may eat throughout the evening. Take the time to eat breakfast. After a few weeks, you won't be able to do without it. Taking time out for yourself will give you time back in improved productivity and you will feel better equipped to handle the unexpected situation.

• During a meal, it takes roughly 20 minutes for your stomach to register to your brain that you are full. If you eat too quickly it does not give you a chance to feel full. Eating regularly including

breakfast allows you to bring more rhythm to your eating, allowing you to pace yourself and taste and enjoy the food.

• Without breakfast, your defense mechanism kicks in. Your body knows that you will feed it only once a day so it compensates by storing more of those calories as fat. It is like the squirrel who "squirrels away" the food for the winter. Just in case you starve yourself again, your body has something to call on.

• The brown fat that keeps the metabolic rate high is not as active without breakfast because you are not eating frequently enough, the result of which is a lower metabolic rate. In other words, it takes less calories or energy for your body to function, your heart to pump, your blood to flow, and your lungs to work.

Eating regularly involves resetting your internal
clock to a regular pattern of meals. Once you begin to
eat breakfast in the morning you will, within a few
weeks, start to wake up hungry for the morning
meal.

By shifting to 3 regular meals a day, you will feel
more energetic due simply to the increased effect of
metabolic rate.

CARBOHYDRATES IN CONTROL

Let's work through this system of empowering you
to make eating choices that make you feel satisfied
longer. Remember those foods that you often cut
back on or cut out when you wanted to lose weight,
those carbohydrates that you feel certain will put
weight on you as soon as you eat them again? Did
you ever wonder why you crave those foods? The
answer is that all carbohydrates break down into
sugar. If you are cutting them back, then your body
makes you crave them as a defense mechanism. If
you cut back on breads, cereals, potatoes, and pasta,
then you will not be able to resist a candy bar or piece
of cake, because your body needs sugar, natural or
refined, in order to function.

Jean lamented, "I just have to look at a piece of cake
and I gain weight." In reality, she was restricting her
natural form of sugar, the carbohydrates, during the
week, causing her to be in a dehydrated state due to
water loss. Going out on weekends, Jean would lose
control at the sweet table.

If you do not take in enough carbohydrates naturally,
then your body will protect you by craving them
from other sources, for example from cakes and
cookies. When reintroducing carbohydrates into your
body, you are rehydrating yourself and therefore the
immediate weight gain that follows is merely water.
It is impossible to gain a couple of pounds of fat
overnight.

Just as your car needs gas to run, your body needs
carbohydrates that break down into sugar to keep
you going, to give you energy. Often people
mistakenly believe that vitamins supply energy.
Excess vitamins will not push the pace of biological

101

reactions faster, just as having a full tank of gas will not make a car go faster than its engine capacity will allow. Vitamins help you extract the energy from the carbohydrates, but the carbohydrates give the energy. Eating in a healthy manner provides you with a sufficient amount of vitamins and carbohydrates.

Protein is a nutrient used by the body to build and repair tissues, hormones, and enzymes. With regard to energy level, protein foods provide you with sustained energy. Foods such as meats, fish, poultry, peanut butter, eggs, and cheese give you stamina just as high octane gives mileage for the car. Protein foods allow you to extract the energy from the carbohydrates at a slower pace rather than all at once. Eating protein foods along with carbohydrates allows

Protein has the effect of making food "stick to your ribs."

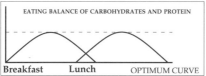

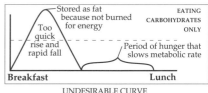

Eat when pleasantly hungry. Waiting till blood sugar level has dropped too low causes overeating and nibbling.

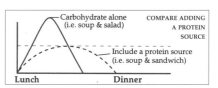

the carbohydrates to break down into sugar at a slower rate, giving you more sustained energy.[5,6] Protein foods slow down the release of sugar from the carbohydrates into your bloodstream. In this way eating some protein along with carbohydrates stabilizes the blood sugar swings that would otherwise lead to binges or feelings of hunger and irritability.

Fat is found hidden in protein foods as well as in recognizable fat foods such as butter, margarine, mayonnaise, or salad dressing. A certain amount of fat is necessary to obtain the essential fatty acids necessary for health and well-being. However, these fats are the most concentrated source of calories and convert to body fat very easily. The HUGS™ style of living gradually cuts back on these foods in meal preparation techniques and food choices without sacrificing flavor. It is important to emphasize to make the changes gradually in order to adopt them as a life-style change.

However, fat is fat, and contains the same number of calories whether it is fat around meat, margarine, butter, or oil. Vary the types of fat to decrease the total amount of saturated fat you take in. If you really like butter, do not cut it out completely. Experience has shown that individuals who cut butter from their diets eventually miss it so much that they binge on it. The result is weight loss followed by a larger weight gain and the starve/binge diet cycle rather than a new-found taste acquired from gradual changes. Attempting to cut out fat too quickly leads only to temporary change.

Learning to balance carbohydrate and protein choices at meals is easy. For example, is anything missing from a tomato and cucumber sandwich?

The principle of healthy eating can be demonstrated as follows:

MATTER OF BALANCE

A balance between carbohydrates and protein is necessary at each meal to feel energetic and hold you over till the next meal.

CARBOHYDRATES	PROTEINS
Give You Energy	Keep you feeling full
GOAL	GOAL
Energize by gradually increasing carbohydrates	*Gradually decrease protein— the next meal is just a few hours away*

Complex Carbohydrates	*Simple Carbohydrates*	
Breads (whole grains)	Milk (natural sugar–	Beef (lean)
Cereals (low sugar)	lactose)	Pork (lean)
Pasta	Starchy vegetables	Lamb (lean)
Potatoes	(carrots, turnips, parsnips,	Chicken & Turkey
Rice	beets, peas, squash, corn)	Fish & Seafood
Crackers	Fruit	Game
Dried peas, Beans &		Eggs
Lentils		Cheese
(soak before cooking,		Peanut butter
discard water to		
decrease flatulence)		

Add other vegetables for color and texture.

Tailor Your Tastes

Experiment with foods and fine tune your cooking to use fat in meals as the accent. Focus on the carbohydrate and protein content of the meal. Learn to appreciate the taste and texture of foods. Taste, savor, and enjoy. . . .

You will gradually learn to listen to your own stomach at meal time and cue in to your physical hunger needs; and then, knowledge about the role of different food choices will enable you to make selections that balance.

103

Be the best you can be!

Dieters have a different attitude to foods labeled "carbohydrates" and "protein." For dieters these are divided into "legal" (those foods that are okay to eat when on a diet) versus "illegal" foods (those foods that are the "no no's" of dieting). The meats and fruits are the "legal" foods and the breads, cereals, potatoes, and pastas are the "illegal" foods that should be eliminated or restricted according to the diet mentality.

Dieters are not used to eating carbohydrates. They are not aware that by taking in more protein sources that contain hidden fat, they are actually "hanging on" to fat and "letting go" of water, along with the carbohydrate restriction. This is one of the main reasons why diets do not last. The HUGS™ concept is a reverse of what dieters expect. HUGS™ shows you that you can eat in a healthy manner and lose body fat, not water. So learn from those former diet experiences and see them for what they are—a ploy to lose weight quickly to keep you motivated. **HUGS™ works on inner motivation that will make you feel better both inside and out. HUGS™ is for the long term.**

"I don't like eating meat so can I use the HUGS™ concept with vegetarian meals?"

HUGS™—VEGETARIAN STYLE
Vegetarian eating is becoming more popular. With the emphasis on increasing carbohydrates and fiber and gradually decreasing fat content, vegetable proteins such as legumes offer those options. The function of protein with regard to health is that new protein is needed daily to allow a constant renewal of body cells and regulators, as well as to repair any damaged tissue. It's a fact that the average person in our meat-eating society takes in about twice as much protein as their bodies need. This excess protein increases the overall fat content of your food intake and if it is above your energy needs for the day, it gets stored as fat.

If you eat more calories than your body needs, the excess gets stored as fat. High-fat foods such as the hidden fat in protein foods gets stored into fat more efficiently than high-carbohydrate foods that contain little fat.

Excess protein		Stored
Excess carbohydrate	>	into
Excess fat		fat tissue

BODY FAT

ENERGY
(calories)

EXCESS
CARBOS

EXCESS
FATS

EXCESS
PROTEIN

Not all proteins are used equally by the body. The protein found in foods is not "ready-made" to be incorporated into body tissues. Instead, the body must break it down by digestion into individual amino acids, in order to build the proteins it needs.

Although there are over 20 amino acids, only 9 are essential for adults. These 9 cannot be made by the body, and therefore, must be available from food sources. Proteins from animal sources such as meat, fish, poultry, eggs, milk, and milk products contain the 9 essential amino acids in the proportions needed by the body. They are called "complete" proteins. On the other hand, vegetable sources of protein are termed "incomplete" and cannot be part of the building process unless they are combined with foods that contain the missing amino acids.

For example, legumes such as soybeans contain the highest concentration of protein in the plant world but cannot be utilized by the body unless combined with either nuts and seeds, grains, or a complete protein. You don't have to combine complementary foods at the same meal to get the effects of a complete protein. If you eat a wide variety of foods, especially if you eat even a small amount of meat or dairy products, you'll absorb a full complement of amino acids on any given day.[7] From the available data, it is reasonable to conclude that protein adequacy can be achieved when different plant proteins are eaten at separate meals throughout the course of the day.[8]

To simplify these concepts and gradually incorporate more sources of vegetable protein into your eating pattern, here are a few tips:

• *Introduce vegetable protein gradually to make it a lifestyle change and to reduce the incidence of stomach distress due to the high-fiber content.* One of my clients was used to living on salads alone (lettuce is low in fiber). When she abruptly added more grains and carbohydrates to her meals, her system became plugged. It is crucial to increase your fiber content gradually so your system can adjust.
Note By increasing your intake of carbohydrates, you are automatically increasing the fibre content of your meals.

105

• *Beans and whole peas must be soaked before cooking because their skins are impermeable; water can only enter through the small end formerly attached to the plant.* (Split peas and lentils do not require pre-soaking.) To prevent gas in your stomach, soak legumes up to 5 hours or overnight. Drain, add fresh water, cook 1/2 hour, discard water. Add more water, cook until tender and discard water a third time. The more often you change the water, the more you will reduce the gas-producing qualities of the beans. You may be getting rid of some of the water-soluble vitamin content of the beans and some of the protein value but more importantly, you are getting rid of the component that is responsible for making you feel bloated. Adding a pinch of ginger may also help. Eat a small amount at a time until your system gets used to the fiber. In this way beans can be enjoyed for their wholesome flavor and nutrition without having the uncomfortable after-effects.

• *Drink plenty of fluids so that the fiber can allow increased movement of the intestine thereby improving regularity and bowel movements.* Fiber acts like a sponge soaking up water. If there is not enough water around, constipation instead of regularity may result.

• *Continue to eat eggs and dairy foods.* Vitamins B_{12} and D are found only in animal products. Plants do not contain vitamin B_{12}. If the above foods are not eaten, soy milk or soy products fortified with vitamin B_{12} could be consumed.

• *Introducing more legumes to your meals is a plus for nutrition and a decrease in grocery bills.* Beans, peas, and lentils are a cheap source of protein. Using legumes is fun. If you don't normally use them, gradually add them to sauces and soups that you enjoy. *Tailoring Your Tastes*, our new cookbook, contains excellent ideas to incorporate legumes into your meals.

• *Meat is a good source of iron.* If plant sources of iron which include legumes, whole or enriched grains, green leafy vegetables, and other vegetables and dried fruits are used, high sources of vitamin C can be used to make more of the iron available to the

106

body. Foods rich in vitamin C include berries, citrus fruits, tomatoes, and broccoli and could be eaten with the meal to enhance the absorption of iron.

FOOD SOURCES OF VITAMIN C		
Food	Portion	Vitamin C (mg)
Orange juice (fresh)	1 cup (250 ml)	130
Grapefruit juice (fresh)	1 cup (250 ml)	94
Papayas	1/2 medium	94
Strawberries (sliced)	1 cup (250 ml)	85
Kiwi fruit	1 medium	75
Oranges	1 medium	70
Green peppers (raw)	1 medium	94
Mangoes	1 medium	57
Cantaloupe	1/4 medium	56
Cranberry juice cocktail	1/2 cup (125 ml)	54
Brussel sprouts (cooked)	4 sprouts	70
Tomato juice	1 cup (250 ml)	45
Grapefruit (white)	1/2 medium	44
Broccoli (cooked, chopped)	1/2 cup (125 ml)	75
Kale (raw, chopped)	1/2 cup (125 ml)	41
Cauliflower (raw, chopped)	1/2 cup (125 ml)	43
Potato (baked)	1 medium	26
Tangerine	1 medium	26
Tomato (raw)	1 medium	34
Turnip greens (cooked)	1/2 cup (125 ml)	25
Beet greens (cooked)	1/2 cup (125 ml)	12
Cabbage (raw, shredded)	1/2 cup (125 ml)	22

If plant foods are your main source of iron known as non-heme iron (heme iron comes from animal-derived foods), then it is crucial that you do not drink tea with your meals. If you do, iron absorption, especially non-heme iron, decreases by 62 percent.[9] More about this in Chapter 11 on fluids.

A vegetarian meal such as lentil soup with bread, will make you full sooner but will allow you to become hungry sooner. Because of the higher fiber and lower fat content of vegetable proteins when compared to animal proteins, it is normal to be hungry more quickly. As long as you understand that you may be eating more frequently throughout the day, this method of eating is an extremely healthy one.

If you use legumes as your protein source, the previous chart, "A Matter of Balance," on p 103 is modified.

CARBOHYDRATES	PROTEIN
Grains:	Eggs
wheat (bread, bulgar)	Cheese
Kasha	Milk
Rice	Peanut Butter
Corn	Legumes:
Oats	dried peas
Pasta	(yellow or green peas,
Cereal	garbanzos or chick peas,
Potatoes	black-eye peas)
Fruit+	Dry beans:
Vegetables+	kidney beans,
	soy beans
	Nuts*
	Seeds*

+Simple carbohydrates such as fruits and vegetables can be added to meals for the feeling of fullness and the vitamins and minerals they offer. However, except for corn, these foods cannot be used to make a protein complete and usable by the body.
* Nuts and seeds are both high in carbohydrate and incomplete as vegetable protein and are also high in fat content. Use them sparingly.

Try using this concept of balance in your meals to give you more energy and hold you over to the next meal. If you feel hungry between meals, have a snack, otherwise overeating may occur at the next meal.

• *Focus on gradually increasing the carbohydrate content of your meals, but include enough protein to keep you feeling satisfied.* Note that due to the lower fat content of vegetable protein foods, you may feel hungry sooner than if you ate a balanced meal that included animal protein. The reason for this is that animal protein contains hidden fat that adds to the feeling of fullness. Remember, carbohydrates digest more quickly, giving you an immediate energy boost. Protein foods take longer to digest and keep you feeling satisfied longer. A balanced meal will probably be sufficient for 3 to 6 hours, depending on fat content.

Allow this period of time between meals and actually

108

experience physical hunger. Constant eating will not allow you this experience. But do not go to extremes. Eating only 3 meals a day could leave you famished by mealtime, decreasing your opportunity to taste and savor your food.

I usually experience a dual reaction in my classes when participants are told that they can have any food they want, including the conventional "forbidden when dieting" list. People exhibit a sense of relief along with a sense of fear. A possible consequence without the new perspective is that a continued sense of restriction may cause them to overeat until they gain the confidence from their developing control over food.

> For some people, keeping a journal of what they eat (no quantities) and how they feel will help them on the process of self-discovery.

WARNING

Giving yourself permission to eat what you want and not following a structured diet does not mean that there is no focus. Trust yourself to find your balance and beware of your pendulum swinging the other way.

Deprivation that occurred due to previous attempts to diet leads to a rebellion to dieting, causing overeating. If this is happening to you, become aware of why it is happening and focus on tuning into your true physical hunger, using the eating guidelines to reduce the number of urges that may occur. Eating more carbohydrates and obtaining natural sugar from them will decrease your urge for sweets. These foods will provide you with your energy source.

> Have the light and dark forces got you teetering to the extremes? Find the balance of normalizing eating habits by learning to think like a nondieter.

CHECK your balance at each meal using the form provided on p110 to indicate the types of food you are eating.

If you would like to check out your understanding of the principles of healthy eating an individual assessment on your journal can be done to determine to what extent your eating habits are in balance. (See end of book for details.)

Many of our present eating habits are in the form of a triangle, that is we eat less during the day and more

109

in the evening. Try to gradually reverse this order. Start with a more hearty breakfast, a more substantial lunch, and even though your evening meal may be large, it probably will be less than you formerly ate.

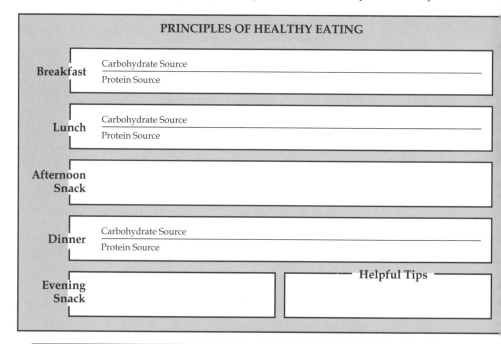

PRINCIPLES OF HEALTHY EATING

Breakfast
Carbohydrate Source
Protein Source

Lunch
Carbohydrate Source
Protein Source

Afternoon Snack

Dinner
Carbohydrate Source
Protein Source

Evening Snack
Helpful Tips

Any weight gain that may occur may be due to one of the following reasons:

- Rehydration of water stores with reintroduction of carbohydrates because carbohydrates are stored with water. This is "water" weight, not "fat" weight.
- Overeating due to "permission to eat."
- Not yet tuned into your natural hunger signals (more about this in Chapter 6).
- Overeating as a result of rebellion to dieting (starvation/binge cycle).
- Overeating since increasing carbohydrates. This implies being "off the diet" and time to binge on those foods long known to be forbidden (i.e. bread). You need to switch out of the diet mentality (see Chapter 6 and 7).
- Retaining water due to insufficient fluid intake (see Chapter 11).
- Retaining fluid due to excessive consumption of foods high in sodium (i.e. salt, convenience foods, carbonated diet drinks, pickles, soy sauce, some snack foods).
- Increase in muscle mass due to increase in activity. A positive outcome!

"I used to skip breakfast and eat very little, if anything, at lunch. This led to a huge supper, and people were amazed at how much I could devour. Then in my mid 20s the weight began to catch up with me. I realized that this style of eating eventually catches up to even naturally slim people. It takes longer in men due to their greater muscle mass as a result of body composition.

The first step in HUGS™ is to learn how to satisfy your physical hunger by balancing your meals with carbohydrate and protein content that best suit your needs. You don't have to purchase a new set of cookbooks or recipe books or spend a lot of time preparing meals by following elaborate time-consuming recipes. Simply fine-tune your present eating habits to ensure that you are including a balance in eating. Turn to Chapter 14 for some ideas to help you accomplish this.

GETTING THE MOST ENERGY OUT OF FOODS
Here are some examples of meals with the right balance.

BREAKFAST   Natural Jump-starters
Carbohydrate   bread, muffins,* fruit, crackers, pancakes, cereal, potatoes, milk, English muffins, bagels.

*Many store-bought or restaurant muffins may be high in fat content and contain up to 400-500 calories (see Chapters 5 and 10). However, fat is being purged from some commercial muffins as consumers become more health conscious. For example, "Mmmarvelous Mmmuffins" have developed tasty low-fat alternatives to please the palate.

Protein   cheese, peanut butter, eggs, meat, crisp bacon.

Try toast with low-fat cheese melted on top (no butter or margarine since there is hidden fat in the cheese). To make it even more special, put onions, tomatoes, zucchini, pepper, or any other vegetable on toast before adding the cheese. Also great for lunch!

Try peanut butter and jam or banana on toast. If you have frozen raspberries on hand, pop in microwave just until defrosted and spread on top of peanut butter for a new taste sensation that is sure to be a hit!

Note No butter or margarine is needed since there is

hidden fat in peanut butter.

Try poached, scrambled, or fried egg (with little fat) on toast. Or try toast with quark, skyr, or ricotta cheese with jam, canned fruit (preserved in its own juice), or fresh fruit cut up on top.

Note Quark and skyr are low-fat cheeses that taste similar to cream cheese. However, they are very bland in flavor and therefore the jam adds just the right flavor stimulation. Try whole grain toast with skyr cheese and cut up strawberries. If strawberries are frozen, pop in microwave just until defrosted but still firm. This is refreshing and appealing! There are also a variety of other low-fat spreadable cheese products on the market (cheddar, garden vegetable, herb and garlic, swiss and almonds, cheddar and port wine, and French onion) that are full of flavor. Of course, cottage cheese is one of the cheeses lowest in fat content. The above cheeses provide variety and alternatives for those who leave cottage cheese to go moldy in the refrigerator.

Try pancakes and cheese. Incorporate your favorite type of fruit into the pancake mix for added moisture. When serving, spread quark cheese on top instead of syrup for some protein source at this meal. Tastes rich.

Add cereal and milk, fruit, or greater quantities of food to the food list to give you a feeling of satisfaction, without being overly full. The examples given will help you to understand the balance.

LUNCH
Gradually increase the carbohydrate content of your meals and gradually decrease your protein content so that you have energy and feel satisfied for a longer period of time. The word "gradual" is emphasized, because human nature tends to make you want everything to happen immediately. Focus on life-style change, not the diet mentality.

Note If you have been restricting carbohydrates in the past, it is normal to gain 3 to 4 pounds (1 to 2 kg) to replenish your carbohydrate stores. The body has to store carbohydrates with water. It takes 3 to 4 pounds (1 to 2 kg) of water to store 1 pound (0.5 kg)

112

FOR A QUICK BREAKFAST CONTAINING A BALANCE OF CARBOHYDRATE AND PROTEIN, TRY THIS:

PUMPKIN CUSTARD

1	egg	1	*Combine all ingredients in a blender*
1/3 cup	canned pumpkin	150 g	*until smooth. Pour into a custard*
1/3 cup	cottage cheese	150 g	*cup and place in a pan of water.*
Dash	cinnamon, allspice, cloves, nutmeg	Dash	*Bake at 350°F (180°C) for 25 to 30 minutes. Bake the night before.*
1 tbsp	honey or sugar or sweeten to taste	15 mL	

If you like a liquid breakfast, milkshakes are easy to make. Try this.

Peanut Butter Milkshake

8 oz	1 percent milk	250 mL
1 tbsp	peanut butter	15 mL
1 small	banana	1 small

Add a little ice cream if you like.

OR TRY THIS.

FRUIT MILKSHAKE

4 oz	1 percent milk	125 mL	*Canned fruit adds texture to the*
4 oz	canned fruit in its own juice (e.g. 2 peach halves plus a bit of juice)	125 mL	*milkshake and makes it thicker, plus it adds carbohydrates, vitamins, and flavor. Egg, peanut butter, and to a lesser extent milk, provide the*
1	egg or	1	*protein. Add 1 to 2 tbs (15 to 30 mL)*
1/4 cup	quark cheese	50 mL	*skim milk powder if you want to increase the protein content or to*
2	ice cubes	2	*make the milkshake thicker.*

If you are using strawberries or raspberries from your freezer, you may need some skim milk powder to give more texture to the milkshake. You could also add a little vanilla ice cream. Add a bit of sugar to taste.

Note Since milkshakes are in liquid form they are more quickly digested and will not satisfy you for a long period of time. They can however, help you get hooked on breakfast and keep up your strength, metabolic rate, and nutrients when you are sick.

of glycogen (stored form of carbohydrates). When people begin to reintroduce carbohydrates into their way of eating, they often feel bloated. They do not recognize this sensation as a normal result of eating sufficient carbohydrates.

Carbohydrate   bread, bagels, pita bread, English muffin, fruit, pasta, potatoes, rice, milk, yogurt, vegetables.

Note Those vegetables that you pull from the ground such as carrots, parsnips, beets, and turnips as well as corn, squash, and peas are the starchy ones. The other vegetables can be used as a filler. They contain vitamins and minerals, and are not considered part of the carbohydrate component of the meal due to high-water content with very little carbohydrate content. Include both complex and simple carbohydrates at each meal. (refer to Matter of Balance for examples p103).

> Croissants may sound light and airy, but they contain twice the fat of a biscuit and 6 times the fat of an English muffin.

Protein leftover meat, canned fish, eggs, peanut butter, cheese, legumes (peas, beans, lentils), milk, yogurt. Gradually try some of the low-fat cheeses.

Sandwiches are great quick lunches. Sometimes people don't care for bread because they haven't given themselves a chance to experiment with the wide variety of tastes and flavors available today. You may like breads that are coarser (whole wheat or any form of whole grain such as cracked wheat or pumpernickel). However, beware of bread that is colored with caramel coloring and has a soft texture. Read the label. This bread probably is not whole grain.

Fillers in sandwiches can be anything. Try leftover chicken, beef, pork, canned tuna, salmon, or other canned fish, cheese, peanut butter, or egg. Luncheon meats are used less frequently because of higher fat content. If using canned fish, try to purchase it packed in water or if packed in oil, rinse, and use less fat to moisten the sandwich. If you use a light mayonnaise mixed with the canned fish, adding butter or margarine to the bread as well is not necessary.

Retrain your taste buds. Consider making toast. You take a piece of bread, toast it, and in this way get rid of the moisture in exchange for texture. Then you add butter or margarine to bring back the moisture and get rid of the texture. Does this make sense? Focus your taste on the texture and flavor rather than the greasy mushy taste.

Often when butter or margarine is cut back or even eliminated on toast and replaced with a protein food such as cheese or peanut butter that contains hidden

114

fat, in 9 out of 10 cases, the fat taste of butter or margarine is not missed. Was it more a habit than a desire? Changing the habit does not instill feelings of deprivation. Focus on progress and life-style adjustments rather than immediate temporary change.

Remember that weight is not necessarily an indicator of health. Alice, a client in her 20s, was referred to me for weight counseling. She weighed 311 pounds (141 kg) and had not been on many previous diets. Every time she even thought about going on a diet, she would crave food and binge so the diets were short-lived. But she was receptive to trying a life-style approach where the focus of success would be improved health. Months later, Alice made a number of remarkable changes: she reduced by half the number of times she had to take ventolin for her asthma, she ate differently because she wanted to, her food tasted better, and she prepared food that had a low-fat content. She began to walk regularly and enjoyed it. Her clothes were a little looser even though her weight was down only slightly. The physical improvement was gradual, not instant.

Alice was much healthier, but by society's measure of success, which is weight, she had failed. Focusing on weight, conventional counselors might have advised Alice to decrease her food intake and increase her activity. She would have been required to work above her comfort zone. This may have had a negative effect on her health.

When Alice followed my advice to focus on her life-style adjustments, this created the momentum to continue with the plan. Her focus was entirely off weight. She accepted that it would take 2 to 5 years to internalize the life-style changes, but she was enjoying the process so time wasn't an issue.

Since both of Alice's parents were large, Alice had an 80 percent chance of being large as well. With life-style changes in place her body will naturally adjust to the weight it is genetically meant to be. Society's expectations that all women should be within a certain range of weights is not the issue here. It is this woman's long-term health that is important. This

115

It is not the quantity that counts, it is the balance in eating and the total fat content that will make the difference. Try adding mustard, light salad dressing, or tomato and lettuce to sandwiches instead of always using butter or margarine.

woman did not fail. She enjoyed striving to be the best that she could be!

Dieters are used to skimping on bread and making open-faced sandwiches, using the thinly sliced bread available in supermarkets. But you can be much more satisfied by eating more bread *without guilt*. If you allow yourself to feel guilty while consuming more carbohydrates, then you are not allowing yourself to experience the excitement of the moment of tasting and savoring your food. This will result in eating more quantity of food in order to feel satisfied.

Making sandwiches with thicker slices of bread makes you feel as if you have something in your hand. It can be very satisfying. Cut thick slices of bread and put enough filler to keep you satisfied or have 2 sandwiches.

Add soup or salad if you like. Try varying types of bread or using pita pockets. Another option that is quick for lunch is a stir-fry made with leftovers from the fridge. Use a teflon frying pan and a cover to maintain moisture which will reduce the total fat content needed. Leftover chicken, beef, potatoes, rice, and vegetables work well. If the mixture starts to stick, add a little liquid such as water, water with bouillon cube, juice, or leftover low-fat gravy.

Soups can be made hearty by adding a protein source such as cheese, leftover meat, chicken, legumes such as lentils, beans, and a carbohydrate source such as potatoes, rice, or barley. Eat the soup with some bread or rolls. If the soup is not substantial enough, you will probably be hungry a couple of hours later. Experiment and learn the quantity that you need.

SNACKS
Some form of complex carbohydrate such as bread, rolls, crackers, cold pizza, bulgur, lentils, or fruit alone, cheese with fruit, popcorn (watch the butter), milk, or yogurt is good for a snack. Milk and yogurt contain some protein as well and therefore may serve as a more satisfying snack. Milk products also ensure that you get enough calcium during the day.

SUPPER

Most people tend to eat balanced meals at supper but they usually emphasize the protein source. Try to ensure that you are increasing your carbohydrate source and gradually decreasing your protein source. However, eat enough protein to hold you over till the next meal. Find the right balance of carbohydrate and protein that works for you.

Carbohydrate   pasta, potatoes, rice, bread, crackers, fruit, milk, yogurt, starchy vegetables. *Note* Milk does contain some protein but it is also very high in carbohydrate. Due to its liquid form and the fact that it is lower in protein content than those mentioned under "protein," it is not as satisfying to be used as "holding over" power. For this reason, it is found under the carbohydrate section.

Protein   lean beef, lean pork, lean lamb, lean chicken, turkey, fish, liver, game, eggs, cheese, peanut butter.

Do not eat only chicken and fish. Beef and pork are much leaner than they used to be (see Chapter 5). Where does portion control or measuring your 3 ounces (85 g) of meat fit into all of this you ask? Rather than becoming preoccupied with quantities, AIM FOR BALANCE.

• As a check for a healthy balance learn to observe what's on your plate. Aim for 2/3 to 3/4 carbohydrates and 1/3 to 1/4 protein content. Learn to recognize the balance that is right for you rather than measuring how much you need. This balance will give you energy and keep you going.

• Tune into your internal signals of hunger and fullness for quantities that you need to satisfy you.

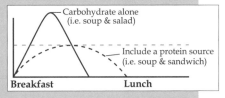

REMEMBER   counting exchanges leaves you preoccupied with food and does not allow you the opportunity to work with your body. Getting back in touch with your body will give you the confidence to listen to it for the quantities you need to maintain energy and health.

COOKING FOR ONE OR TWO

Make a larger roast or cook greater quantities of food (more pork chops, larger chicken, more hamburgers) plus more rice, potatoes, or pasta. Portion meat in freezer containers, cool, add gravy (use ice cube tip as explained in Chapter 5), package, and put in the freezer for those rushed days or those "I don't feel like cooking days."

Note Pasta and rice will freeze but potatoes do not freeze well. Reheat leftovers for breakfast or lunch. Add vegetables or a salad.

Note Meat and carbohydrates (pasta and rice) keep a few days in the fridge. Freezing them just gives you more variety, the easy way.

CARBOHYDRATES FOR THE MOST ENERGY

Even if you don't like vegetables you can acquire a taste for them if you introduce them gradually.

Balance and variety are important to gradually introduce more vegetables as you experiment with foods. A way of eating that is rich in fruits, vegetables, and grains may protect you against many kinds of disorders including cancer. Promising research suggests that the so-called antioxidant nutrients such as beta carotene (which the body converts into vitamin A), vitamin C, and other substances in fruits and vegetables may help ward off certain cancers.

When Rod started the program, he didn't like vegetables. In balancing carbohydrates and proteins, he would choose more grains than fruits and vegetables. Then gradually, without being forced, he acquired a taste for some of these other foods. By the end of the program, he was discovering the new taste sensations of vegetables for himself.

Try the darker green leaf lettuce. The darker the leaves, the more nutritious. For example, romaine lettuce has about 6 times as much vitamin C and 8 times as much beta carotene as iceberg lettuce.[10] Be adventurous. Eat "cooking greens" raw sometimes (see vegetable dip in Chapter 14 to go along with the raw vegetables) and salad greens cooked (try recipe for wilted lettuce in Chapter 14).

Normally if you eat only carbohydrates at a meal, you will feel hungry very soon since carbohydrates are digested and absorbed into your bloodstream

118

Now you have discovered a way of eating that gives you more
energy by providing a balance of carbohydrate and protein while
gradually decreasing fat. The carbohydrate source gives you the
energy to fuel your body; adding in the protein allows you to
sustain your energy. The protein slows down the release of sugar
into the bloodstream. In this way, instead of having a burst of
energy from your food, you get the energy in continued spurts
that keeps you going for a longer period of time.

quickly. But what about snacks? Carbohydrate foods
make ideal snacks where the purpose is simply to
hold you over to the next meal. However, when
eating carbohydrates alone, you would like to
prevent the immediate rise then fall in blood sugar.
This effect of low blood sugar will make you feel
tired and hungry again. To prevent this, choose those
carbohydrates that give you a more gradual rise in
blood sugar and are therefore more effective in
holding you over till the next meal.

The complex carbohydrates (breads, pasta, potatoes,
rice, legumes) consist of a longer chain molecule.
Chemically, they take longer to break down than the
simple carbohydrates (milk, vegetables, fruit, sugar,
honey). Using this theory you should focus on
consuming more complex carbohydrate foods.

The entire focus up to this point has been to increase
the quantity of carbohydrates that you may be
consuming. This has been done by including a
variety of both complex and simple carbohydrates.
With meals, a source of protein has been included to
provide a better balance. In the process you may have
discovered that certain carbohydrate foods are more
effective than others in keeping you satisfied at snack
time. Why is this?

Tests have been done using different carbohydrate
foods to discover how these foods would affect blood
sugar physiologically. Normal individuals ingested
1-ounce (28-g) portions of carbohydrate foods and
were tested to see the effect this had on blood sugar
levels. A glycemic index table was the result. This
table provides a method of rating selected carbo-
hydrate-rich foods according to how high they
elevate blood sugar levels. The higher the glycemic

119

index, the more the food elevates blood glucose levels, thereby releasing glucose (sugar) more quickly into the bloodstream.

The glycemic index indicates that your blood sugar will shoot up faster following a snack of potatoes, carrots, or bread, than after a snack of fruit, legumes (beans, peas, or lentils), nuts, or pasta.

FASTER

THE GLYCEMIC INDEX[11]
(rated from quickest glucose release to slowest)

baked potato (russet)
honey
corn flakes
instant potatoes
millet
white/whole wheat bread
corn
Mars Bar
white rice

___

brown rice
raisins
wheat crackers
sucrose (table sugar)
frozen peas
porridge-style oatmeal
banana
buckwheat
sweet potato
pasta
oranges

___

orange juice
whole grain rye bread
apples
dairy products
beans/legumes
plums
cherries
fructose (fruit sugar)
peanuts

SLOWER

Some high-fiber foods can keep blood glucose from soaring after a meal by releasing glucose, our form of energy, in small doses. This prevents blood sugar from going on a roller coaster ride that will cause energy levels to dip. **High-fiber foods achieve this by
1. delaying food release from the stomach, and by
2. slowing the digestion of starch and sugars in the intestine.**

With a slower release of glucose into the blood-stream (flatter glucose response), you have a more sustained energy level.

Other factors that affect glycemic response are
• the amount and type of fiber,
• the form the food is in (i.e. the smoother the texture, the higher the glycemic response),
• the degree to which the food is cooked,
• the speed of eating, and
• timing the consumption of liquids.

THE "HOW MUCH" AND "HOW-TO" OF FIBER[12]
We used to hear a lot about wheat bran and bran muffins. Lately the emphasis has switched to oat bran

and its effect on cholesterol. No need for confusion. Both of these foods contain fiber. However, the type of fiber and its function are different. Water-insoluble fibers, such as wheat bran, can improve bowel regularity. Water-soluble fibers become gel-like during digestion; they are the ones that seem to help keep blood glucose and cholesterol levels in line.

Ensure the gradual increase in fiber content to minimize stomach distress, bloating, and discomfort as well as the focus on lifestyle change. Drink plenty of fluids, especially with insoluble fiber so that it will be able to perform its function of regularity.

SOURCES OF DIETARY FIBER

SOLUBLE	INSOLUBLE
High in pectins and gums	*High in cellulose, hemicelluloses, and lignin*
dried peas, beans, lentils	bran cereals
seeds	whole grain cereals
nuts	whole grain breads & rolls
raw fruits	whole grain crackers
dried fruits	whole grains
raw vegetables	brown rice
cooked vegetables	cracked wheat
oat bran	bulgur

Fructose is a major carbohydrate component of fruits. It takes much longer to release glucose into your system than table sugar (sucrose) because the body must first convert it to glucose before it can be used or stored. In particular, fruits and vegetables high in natural pectin are lower on the glycemic index.

Pectin is a gel-like substance that delays emptying of the stomach. In this way, it makes you feel fuller longer, causing a slower release of glucose into the bloodstream. Fruits and vegetables high in pectin are high in soluble fiber. Fruits and vegetables high in pectin are squash, apples, cauliflower, citrus fruits (grapefruits, oranges), green beans, cabbage, carrots, strawberries, potatoes, legume dried peas.

Dried fruit may be high in soluble fiber but it also contains a concentrated sugar source because the moisture has been taken out. Fresh fruit or fruit canned in its own juice would be a more refreshing choice that would satisfy both hunger and thirst. Even though nuts and seeds are high in soluble fiber and contain some vegetable protein, they are also high in hidden fat. It is easy to eat a cup (250 mL) of peanuts at once without even realizing it. However,

121

along with the peanuts, go 900 calories of which 684 calories come from fat. Why did you eat them? Much of this eating may even be unconscious eating where you are not even tasting the food. A more satisfying choice at roughly 170 total calories would be 1 slice of bread with a tablespoon (15 mL) of peanut butter. By adding the carbohydrate source, the total fat content is essentially reduced and a better balance exists. Only 81 calories or 47 percent of the calories come from fat as opposed to 76 percent of the calories coming from fat by eating the peanuts alone.

Increasing soluble-fiber content such as fruits, vegetables, and oat bran causes a total decrease in the amount of saturated fat in your total eating pattern. Saturated fat is often used in convenience foods in the form of hydrogenated vegetable oil to improve the shelf life of the product. It has the effect of elevating cholesterol levels. However, soluble fiber forms a gel-like substance as it is digested, and it stays in your stomach longer, keeping you full for a longer period of time. It is for this reason that a breakfast consisting of oatmeal porridge may be just as satisfying as a breakfast containing a protein source. You can add fruit and some milk to the porridge to add more fiber as well as a little protein.

Oat bran does not have any flavor of its own and dissolves in liquids. To help incorporate more fiber into your meals, try adding oat bran to the following dishes:
• in hamburgers as a binder instead of crackers or bread crumbs (wheat bran can also be used),
• in muffins,
• in spaghetti meat sauce, stews, or soups as a thickener,
• as toppings on canned fruit, yogurt, or puddings,
• in chili, sloppy joes, meat loaf,
• in batters for pancakes, waffles, muffins, and quick breads.

FOOD FORM
The form the food is in has a bearing on how effective it will be in satisfying you. Insoluble fiber such as that found in whole grain products adds *texture* to food. Since it needs to be chewed more and takes longer to

122

eat, it helps to extend the meal. Pasta is lower on the glycemic index indicating that the sugar is released more slowly into the bloodstream. The compact nature of the starch in pasta reduces accessibility of the starch to digestive enzymes that are involved in breaking down the starch molecule. It takes longer for the starch molecule to break down into sugar and this causes the slower release of the sugar into the bloodstream.

Whole grain rather than whole meal products result in flatter glucose responses keeping you satisfied longer. You can achieve this by
• parboiling wheat to form bulgur,
• parboiling rice to reduce the gelatinization of the starch (the bonus is that this parboiled rice known as converted rice involves a process by which the nutrients are pushed back into the grain resulting in a greater retention of minerals and vitamins in the cooked grain),
• use of whole cereal grain in pumpernickel bread, a whole grain rye bread.

Note **Flour made from whole wheat grains will produce brown-colored bread. But a coloring agent could be used to make brown bread from white flour. To make sure, check the list of ingredients on the label. When brown bread is not made with whole wheat flour, that is when molasses or caramel is used to color the bread, the words "made without whole wheat flour" or "colored with..." must appear on the label according to law.[13] Read your labels!**

Note Potatoes have a greater response on blood sugar levels than rice, spaghetti, or lentils because of the food form. Using whole potatoes with the skin rather than mashed potatoes can change this response. When making french-fried or mashed potatoes, try leaving the skin on for the added fiber and color.

Grinding or cooking a starchy food as in mashed potatoes speeds up the food's absorption in the intestine, causing blood glucose to rise more rapidly.

COOKING FOOD
Try to eat more raw vegetables and fruit. Cook vegetables only to the crisp stage. When foods are

raw, the cellulose cell walls are not completely disrupted by chewing. These prevent access of digestive enzymes to the starch within the cell. Cooking swells the starch within the cell, bursting the cell wall and potentially making the starch more available for digestion.

SPEED OF EATING

Eating slowly maximizes your enjoyment of food and provides an earlier feeling of satiety for a given quantity of food consumed. Slow eating will slow down the release of sugar into your bloodstream. Eating quickly minimizes your enjoyment of food and fools your body's defense against eating too much. It takes roughly 20 minutes for your stomach to tell your brain it's full.

TIMING CONSUMPTION OF LIQUIDS

When liquids are ingested along with solid foods, they empty more rapidly from the stomach into the small intestine. So if you are consuming liquids containing sugar, drink these fluids after a meal. Better yet, keep on diluting those liquids whether they are juices or drinks. You will end up with a beverage that is more refreshing and does wonders for quenching your thirst.

If you find a particular carbohydrate food makes you hungry when eaten alone, try adding a source of protein.

By focusing on increasing the carbohydrate content of your meals, you already have decreased the overall fat content. The next step will be to learn ways to gradually decrease the fat content by preparing foods tastefully with less fat.

> **Ensure that you are eating a variety of sources of carbohydrates to get the benefits of regularity, satiety, and a sustained energy source.**

5
Tailoring Your Tastes

Taking the focus off fat

Is the obsession moving form counting grams of carbohydrate, calories, or exchanges to counting grams of fat? Is this simply a repackaging of the same old diet message where the focus is still on numbers rather than fullness and enjoyment of taste and texture? The answer is yes. Look around you and begin to critically evaluate the new language people are using, the talk in the lunch room, the commercials on television. This is not about a new life-style . . . this is the same message repackaged to attempt to fool the consumer that the intentions of the weight loss industry are real and valid. The fear of fat on your body is now transferred to a fear of eating too much fat in food. Yet, rigidly restricting fat in the way you eat, or replacing an obsession with body fat with counting the amount of fat grams in your food, is adding to your health problems.

Take a look at how *you* feel about fat in the food you eat. Ask yourself these questions:
1. Am I counting the number of grams of fat in the food I eat?
2. Do I base decisions about what foods to eat on the amount of fat in the food?
3. Am I attempting to cut out all fat in my food?
4. Am I afraid of fat on my body and fat in food?
5. Am I buying into society's culture of adopting this behavior as normal and healthy?
6. Does my conversation revolve around food, fat, and fiber?
7. Is this way of thinking causing me to obsess around numbers, calories or fat grams or make me feel bad about myself?
8. Am I restricting my fat intake by too much, resulting in hunger, cravings, and feelings of deprivation?
9. Do I binge on high-fat foods when I get the chance?
10. Do I deny the need to eat some fat for my physical health and enjoyment of food?

If you answered yes to one or more of these questions, then you need to recognize that you can decide to choose to buy into this way of thinking or make some changes.

WHY DO WE NEED TO EAT SOME FAT?
Healthwise, a small amount of fat daily in our daily
126

eating pattern is needed to give us the essential fatty acids we need. Fat is also necessary to act as a carrier for fat soluble vitamins.[1] Just as importantly, fat helps our food to taste and feel good. It makes us feel full and helps to keep us full for a longer period of time because it takes time for us to digest it.

Why the concern about the fat in food? In the past, foods with a higher fat content were prized because they were not as easily found in nature. We have come a long way since that time. Today convenience foods, which are generally higher in fat content than foods prepared from scratch or in their fresh form, are readily available. In recent years investigators have found evidence that the body may be able to convert dietary fat into body fat with greater ease than it can convert carbohydrates (starches and sugars) into body fat. [2-4] In other words, it takes more energy to convert carbohydrates into body fat than to convert fat calories into fat tissue.

In class, when Barbara heard this, she felt she had to cut back her fat intake even more. She was consuming very little fat to begin with—only a little bit in cooking and on her salad. Eating too much fat is not desirable for overall health but dieters can actually restrict their fat consumption too much. Remember those days when people used to restrict carbohydrates, those foods that contain natural sugar like breads, potatoes, and pasta, only to crave those foods later on? The same process may be occurring with fat. Denying yourself fat can lead to feelings of deprivation, increased cravings for fat and eventually bingeing on the food or foods restricted. The purpose is not to go down to the bare minimum of fat, which is the diet mentality. You might end up feeling psychologically deprived and bingeing on higher fat items. Take it gradually. The taste for the lower fat way of eating will come with time.

Today people are more conscious of their fat intake and are consuming less butter and meat. However, the total fat content of their daily intake has not decreased. How could this be? Even though people are eating less meat, trimming the fat off the meats they do eat, and consuming less butter, their fat intake often remains high because there has been an increase in the purchase

127

of specialty foods such as premium ice cream, gourmet soups, and convenience foods such as processed meats. These items are high in fat. If you eat them often you have not learned to enjoy the taste and texture of lower fat foods, you have simply shifted the source of your fat consumption. The visible type of fat is being traded for the hidden fat you don't actually see.

WHERE DOES MEAT FIT IN?

Eating more grains, legumes, fruits, and vegetables instead of convenience foods and protein foods such as prepared meats gives better health and the bonus of a reduced grocery bill. However, some consumers have cut down on beef and pork and are eating more fish and poultry thinking that these items are leaner. Not so, because modern meat sources contain less fat than animals raised years ago.[5] In fact, round steak has the same fat content as the white meat of chicken breast with the skin removed.

Note The type of fish and preparation method will determine whether the fish has a high fat content. Vary the types of fish you eat since fish such as salmon, herring, sardines, mackerel, tuna, and trout contain a higher amount of omega-3 fatty acids which seem to have an effect of lowering blood cholesterol levels.

MAKE ROOM!

Ann would not eat pork and beef because she thought they were too high in fat. But her lunches would often consist of deep-fried chicken or fish burgers, garlic toast, and fries with gravy. All these items are high in fat and Ann added even more fat by topping them with greasy gravy. Was she compensating for the fact that she liked fat and was cutting it out too quickly by eliminating pork and beef? Adding gravy to fries did not allow her to tune into the crispness (texture) of the fries. The idea is not to eat one way at home, "being good all week," only to binge on high-fat foods when you go out, or on weekends, as "your reward." You are not dieting. You are developing a new life-style where your new-found preferences help you to make healthier choices more frequently.[6]

In another situation, Donna decided to use margarine instead of butter as she enjoyed the taste of butter but did not care for margarine. Her thinking was that if she

128

didn't like margarine she would not eat as much of it and therefore decrease the amount of fat she was taking in. This is in fact what happened in the short term. She did eat less margarine and therefore less total fat, but a few months later her craving for butter became so strong that she ended up bingeing on butter. Sudden decreases in fat content are recognized as being part of the dieting process. Attempts to restrict higher fat foods while people still have a preference for these foods result in feelings of deprivation and may cause a higher intake of fat than would normally be consumed.[7]

Thus, the starve/binge cycle that occurs with sweets is now also occurring with fats. Part of the reason for this increase is the tendency to make changes in your eating patterns, in this case, fat intake, too quickly. Sudden changes may turn out to be only temporary changes.

Compare the big jump to the smooth slide in the chart on p130 and decide for yourself which you prefer.

Jane, who is a longtime dieter, ate cottage cheese and fruit every time she was on a diet. The problem was that she did not like the taste or texture of cottage cheese so her new way of eating did not become a life-style change. It was only something temporary she did in order to lose weight. Resuming old habits of eating once the weight has been lost leads to weight gain. And then the cycle brings you right back to the same ineffective and unappetizing eating habits in order to lose weight. To succeed, break the diet cycle.

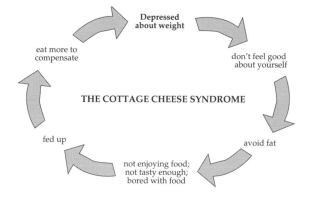

The best plan is to fine-tune your present eating habits.

THE **BIG** DECISION

"I've decided that our whole family is going to move to healthier eating."

	THE BIG JUMP	THE SMOOTH SLIDE
First action on decision	BRACE YOURSELF. Quickly eat all of your favorite foods because they won't be part of your diet tomorrow.	LOOK AT YOURSELF AND FEEL GOOD ABOUT YOU! Feel good that you have made the conscious decision to start making slow changes that will reflect a healthier life-style.
First shopping trip for healthy food	Stock up on foods that say "light," "low fat," and/or "diet" on the labels regardless of whether you enjoy them. Your family likes whole milk but now that you've made the decision to "eat healthy," you buy skim milk.	Stock up on a wide variety of foods that you and your family enjoy, paying more attention to moving towards more carbohydrate foods and less protein. Buy a few herbs to highlight the flavors of your foods. Your family likes whole milk, so now you buy some 2% milk and plan to serve it to your family. If they don't like it at first, you can mix it half and half with whole milk till they prefer the lighter mouth feel.
Feelings of cook after 1 week	Frustrated and overwhelmed. Food is drier than the family enjoys. You still have a strong resolve to eat healthy, even if rest of family isn't as enthusiastic.	Encouraged by how easy it has been to make small changes to the foods, cooking techniques, and carbohydrate/protein balance that the family already enjoy. Surprised that the family hasn't complained or even really noticed the changes. Notices that the foods have a nicer color and texture with all the taste they had before.
Reaction of family after 1 week	Concerned that the food will never be "tasty" anymore. Tired of the new chewier, drier tastes and textures of these new foods. Longing for last week's menu. Quite agile at slipping food to grateful canine under table. Wishing that the budget allowed more order in or eat out foods for next week. Snacking and eating away from home as much as possible.	Surprised that even though the decision to "go healthy" was made, they still get to eat the foods they love! Notice that the foods they loved have more color and just as much, if not more, flavor than before. Feel more energized after they eat rather than tired and overfull.
Feelings of cook at 1 month	Almost ready to give up because no one (including the cook) is enjoying the food that is prepared. Disappointed and feeling deprived. Misses cooking and eating all the foods that the family used to eat. Wishes that cooking wouldn't be such an overwhelming chore. Sneaking "favorites" more and more often.	Excited that the process is still so enjoyable; not even thinking about quitting; having more and more fun experimenting with old and new recipes; pleased with the results, flavors, and textures.
Feelings of family at 1 month	Ready to move to the neighbors during the meal time. Wishing the "health kick" that hit the house would stop kicking. Eating out or ordering in as much as possible and when eating foods they enjoy, really eating lots. Snacking and sneaking foods that they love on a more frequent basis.	Still enjoying the food that is on the table. Asking for certain favorites more often, "When are you going to make that great bread again?" Noticing that they aren't hungry between meals as often.
Situation after 3 months	Disillusioned with the "health movement." Feeling disappointed and a little guilty, they give up and return to the old ways of eating and cooking again. Some of the family only feels "joy" because they finally get to eat what they love!	Feel good about themselves and their new ways of eating and preparing foods. Energized by the successes, the whole family wants to keep moving on the smooth slide toward healthier eating. They are surprised and pleased to find that they actually like the new ways better. They prefer the new flavors, textures, and tastes and don't want to go back.

© 1995 *Tailoring Your Tastes* by Linda Omichinski, RD and Heather Wiebe Hildebrand, RN

Start from where you are right now and implement gradual changes to allow your entire family to acquire a taste for a healthier way of eating. Begin by ensuring that you have a balanced menu and then gradually make changes to bring out new flavors and textures.

Many people are enthusiastic about a new way of eating at the beginning of the program but then give up because trying new ideas seems too much trouble. This process is actually easier than switching to all new recipes and foods. You don't have to spend time gathering new recipes and buying new ingredients to get on the road to healthier eating. When you try to alter your recipes drastically, you are switching back into the diet mentality. It is better to adjust your present recipes while retaining, even enhancing, the flavor and texture you are used to. Otherwise, you may bake and eat flavorless cookies which do not satisfy you, and this inevitably leads to bingeing on the cookies you do like. When you are out of the diet mentality, you will eat only 1 or 2 cookies at a time instead of 6 or the whole box of cookies. Making a diet recipe that contains half the calories and eating twice as much is not the way to change your tastes and listen to your body.

Putting the HUGS philosophy into practice by gradually cutting back fat content does not mean eliminating fat. Gradual is the key. Otherwise you will miss the flavors you enjoy, feel deprived, and become very discouraged.

Sylvia had a hard time accepting the idea of gradual change. "But I have a friend who eats in a healthy way and exercises regularly and she looks great. So why can't I do it too?" She wanted immediate results. I eventually discovered that Sylvia's friend puts all her efforts into looking good and doing things just right. Then she gets fed up and reverts to her old behavior. Apparently she does this several times throughout the year. If you constantly compare yourself to others, you will be wasting your energy on wishful thinking rather than action. Remember, you are doing this for yourself for a lifetime. Do it gradually, one step at a time, and never mind what others think.

131

SELECTIONS THAT SATISFY

Part of the philosophy of listening to your body and tuning into taste and texture involves making gradual changes, one step at a time. If you are getting cravings for foods high in fat, it may be a sign that you are not eating frequently enough or that you are restricting your fat intake too much. You will gradually acquire a taste for new foods with lower fat content. Remember, the new way of eating is for life! You do not want to feel deprived while you are acquiring your new tastes.

You are listening to your body if:
1. You are tuning into the texture, taste, and satiety value of the meal.
2. You are enjoying the energizing feeling of balanced meals. Higher fat meals make your mind and your body sluggish by slowing circulation and reducing the oxygen-carrying capacity of the red blood cells. Meals too low in fat will leave you feeling hungry and thinking about food.
3. You are accommodating your present taste preferences by only making slight changes in your eating pattern.
4. You are checking the regularity of meals and the type and quantity of food eaten if you are experiencing cravings.
5. You are paying attention to the experience of eating and allowing yourself to taste, savor, and enjoy your meal.

If you answer no to some of the above questions, reassess if you are eating too low fat and therefore need to readjust to a more normal and natural way of eating. A low-fat way of eating is not desirable for everyone all the time. If something does not feel right, make adjustments and go slower in the process of moving towards healthier eating. Recognize that any change is progress. Striving for a particular endpoint is falling back into the diet thinking. Use improved health as your guide. Tailor your tastes to appreciate the slight subtle differences in the taste and texture (the "mouth feel") of healthier foods. If they are not becoming choices you make because you prefer and enjoy them, then you are returning to the diet mentality.

132

Let's look at some examples.

If you need a snack, eat it; otherwise, you will be too hungry by the next meal and will eat too quickly and not enjoy your food as much. Eat regularly, being guided by your physical hunger and appetite. Try introducing more carbohydrates and do not restrict yourself to salads alone. They do not have much substance and may lead to bingeing later on. While a salad may fill you up more quickly because of the high water content of the lettuce, there is little substance and few nutrients in the meal. In fact, there is almost twice as much fat in a caesar salad as a roast beef sandwich. A meat sandwich, on the other hand, will provide you with more carbohydrate for energy, nutrients, and holding power, not to mention the feeling of satisfaction and taste. *The aim is to focus more on the satisfaction, taste, and hold-over power of foods and meals rather than the content of fat and calories.*

Compare fast food at home to a fast-food meal in a restaurant. A typical fast-food chicken dinner has over four times the amount of fat as a well balanced 20-minute home-made chicken dinner. Those of you familiar with fast-food fried chicken will remember the grease marks on plates and napkins, the greasy fingers and lips that require a soap and water wash after eating, the thirst produced by the extra salt needed to cut through the fat flavor, and the full and bloated feeling after eating. In contrast, the home-cooked chicken meal has a variety of colors, tastes, and textures, and leaves a refreshing, satisfying feeling.

FAST FOOD AT HOME
Twenty-minute home-cooked dinner (for four)
Baked breaded chicken
Rice
Peas with green onions
Sliced tomato
Milk (2%)
compare this with:
Fast-food fried chicken dinner
1 piece side breast
French fries
Coleslaw
Milk (2%)

TAKING THE FOCUS OFF FAT ADDS PIZZAZZ TO MEALS

"My partner is a great cook and it tastes so good. I agree with the saying 'butter makes it better.' Doesn't it?"

Maybe not. The true chef can use herbs tastefully without a lot of fat to bring out the flavors in a meal. (See Chapter 14 for more details.) Changing to a lower fat way of eating can be a simple matter of adapting the foods you normally enjoy. Lower fat eating can still mean eating very well, especially when foods are prepared at home. Food can be moist, tasty, and have flavor and texture without being heavy with grease.

In order to acquire a taste for foods and meals lower in fat, you have to learn how to make gradual changes to your food preparation techniques so that you will enjoy the end product. The traditional way of frying with fat and no lid leads to moisture evaporation and food sticking to the bottom of the pan. Adding more fat results in a meal loaded with fat and grease, which is heavy on the stomach and difficult to digest. Instead of feeling energized, you feel drowsy.

Choosing meat with less marbling (the streaks of fat seen throughout a cut of meat) and trimming all visible fat off meat before cooking can sometimes result in a drier, less tender product. Try using a non-stick frying pan with a lid to retain the moisture. Trim the fat from the meats, sear the meat in a non-stick frying pan with a light coating of oil or non-stick cooking spray, turn the meat over, brown, and add the lid while the meat cooks. When the oil has been heated, add onions, garlic, and fresh or dried herbs for more flavor prior to adding the meat. If meat sticks to the pan, deglaze with wine, alcohol, milk, or vegetable or fruit juice, water and herbs, or broth or water with a bouillon cube to brown the meat nicely. The liquid will gradually evaporate and it can be thickened to make a gravy, if desired. The alcoholic content does not remain.

You can brown meat in the oven instead of using a frying pan. Just coat the meat lightly with seasoned flour and place it on a rack set over the pan to catch the drippings. Bake at 350°F (180°C) for 15 to 20 minutes. Chops can also be done in the oven on a rack in a

134

covered dish. Add seasonings instead of fat flavor.

Roasting can be done on a rack in a covered roaster. The rack prevents the fat drippings from coming into direct contact with the roast, so the roast will be less greasy. Use lower temperatures when cooking a roast, 325°F or 160°C (for tender cuts) and 275°F or 130°C (for medium tender cuts). This process retains the moisture, reduces shrinkage, and prevents the fat from going back into the roast. Gravy can be added for flavor, color, and moisture. Remove the roast, then put ice cubes in the fat drippings to allow the drippings to cool quickly. The number of ice cubes added will depend on the volume of juices. Ensure that sufficient ice cubes are added so all the fat rises to the top as it cools. Remove fat and thicken juices with flour or cornstarch. Lump-free gravy thickeners are also available to make the job easier. Quark cheese, yogurt, or oat bran can also be used as thickeners. Add extra seasonings such as garlic or onion powder or milder herbs and spices to add new flavors. *Note* If time permits, placing the gravy in the freezer or refrigerator will allow the fat to float to the surface for easy removal.

> Use sauces as accents to meat, not the main feature. Tune into texture and natural flavor.

Less tender cuts of meat are best cooked in liquid (braising, stewing, or pot roasting) to create succulent, tasty dishes. Marinating meat helps to tenderize and add flavor. Marinating liquids include wine, vinegar, seasoned vinegars, soy sauce, citrus juices, beer, yogurt, and oil. The acidic ingredients soften the tough connective tissue and the oil lubricates. Often the oil can be eliminated. Don't use salt in a marinade because it draws out the moisture.

When microwaving beef, it is not recommended that beef come to room temperature before microwaving. It is best to slightly undercook beef. Remember, cooking continues during standing time. Large dense items need a standing time of 10 to 20 minutes. Overcooking or cooking at too high a power level causes the meat to be dry and tough.

Steaming, microwaving, or stir-frying vegetables retains the flavor, texture, and color. If you sauté vegetables, cook them over lower heat and add white wine or water to help soften them. The addition of fresh or dried herbs can heighten the flavor. Use herbs such as dill, rosemary, thyme, and garlic instead of salt for flavor. Thyme is a mild herb that works well with any dish and the bonus is that it is high in iron. A small amount of a simple white sauce (below) will enhance the natural flavor of vegetables.

White sauce Place a teaspoon (5 ml) of oil in a non-stick frying pan. Add fresh or dried herbs to hot oil to extract the flavor of the herbs. Add chopped onions, if desired. Add skim or 1% milk or yogurt and heat. Thicken with flour or cornstarch, or for convenience, add white instant gravy thickener. If you prefer a cheese sauce, add a hint of your favorite cheese to accent the flavor of the vegetables (too much cheese will mask the vegetable flavor).

When using oil to saute foods, use a heavy non-stick pan so that a light coating of oil will prevent the food burning. Make sure the oil is hot before adding the ingredients in order to reduce the amount of oil that soaks into the food.

Roasted french fries Crisp, tasty french fries can be made without them tasting and feeling greasy. Cut potatoes into french fry strips, toss lightly with a bit of oil to coat the potatoes lightly, and add seasoning, if desired. Cook in a hot oven (425° to 450°F or 210° to 230°C) on a non-stick baking tray brushed with a very thin coating of oil to prevent potatoes from sticking as the starch is released. Cook for 15 to 25 minutes, turn and cook for another 15 to 25 minutes, or until brown.

Seasoned rice The cooking instructions on the rice box may call for butter or margarine. Since minute rice is so overly processed it needs extra fat or spices to give it flavor. Use converted rice instead. It takes only 20 minutes to cook, has more nutrients than even long grain rice, and you end up with rice that does not stick together. Add a bouillon cube or juice to water to add flavor to rice. Chopped vegetables such as celery, mushrooms, onions, and herbs and spices make a very nice rice pilaf. Brown rice is now available in the converted form (the rice is parboiled and some of the nutrients are pushed back in). Note that packaged seasoned rice is costly and is often disappointing and

TIP To microwave your vegetables so they are crisp and not mushy, put a consistent quantity of vegetables cut uniformly on to a plate, cover with plastic wrap, and watch for it to fill with air. When this happens the vegetables are cooked but still crisp.

Note Potatoes do not need to be peeled. Peels add color and fiber to the potatoes and most of the vitamins are right under the peel. Add paprika or your favorite seasoning. These potatoes are a real treat for the whole family.

136

A small amount of the real thing may be more satisfying than a large amount of something artificial. The substitute is okay, if you can enjoy the taste.

artificial tasting, so go with the real thing!

Flavor enhancers   Herbs and spices are natural flavor enhancers (see Chapter 14 for more details). Substitutes for high-fat products are effective only if you enjoy the replacement. For example, if you enjoy butter on your potato and you replace it with a lower fat product such as light sour cream or yogurt, which you don't really like, then eventually you will crave the butter. The true butter connoisseur might try gradually using less butter as an accent to the meal. On the other hand, if you enjoy the replacement, then the substitute will work. Low-fat substitutes, such as diet margarines or diet butters, are high in water content. For this reason, they cannot be used for frying. If you try to fry with them, you will notice that the pan soon becomes dry because the water from the product evaporates as soon as it is exposed to heat. The high water content of these products can make hot toast soggy. Experiment and do what works best for you.

If you are drinking whole milk, try diluting it with 2% for several weeks until you get accustomed to this taste. Then try 2% milk for several weeks. Work your way down to mixing 2% and 1% and then finally switch to 1%. You may decide to stop here or to mix 1% and skim and finally drink only skim milk. Skim milk has a fuller body than it did years ago due to the higher solid content. As you become aware you will gradually acquire a taste for foods with a more refreshing, less thick texture. This is much easier and more enjoyable than the diet approach of going from whole milk to skim milk all in one swoop.

Cheese has a high hidden fat content. If you like cheddar cheese and go straight to cottage cheese, you may find it difficult to adjust to this sudden drop in fat content. If you don't like cottage cheese because of its taste and lumpy texture, then you will eat it temporarily because you think you should and then go back to what you were doing before. If you prefer the taste and texture of cheddar cheese, try mixing it with skim mozzarella or a lower fat cheddar cheese to gradually reduce the greasy feel and still savor the cheddar taste. Eventually you may prefer the lighter taste of the lower fat cheese.

137

WHY THERE AREN'T NUMBERS (CALORIES OR FAT COUNTS) IN THIS BOOK

Focusing on numbers can take the enjoyment out of life and it doesn't help us to become healthier, happier people. We exercise to lose weight or burn calories rather than to enjoy the outdoors or feel the improved energy and self-concept that activity brings. We feel good about ourselves on the days when we weigh the "right" amount and feel depressed and forlorn when we are above that number. Often we choose foods because they are lower in fat or have fewer calories rather than because we enjoy them. But when we get tired of counting we crave the familiar flavors, tastes, and activities we enjoyed before, and we return to old eating habits and patterns. None of these numbers help us to become healthy and numbers didn't help us to learn to enjoy the flavors and textures of foods lower in fat, sugar, and salt and higher in fiber. Numbers just provide a rule book of what is good and bad to eat.[8]

So let's look at food in another way. What are the flavors and textures of the foods we enjoy? What is it about food we enjoy? Can we slowly change our preference for familiar flavors and textures to reflect healthier eating patterns without becoming obsessed with numbers? We know we can! The charts on pp139 and 140 illustrate how the tastes and textures of familiar foods prepared and served in the usual ways can slowly be replaced by an appreciation of foods and meals with more refreshing and energizing qualities. It isn't important to know the exact calorie or fat content of food. What is important is that you enjoy what you eat.[9]

Tailoring your tastes to enjoy new flavors and textures is a slow, pleasurable process. Over time, your new choices will become preferences. You will choose techniques and foods which are lower in fat, sugar, and salt and higher in fiber because you *prefer* them, not because you think you *should* eat them. When you prefer something, you repeat it. Repeating healthier lifestyle practices leads to healthier living. You can find more information regarding these areas in *Tailoring Your Tastes*.[10] (See order form at back of book.)

THE PROCESS OF TAILORING YOUR TASTES

	TRADITIONAL	NEW EXPERIENCE
Appearance	Grease may be seen or is floating on top of sauces, salads, or soups. Washed out colors of vegetables. Thick beverages. Grease leaves a mark on napkins.	Refreshing, clean looking. Sauces, dressings, and garnishes provide a colorful accent without overwhelming the food. Exciting colors and textures.
Taste	Subtle flavors not noticeable. Flavors masked by fat taste. Sauces, dressings, or garnishes overwhelm the food. Needs more salt or sugar to bring out flavors masked by fat.	Natural flavor can be tasted. Less salt and seasonings needed. The more you taste it, the better it gets; taste is subtle and builds gradually. Sauces, dressings, and garnishes enhance flavor without overwhelming it.
Texture	Mushy, gooey, soft, dense, greasy.	Crunchy, crisp, chewy, cleaner.
Mouth feel	Coats mouth, greasy; beverages leave mouth more dry, coated with fullness of beverage.	Experience the variety of textures and consistencies. Beverages feel refreshing and go down easily.
Body response	Heavy feeling as it goes down. Feel tired and bloated when finished. Beverages leave you feeling still thirsty.	Refreshing, satisfying feeling as it goes down. Not overfilling. Leaves you energized. Beverages quench your thirst.

Broken down into food categories, the above chart would look like this:

Soups & Appetisers	Rich, creamy mouth feel, coats top of mouth, overpowering with first mouthful, subtle flavors not noticeable, real taste is masked, heavy feeling as it goes down.	Real flavor can be tasted, less salt or seasonings necessary, the more you taste it, the better it gets; taste is subtle and builds gradually, refreshing, satisfying feeling as it goes down. Coarser texture; garnishes used only as accents, don't overpower.
Salads & Dressings	Heavy, salad is drenched so that crunch and texture is not noticed; color is washed out.	Dressings provide a colorful accent and bring salad to life; salad remains crunchy and colorful.
Bread & Bread Products	Soft, cake-like texture; no coarseness; a greasy feel on fingers and mark on napkin.	Experience the chewier texture, the satisfying mouth feel of the grains. Breads have a coarser look, and variety in color and texture. You are able to taste the flavor and feel the moisture without masking it with fat.
Vegetables	Gooey, mushy, washed out, needs butter or margarine on them for any flavors; sauce overpowers vegetables.	Crisp, subtle flavor that adds life to the plate; crunchy; herbs, spices, and sauce enhance without drowning flavor; vibrant colors.
Main Dishes	Heavy, greasy, rich sauces; too full feeling; feel tired and bloated when finished.	Natural flavors more pronounced; a balance of carbohydrate and protein; exciting colors and textures; satisfying, not over full.
Fluids (full strength)	The "pucker" experience that leaves mouth more dry, coated with fullness of beverage, stark in color, still thirsty afterward.	*(water added to beverage—refer to chapter 11)* Refreshing feel, goes down more easily, leaves your thirst quenched and satisfied, a hint of color, subtle flavor.

Desserts	Rich, creamy, dense texture heavy feeling once you have eaten; garnishes overpower it, fat masks other flavors.	Airy, fluffier texture; taste true flavors of ingredients, garnishes used as accents, a pleasant ending to a meal.
Snacks	Rich, greasy, leave a ring on the napkin and greasy fingers.	Crunchier, flavorful, and chewy; a more substantial, satisfying feeling.

MODIFYING RECIPES TO SUIT YOUR NEW TASTES

Getting in tune with the HUGS philosophy does not mean turning to special low-fat versions of recipes and spending a lot of time preparing new foods. It means modifying your present recipes and learning what you can do to enjoy new flavors and textures which are not masked by fat. Use your own recipes, and let your creativity and new-found knowledge allow you to make slight changes so that you produce a product that is moist, tasty, and lower in fat and sugar content.

Muffins

Function of fat — moisture, flavor
Function of sugar — tenderizer, flavor (sweetness); need sugar for egg to coagulate at a higher temperature, allowing muffins to rise. Cutting out the sugar completely will result in small muffins.

> **Take time to adjust to new taste before making more changes.**

Initially, decrease sugar and fat called for by 1/4. Next time you make muffins, you may be able to decrease the sugar and fat a little more. Enhance the new flavors by using sweeter spices such as cinnamon, mace, lemon extract, vanilla extract, lemon or orange peel, or your favorite spice. If the recipe already contains one of these, try doubling the amount.

Retain the moisture by adding milk, yogurt, or light sour cream. Applesauce, pineapple, juice, blueberries, shredded carrots, or chopped raisins can add back moisture and some sweetness. Raisins are a concentrated source of sugar, so a small amount goes a long way.

Replace leavening by adding more baking powder and baking soda with the sifted flour (1/2 tsp or 2 ml baking soda and 2 tsp or 10 ml baking powder). Ensure that you sift the baking powder and baking soda with the flour; otherwise lumps of these ingredients may

140

appear in your muffins. If you can taste the soda and do not like it, then add a little more sugar the next time and slightly cut back on the baking soda content of the recipe.

Cookies
Function of fat — to allow creaming effect of ingredients, flavor
Function of sugar — sweetness, allows creaming effect.

Sugar, flour, and fat are the main ingredients. Cutting back on sugar and fat too much does not allow the creaming effect to occur. Sugar also adds to the sweetness of the cookies so you may be able to cut back by about half and replace with some sweeter spices such as nutmeg and cinnamon. Fat content can only be cut back slightly (by 1/4). Cutting the fat content too much will change the nature of the cookies. A crispy oatmeal cookie may become a chewy oatmeal cookie that, with time, will go hard. To keep cookies moist, add milk to replace the moisture taken out by cutting back the fat content. Applesauce or blueberries can also add back moisture to cookies or brownies. Try storing cookies in a tight cookie jar with a slice of apple. This will help retain some moisture.

Less fat in a recipe may reduce cooking time by around 25 percent. Overcooking will result in a dry product.

The idea is to modify your present recipes so that they still taste good and you will enjoy them. The purpose is to learn to taste and savor more wholesome foods. *Learn to tune into the texture and wholesome flavor to ensure the end product is enjoyable.*

CAKES AND QUICK BREADS
Try replacing the butter in your recipe with sour cream. If this works, the next step is to try to replace some of the sour cream with plain low-fat yogurt and eventually to move towards using more plain low-fat yogurt.

Use the concept of replacing oil with fruit juice to give moisture and flavor to all your cooking. Chicken fingers made this way are moist and tasty. Use a deboned chicken breast, dunk slices in concentrated orange juice and then bread crumbs or crushed cornflakes. Bake in the oven. Makes a tasty meal or an innovative snack! Let your creativity take hold for your own creations.

141

TIPS & TECHNIQUES FOR LOWER FAT COOKING

When you move toward lower fat foods you will find that there are some techniques and ideas that will make the move more enjoyable. Try the following suggestions. You can use these ideas and techniques in your own recipes.

These techniques help to make baked and cooked foods tastier, moister, and more enjoyable when using less fat content. Some of the techniques are a little more time consuming than traditional methods of cooking. Once you begin to incorporate these skills into your way of cooking, they become a more natural quick process. The end results are worth the extra effort. Enjoy the gradual process of change. Make meal preparation a fun part of your day by including your family.

Browning ground beef
• Ground beef can be browned alone or with onion and garlic in a microwave oven. Place beef, onions, and garlic in a microwave-safe sieve. Put the sieve in a microwave-safe bowl.
• Microwave uncovered on high for 2 to 3 minutes at a time. Take the meat mixture out and stir. Return to microwave again.
• Repeat this procedure until the meat is completely browned. The sieve will allow fat to drip to the bottom of the bowl, so you aren't cooking the meat in the fat.

Sautéing vegetables
• Replace some or all of the sauteing oil with dry white wine to add moisture to vegetables. You may need a greater amount of wine than oil because the liquid cooks out of the wine faster than the oil. Adding about 1/4 cup (50 ml) white wine increases the sugar content to the equivalent of approximately 1/4 tsp (1 ml) white sugar. The increase is very small and compensates for the decrease in fat content.
• Cheaper white wine found at liquor stores is a good choice. Using a bottle with a screw top makes storage easier. Remember the alcohol content is removed during the cooking process as long as the wine boils (which it does when sautéing).
• Using wine to saute vegetables results in a lower fat

142

food that has a lovely tangy flavor. And the aroma of vegetables cooking in white wine is very appealing.

Separate eggs and whip the whites
• Use this technique for a lighter fluffier texture, when baking lower fat cookies, puddings, cakes, or muffins.
• Separate egg whites and beat until they are white and hold their shape. Add egg yellows to other ingredients as outlined in the recipe. Follow the recipe as instructed, leaving the egg whites until the end. Then gently fold the beaten egg whites into the remainder of the ingredients until completely blended.

Underbake cookies
• Cookies have a nicer texture if they are slightly underbaked and this is essential when the fat content is decreased.
• Never bake a lower fat cookie much longer than 8 minutes in a 375°F (191°C) oven (time will vary depending on the oven).
• When the outside of the cookies start to get firm, the middles will still look soft and unbaked. However, once the cookies have cooled they will be moister than if they are overbaked.

Tips for storing lower fat baked foods
• Most lower fat baked foods taste best fresh. If you want to store them, use an airtight container. Store them in your freezer and remove only what you want to eat at one sitting.
• Lower fat baked foods can be stored on your counter in an airtight container for a few days. However, lower fat foods don't taste as good the second day. Freezing everything not used the day it is baked is preferable.

Using low-fat yogurt
• Plain or plain low-fat yogurt (.9% M.F. or less) can replace some of the oil, shortening, or butter/margarine in cakes, cookies, or muffins.
• Adding yogurt to a baked food replaces some of the moisture lost when fat is decreased.

Using honey, corn syrup, or molasses to sweeten lower fat foods
• These products can be used in baking when you

are decreasing the fat content to replace all or part of the sugar content in recipes.

• These three sweeteners replace moisture that is lost when decreasing oil and fat and add lovely flavors to foods.

• Honey, corn syrup, or molasses do not have the same sweetening capacity as table or brown sugar, so you can't replace them cup for cup in a recipe. Here are some guidelines for the same amount of sweetness:

—**Honey** about *3/4 cup (175 ml) honey to 1 cup (250 ml) sugar*

—**Corn syrup** *3/4 cup (175 ml) plus 2 tbsp (30 ml) corn syrup to 1 cup (250 ml) sugar*

—**Molasses** *1 cup (250 ml) molasses to 1 cup (250 ml) sugar*

• Honey, corn syrup, and molasses give foods an added soft texture when used in place of sugar. Molasses has a distinctive flavor and dark color.

• If you substitute honey directly for table sugars, you will actually be consuming more sugar than you were originally.

• When making changes to your recipes do so gradually. If you make changes too quickly you and your family won't enjoy the flavor changes. Slower changes last longer.

Unsweetened applesauce adds moisture to lower fat foods

• Unsweetened applesauce adds extra moisture and sweetness to recipes so you won't notice the decrease in sugar and/or fat in lower fat cooking. You may want to decrease the sugar content when using this product in baking to replace some of the fat. Otherwise you will end up increasing instead of decreasing the total sugar content due to the natural sugar in applesauce.

• Do not use unsweetened applesauce in the same recipe you are replacing the sugar content with alternate sweetening agents such as honey, molasses, or corn syrup. The end product will be too moist and won't hold together.

• Unsweetened applesauce has a much less sweet taste than table sugar. Use *1/2 cup (125 ml) unsweetened applesauce to 1 tbsp (15 ml) white sugar* for the same amount of sweetening power.

6

When to Eat, How Much to Eat

Tune into your natural hunger signals. Eat whatever you want whenever you want, as long as you are physically hungry.

THE HUGS ™ PROGRAM OFFERS NO SET DIET.

The positive result of a lack of structure is flexibility. You can replace your old way of eating with an improved and more healthful eating style. If you have been accustomed to following a diet, you may think that this method cannot work since there is no rigid pattern to follow. However, focus and flexibility can replace structure.

The focus is getting you to deal with the cause of your poor eating habits. Why did you get to this stage in the first place? The focus is to show you how to eat in a way that gives you more energy and keeps you satisfied. HUGS™ is a new concept of healthy eating and healthy living.

Follow the HUGS™ guidelines and balance your carbohydrates and protein sources, gradually cut back the fat content in your food choices and food preparation methods, and note when you are actually physically hungry. If you eat all the time, you won't give your body a chance to experience hunger. If you are used to dieting and starving, you may be out of tune with what real hunger is, especially if you have been ignoring it for a number of years. If you have recently stopped smoking, you too will be out of touch with your internal hunger signals. If you wait until you are too hungry, there is a danger of being famished, "gobbling" your food, and overeating. In these situations it's unlikely that you are tasting your food.

HUGS™ gives you permission to eat. The danger is that you may swing the other way and eat everything in sight. Can this happen? Long-term denial and deprivation of food can lead to a rebellion against dieting, whether you or someone else gives you the permission to eat. Permission to eat can be frightening because of the lack of rigid control. With HUGS™ you are taking charge. Rather than someone else learning to ride the bike for you, you are actually learning to ride it yourself. You are learning a new skill.

When you feel you can't or shouldn't have

146

something, you often desire it more. On the other hand, if you know you can have it, you might not want it as much. Realize that you are striving to bring the pendulum back to the middle so that you learn to eat like a nondieter, that is, someone who eats when he or she is physically hungry. Check how you feel 3 to 4 hours after eating to help you to tune into your natural hunger.

DO DIETERS THINK DIFFERENTLY?

Do you think like a nondieter? Two psychologists, Polivy and Herman, from Toronto,[1] gave 40 dieters and 40 nondieters 2 milkshakes each to drink followed by an offer of ice cream as part of a controlled study.

ALL DONE !

The dieters finished their milkshakes and ate the ice cream too. The nondieters ate very little ice cream once they finished the milkshakes. Why is there a difference between the actions of the dieters and the nondieters? The dieters' thinking is all-or-nothing thinking. "I blew my diet anyway, so I'll go for it and eat it all. Since I'll go back to dieting and depriving myself tomorrow, I'd better get my fill." Dieters either diet faithfully or not at all. Once they have been deprived for so long, they may not be able to control themselves. The pendulum has swung the other way.

Continue to observe nondieters and children. They are in tune with their natural hunger signals and those that signal appetite and fullness (physical satisfaction). What are they doing in order to eat when they are hungry and stop when they are full? Try to model their actions.

Often dieters are perfectionists and their "absolutely perfect" mentality transfers to other aspects of their life as well. "I'll clean the house completely or not at all. I'm that type of person." It is this all-or-nothing thinking that can lead to frustration when something doesn't proceed perfectly. This type of rigid thinking does not allow a person to be human.

There is flexibility in the nondieter's thinking and this is how it differs from the dieter's thinking. The nondieters, once the milkshakes were finished, chose to eat very little ice cream because they were in tune with their bodies' feelings of hunger and fullness. They were satisfied with the milkshakes and were no longer hungry. The added fact that they knew they could have more ice cream when they wanted it decreased the need to have it immediately. The nondieters were tuning into their internal cues of

147

hunger. The dieters responded to the external cue of sight. "I see it—I want it!"

The second part of the Polivy and Herman study dealt with both groups being given no milkshakes, after which both groups were offered ice cream. This time the dieters ate no ice cream. The "all-or-nothing" response was: "I'm still on my diet, so since I did not start to eat anything illegal, I'll be able to forgo the ice cream. I have the willpower to say no."

The nondieters who did not have milkshakes but were offered ice cream ate a lot of ice cream. They were tuning into their internal hunger signals. The nondieters were physically hungry and therefore ate the offered ice cream.

DIET THINKING	NONDIET THINKING
"all-or-nothing"	listens to the body's needs
I will have it all or nothing at all	is flexible
perfectionist attitude	human—goes with the flow
responds to external cues of sight, smell, and power of suggestion	responds to internal cues— eats when hungry
out of touch with physical hunger—may eat in response to psychological hunger, i.e. when under stress	in tune with body's internal cues of physical hunger; listens to body, does not turn to food when dealing with problems such as stress
diet is in control	person is in control and decides when and what to eat
asks self, "Should I have it, do I need it?"	asks self, "Do I want it?"

How do you shift your thinking to be a nondieter? The first step is to acknowledge what you are doing and accept it, just as you accepted yourself as you are without condition. Without acceptance of yourself, too much energy is diverted toward feeling sorry for yourself and feeling negative.

An illustration of this is a neglected plant that grows tall, thin, and straggly as the energy is diverted upward. With a little caring, by snipping it, the

148

energy is no longer wasted but rather the nutrients and energy are used where they are most needed, for growth.

By accepting yourself, you use your energy to take care of yourself rather than divert your energy by criticizing yourself.

HUGS™ wants you to grow from within and burst forth with new shoots, as the plant does. So don't waste your energy being negative. Go with the flow and learn from your mistakes. *Care about yourself enough to listen to your body and find out what is really causing you to eat.* Ask yourself what is happening that you need to distract yourself by eating or worrying about your eating? Take a moment to reflect on reasons why you are eating.

When you eat for these reasons, are you really tasting your food or are you eating to drown your sorrows? Does food give you a temporary lift? Does it deal with the problem? It's time to replace this dependency on food. Have confidence in yourself, trust yourself, believe in yourself. Only you can uncover the reasons for your eating and learn new techniques to deal with them more positively. Remember that if you feel you were not successful in the past, it is not you that failed but the diets that failed you. *Diets don't work.* You can succeed by getting rid of the diet and the diet mentality. As you begin to discover yourself, you will be drawing on your inner self, that is, you will be internally motivated. Remember, *action creates motivation. Once you have discovered why you are eating, take action.*

Reasons For Eating
- boredom
- loneliness
- frustration
- stress
- anger
- rushed
- comfort food
- tension
- social occasion
- everyone else is eating
- happy
- sad
- "see-food" diet ("I see it, I want it")
- tired
- insomnia
- PMS

149

Now that you have discovered why you are eating, what do you do about it? Meet the causes of your eating head on. Eating only provides temporary relief from thinking of your other problems. These problems will recur if you don't deal with them and so will the eating. Catch yourself as you are reaching for the food and ask yourself, "Do I really want it or do I think I want it simply because it's there and everyone else is eating?" If you just follow the crowd then the calories are wasted and will end up on the waist. Part of life-style change is acquiring a taste for less fattening foods and learning to eat until you are satisfied, not stuffed. Eat only those things that you really want and only if you are hungry.

When you eat because of a happy event to celebrate something that you accomplished, the food becomes a reward. It is a social custom to eat at such times and this is why you feel that you need something as an external reward to complete the happiness. Try not eating and allow yourself to experience the pleasant feeling of accomplishment for itself.

Eating because you are sad, depressed, or angry may provide a temporary comfort that you are searching for. But the problem that brought on these feelings remains and must be dealt with. Do you feel that you must always be "up" and happy? What's wrong with allowing yourself to experience sad or frustrating emotions and working them through? It is part of normal life to go through these "ups and downs." Try to deal with the issues at hand. This will help to level off the roller coaster ride of emotions.

Loneliness and boredom and television seem to trigger the food munchies. Social occasions where there is drinking also empties many peanut bowls. Suddenly you are out of control, the peanut bowl is empty, and you don't even remember eating them.

Loneliness is often tied to not fully appreciating our own company. Nancy always goes into the "tea and toast" syndrome when her husband is away. After all, she has no one to cook for or to try to please. She reaches for the sweets to keep her company and to comfort her.

150

Wait a minute! You are worth the little extra effort to prepare a sit-down meal for yourself, and maybe even a candle to go with it. This is your free time; you can do whatever you want. It's your own time to reassess your goals and redirect your life, time to think things through or maybe just relax, clear your mind and enjoy some peaceful moments. Don't waste the moment by feeling sorry for yourself. You are special too!

You come home from work, tired. You eat, clean up, and then plunk yourself in front of television. There is nothing else to do so you might as well eat. Stimulation is in order. People tend to get into an everyday humdrum routine, taking the safe and easy route in life. Well, this route is also the boring route. Try to incorporate a little risk, a little excitement, a little adventure into your life. One of my favorite years of married life was the year we didn't have a television. We made our own fun and enjoyed simple things. Sure we need goals and direction to get somewhere in life, but we also need to make room for spontaneity and fun — even a little adventure now and then! When we grow up, we become more serious about life. Observe children once in a while and then attempt to bring out the child in you.

It's easy for food to become the center of attention, even for animals! When we first got our new kitten, we played with her frequently. In a couple of months we stopped. All of a sudden, before our very eyes, she became fat. We were told by our veterinarian to put her on a diet because she was too fat for her health, especially at such a young age. Of course dieting is totally against my philosophy. I would never put a child on a diet. Are animals different?

My husband and I decided to try an experiment. We began to play with the cat more. I play a version of floor hockey in the kitchen with her and Mitchell plays hide and seek. We enjoy it. It's therapeutic to play with animals. These days Dynamite is dashing around getting in her aerobics in her own way.

She has slimmed down naturally. Food is no longer the center of her attention. She eats, but she doesn't

151

only eat. Food has a new perspective for her. Dynamite lives by the HUGS™ philosophy now. She has interests other than food! So find that little excitement in life that can rejuvenate you. Observe others who have other hobbies and see how food fits into their lives.

Overeating at social occasions once in a while isn't an issue. It's part of being normal. The type of thinking to watch out for is dieting during the week, only to allow yourself to binge on the weekend. This is the diet mentality. Try eating the foods you desire more regularly, then when someone offers your favorite onion rings, you can eat a few and not crave them so much that you stuff yourself. Taste and savor and enjoy *without guilt* and you will be satisfied with less. You may slip back into the diet thinking from time to time. After all, it was part of you for many years. But if you are aware of this, you can overcome it.

If you can't sleep at night unless you get up for cookies and milk perhaps you shouldn't go to bed hungry. One of my clients, Betty, frequently had trouble sleeping. At 2:00 a.m. she got up for her snack and then went to sleep. Avoiding a snack prior to bed did not help her reduce her overall caloric intake. Rather, it prevented her from sleeping and she had to have a snack at an inconvenient time of the morning. If it has been over 3 to 4 hours since you ate supper, consider a little snack before going to bed. A small snack will not ruin your hunger for breakfast the next morning.

Experiment and find out what works best for you. Listen to your body!

Karen was tired early in the evening but believed that she could stay up with the rest of the family. She ate to keep herself awake. Since she physically had no energy, she attempted to retrieve energy from food. Perhaps Karen's best action would be to go to bed early once in a while and realize that it is normal to be tired on some days. However, if the tired feeling persists, she should make an attempt to incorporate more activity and regular meals into her eating pattern to give her energy level a boost!

152

Enough sleep is essential. It's a basic physiological need. Being sleep-deprived is not an indication of strong character or willpower. It is harmful to your health. Yet in this fast-paced, competitive society, sleep is often undermined and sacrificed. It's considered a waste of time in an age when people are valued for what they do, not who they are. The danger is that we may become workaholics, attaching our self-worth to tremendous achievements. Our goals may be impossible as we're driven to prove ourselves, to be dynamic with boundless energy. This affects our mental health, sleep, and eating patterns.

Learn to take everything a step at a time. Keep your goals within comfortable reach and build in balance along the way. Be satisfied to be the best you can be and don't push yourself beyond your capacity.

If your schedule is so busy that you can't take time for a meal, bring along handy snacks such as cheese, crackers, bread, rolls, fruit, or yogurt. Healthful snacks are not only a wise alternative to a skipped meal, but they can help you make the transition to taking the time to eat. Building in some relaxing "time out" from your rushed schedule gives you a chance to nourish your body and refuel your energy reserve. Your productivity will increase because you will be more alert. You will have a clear mind to keep you working those extra hours. Try it and feel the difference! Pausing to eat can help you to deal with stressful situations better than when your blood sugar is low.

Sufficient restful sleep, proper nutrition, physical activity, relaxation, building in time for yourself, and knowing when to pull back helps you to deal with stress more easily. Ignoring your body's signals and not taking care of it may result in burn out and time off work. Think about it and re-adjust your life accordingly.

If you eat when you are under stress this kind of eating is strictly automatic. You are trying to solve your problem while eating and you are definitely not focusing on the food. Once again, wasted calories are ingested. Dealing with the issue is the answer for you.

153

Premenstrual syndrome known as PMS is a normal biological occurrence that bothers many women prior to the onset of the menstrual period. Realize that you may be hungrier more frequently due to the peaking hormone level of progesterone which causes the level of your blood sugar to drop down. Because of this, hunger strikes more often. The answer is to eat more frequently, and understand that giving in to those cravings for caffeine in the form of chocolate or coffee may aggravate your blood sugar swings.

Don't deny yourself the foods you like. If you eat according to the HUGS™ balance you can leave room for these foods, but you will have them on a fuller stomach rather than an empty one. If you have these cravings, you may simply be hungry. Don't ignore your natural hunger signals that occur more frequently during this time of the month. Stay tuned to your body's changing needs and observe to find out what your body needs.

The "I see it, I want it" mentality will occur less frequently as you switch into the nondiet thinking and normalize your eating and life-style habits.

Try to get rid of the diet mentality and learn to think like a nondieter. If you like butter don't deny yourself. When Donna replaced butter with margarine, she initially used less, because she didn't like the taste. Eventually, she felt deprived. Once she resumed eating butter, she binged on it. Donna's diet thinking, which indicates substitution of foods for less enticing items, was wrong for her. Dieters feel that if they don't like the substituted food, they won't eat as much. That may be true temporarily, but eventually the dieter feels deprived and binges on the forbidden food.

The HUGS™ way involves eating what you like but gradually cutting back the quantity of fat foods, so that you are eating bread with butter, not butter with bread.

Fat adds flavor but tends to take away the texture by making the food soggy. You can experience both. Use a little less butter and eventually you will enjoy the real taste of bread without the grease. Experimenting with different types of whole grain breads will allow you to discover a new dimension in eating. Or add a protein source to give you some moisture and more nutrient content with less "fat" calories.

Take the case of 9-year-old Paul who butters his toast only in the center because that's the way he likes it. Along comes Mom who says, "No, no, Paul, that's not the way you butter toast. Spread the butter out to the sides, otherwise it will be too hard." Like Paul, most children naturally have a taste for less fattening foods until we as parents impose our own preferences on them—just as our parents likely did to us.

Does HUGS™ say that because "fat goes to fat" you shouldn't eat the potato the way you like it—loaded with butter? Certainly not. HUGS™ encourages more carbohydrates and potatoes have carbohydrates. Try to acquire a taste for the potato with butter rather than butter with the potato. You can use substitutes (margarine); however, margarine contains the same number of fat calories. Sour cream is a lower fat choice. But if you really miss the butter, then use it and gradually decrease the quantity. Within a few months, you will enjoy your potato with less total fat content and not feel deprived. Gradually you will acquire a taste for less fattening foods. Low-fat gravy is also an excellent choice. It is full of flavor. Experience it and you may be converted!

The diet mentality of all-or-nothing thinking instead of gradual change hampers the progress you are making. Debbie had a sandwich for lunch without fries and then had a chocolate bar. She thought that she had failed because she gave in to her craving. But it was the time of month that her hormonal change caused her to crave chocolate. On pursuing this instance, we discovered that normally Debbie would have eaten a sandwich and fries followed by 2 chocolate bars. She realized that she was progressing! Note the positive changes you are making. When you occasionally fall into the all-or-nothing thinking, don't be too hard on yourself.

155

Kick your mind into gear and shift into thinking like a nondieter. What about those chocolate almonds or candies that you cannot refuse at a party. Other people take one or two and are satisfied. Why can't you? Have you been denying yourself these foods, regarding them as special treats only to be eaten at certain special occasions? Remember that denial leads to the eventual binge. *Do you really taste these chocolates or is it automatic eating?*

You may be eating them for one of the following reasons:
1. **because they are there, an external cue,**
2. **because you think you may not have them again for a while, or**
3. **because it's a special occasion so it's all right to eat on a special occasion.**

Dieters have difficulty distinguishing between "should," "need," and "want." Dieters may feel that they always want a dessert after a meal because it is part of the meal. Habit may be confused with the real desire to have it. However, realizing that you can have it later on and accepting this fact will help to clarify the difference between "want" and "need." Just because it is there and you see it is no reason to eat it. Eat it only if you are physically hungry for the food.

Should I have the cookie? Do I need the cookie? These questions reflect the diet thinking. Replacing this question with "Do I want the cookie?" gets you on the road to nondiet thinking.

Phyllis, when on a diet, used to eat the raw cookie dough when she was making cookies because cookies, the finished product, were on her "illegal" list of foods. With her new way of thinking, she allows herself to have the cookies but often chooses not to, simply because she doesn't want them at the time. After all, she can have cookies later on if she wants. What a relief to no longer have that mind struggle with food!

If, after using these techniques for a while, you still

156

feel the urge to eat the entire box of cookies, you may still be partly in the diet thinking. You may feel you want the cookies, but still are getting mixed signals.

When confronting the urge to eat a particular food, practise your new skills in nonstressful situations so that you allow this powerful skill to work for you when you need it. Being preoccupied with confrontation does not allow it to happen naturally. To help it happen naturally, ask yourself "Do I really want it or do I think I want it because it's there and I like it (partly out of a habit)? I know I can have it later on if I want it. And if it is no longer there, I can buy or make some more."

WHAT DOES IT MEAN TO FEEL HUNGRY?

What does it mean to feel hungry? What does it mean to eat till you're satisfied and not overly full? Once again observe nondieters and notice what they do to tune into their natural hunger signals.

To begin to eat normally and think as nondieters do who eat when they are hungry and stop when they are full:

Ask yourself, **"Am I eating because I *really* want it or because I feel it will no longer be there tomorrow?"** Eating "normally" for most dieters suggests being "off the diet." They think they have to "pack it in" before going on a diet again. Tell yourself, "I don't have to overeat. It will be there later on."

Ask yourself, **"Am I eating because it is there and I see it (automatic eating) or do I really want it?"** If you are not tasting and savoring your food and consciously eating it, then it is "waisted" calories. Tell yourself, "I want it only if I am physically hungry. If I eat for other reasons, I will not focus on my food while eating, tasting, and savoring my food without guilt. In this way, I will eat less food and 'waist' less calories."

Ask yourself, **"If I eat a piece of cake because I want it, and I can't stop at one piece, what is happening when I lose control?"** Perhaps you think you want the piece of cake simply because you haven't eaten for a while and your blood sugar level is low (this means you are hungry). Tell yourself, "This is a normal reaction. I will eat when I am pleasantly hungry. Waiting until I am too hungry causes me to desire the quick sugar and to overeat on these foods."

157

Eating regularly keeps you from binging because of insatiable hunger. Often people binge for a number of reasons, either because they have been deprived or they allow themselves to get too hungry.

Let's look at a scale of hunger as defined by HUGS™ that will help you to determine what it really means to feel physically hungry:

HUGS™ states that you do not want to let yourself get past number 3 on the scale (p159). At that point you no longer care what you are eating as long as you are fed. HUGS™ shows you how to eat to keep your blood sugar from the "hills" and "valleys" that can occur with improperly balanced eating habits. It shows you how to eat so that you can get more sustained energy from foods. It advocates the balance of carbohydrate and protein that allows the sugar to be released into your bloodstream at a more gradual rate. In this way, physical hunger will not overtake you so quickly. When you eat balanced meals (a balance between carbohydrate and protein), physical hunger will not set in for 3 to 6 hours after a meal.

If your hunger level is under 5, you are consuming food as a fuel source and feeding your physical hunger. If you are above 5 you are dealing with the social pressure to eat. This psychological eating feeds the head rather than the body and you are no longer in control.

One of my clients was a constant nibbler. She never gave herself a chance to get hungry. By allowing more time between eating, she discovered what it feels like to be hungry. On the other hand, if you diet below your weight set point (the point your body deems normal for you), you may always be hungry. It's your body's way of protecting you from going below your natural weight. The starvation way of losing weight seems to trigger the body to binge as a protective measure to bring the body weight back to normal or the set point. This method of starving and binging does not allow you to tune into your internal hunger signals. HUGS™ shows you how to eat in a normal way.

When psychological satisfaction = physical satisfaction, you are eating like a nondieter.

TIP: Before shopping for food, eat a snack if your meal will be delayed. Shopping when hungry can easily run up your bill on high-sugar, high-fat foods. These are particularly tempting when your blood sugar is low.

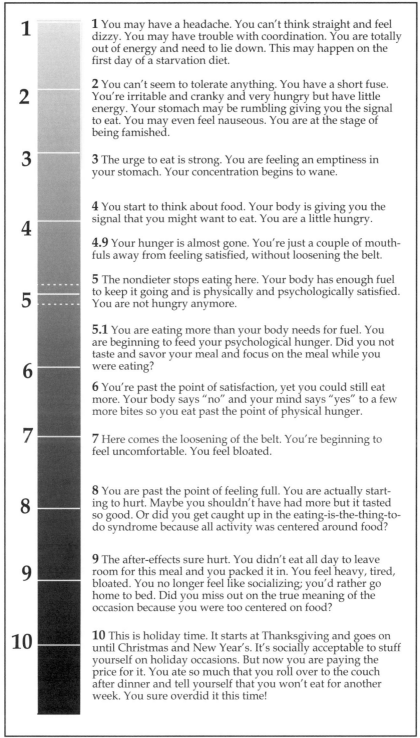

1 You may have a headache. You can't think straight and feel dizzy. You may have trouble with coordination. You are totally out of energy and need to lie down. This may happen on the first day of a starvation diet.

2 You can't seem to tolerate anything. You have a short fuse. You're irritable and cranky and very hungry but have little energy. Your stomach may be rumbling giving you the signal to eat. You may even feel nauseous. You are at the stage of being famished.

3 The urge to eat is strong. You are feeling an emptiness in your stomach. Your concentration begins to wane.

4 You start to think about food. Your body is giving you the signal that you might want to eat. You are a little hungry.

4.9 Your hunger is almost gone. You're just a couple of mouthfuls away from feeling satisfied, without loosening the belt.

5 The nondieter stops eating here. Your body has enough fuel to keep it going and is physically and psychologically satisfied. You are not hungry anymore.

5.1 You are eating more than your body needs for fuel. You are beginning to feed your psychological hunger. Did you not taste and savor your meal and focus on the meal while you were eating?

6 You're past the point of satisfaction, yet you could still eat more. Your body says "no" and your mind says "yes" to a few more bites so you eat past the point of physical hunger.

7 Here comes the loosening of the belt. You're beginning to feel uncomfortable. You feel bloated.

8 You are past the point of feeling full. You are actually starting to hurt. Maybe you shouldn't have had more but it tasted so good. Or did you get caught up in the eating-is-the-thing-to-do syndrome because all activity was centered around food?

9 The after-effects sure hurt. You didn't eat all day to leave room for this meal and you packed it in. You feel heavy, tired, bloated. You no longer feel like socializing; you'd rather go home to bed. Did you miss out on the true meaning of the occasion because you were too centered on food?

10 This is holiday time. It starts at Thanksgiving and goes on until Christmas and New Year's. It's socially acceptable to stuff yourself on holiday occasions. But now you are paying the price for it. You ate so much that you roll over to the couch after dinner and tell yourself that you won't eat for another week. You sure overdid it this time!

HUGS

It's wondrous what a hug can do,
A hug can cheer you when you're blue.
A hug can say, "I love you so,"
or, "Gee! I hate to see you go."
A hug is, "Welcome back again!"
and, "Great to see you!" or
"Where've you been?"
A hug can soothe a small child's pain
And bring a rainbow after rain.

The hug! There's just no doubt about it,
We scarcely could survive without it.
A hug delights and warms and charms,
It must be why God gave us arms.

Hugs are great for fathers and mothers,
Sweet for sisters, swell for brothers,
and chances are some favorite aunts
love them more than potted plants.

Kittens crave them. Puppies love them.
Heads of state are not above them.
A hug can break the language barrier,
And make the dullest day seem merrier.

No need to fret about the store of 'em.
The more you give, the more there
are of 'em.
So stretch those arms without delay
and give someone a hug today.

Author Unknown

7
Automatic Eating: How to Take Charge

Eat until you are physically satisfied, not overly full

Automatic eating refers to eating that occurs unconsciously. Suddenly, the cookie jar is empty and you didn't even realize it. Studies have shown that urges to overeat are like waves, they gradually build, peak, and then decline. When you have an urge to eat, note whether it is actually physical hunger because you have not eaten for a while or perhaps it is for one of the other reasons discussed previously (p149).

Often people feel the social pressure to eat when they go to visit at someone's house. They eat to be sociable or polite, rather than to satisfy their inner needs of hunger. Individuals who have low self-esteem need to find acceptance by pleasing others. *Ask yourself if you are eating simply because everyone else is eating or if you really want to eat because you are hungry.*

Studies have shown that the most satisfaction from eating comes from the first and last few bites and that the middle bites are automatic.

This means that you eat the middle bites because they are there, not because you are actually tasting and savoring the food. These calories are packed on the waist and the food is not really being tasted. Does this just translate into cutting back and taking a smaller portion? How is the HUGS™ method different from conventional diets that advocate smaller quantities and eating in moderation?

Bonnie walked into the Dairy Queen with a couple of friends who were on diets. She wanted a Blizzard so she ordered one. Her friends, on the other hand, may have yearned for a Blizzard and since they were on diets, they chose not to have one. Bonnie enjoyed the treat without guilt. She tasted and savored it and then a third of the way through she was satisfied and she left it unfinished. She knew she could have another Blizzard any time she wished so she had no need to binge.

Why did she leave part of it? Not because she felt pressured. Not because she had to eat in moderation and cut quantities. If you remember the Polivy and Herman example (p 147), dieters, once they start

162

eating something, cannot stop until it is finished.
Dieters say, "I blew my diet anyway, therefore I will
eat the whole thing and diet tomorrow." Or dieters
may eat the treat with guilt or in secrecy or too fast,
and not feel totally satisfied, ending up binging on
another Blizzard. Or they may eat several because of
the feeling of being deprived. My client was exhibiting the nondiet mentality. She no longer felt satisfaction from the Blizzard so she left it. It is true that the
most satisfaction comes from the first few bites
because you look forward to the taste, and the last
few bites because you won't have it again for a while.
The middle bites give you no greater satisfaction.
They are eaten by dieters because of the external cue
of seeing the food. *Nondieters are selective and eat only
what they really want.*

What did the dieters who just ordered coffee or diet
drinks do when they got home? They binged on
everything in site. They felt deprived and they wanted
the Blizzard but it was an illegal food for the diet.
When they got home they tried to find something that
would satisfy their craving for a sweet. Usually these
people eat more calories in the replacement food than
if they had eaten the Blizzard. For them, calories don't
count if no one else sees you eat it. This is diet
thinking that contributes to you
eating more, not less. *The extremes
of dieters are denying themselves on
the one hand and hanging on the fridge
door later on.*

Constant caloric restriction
followed by binging on foods
plays havoc with your metabolic
rate. Every time you starve and
binge, your metabolic rate drops,
which means that less calories will
be burned at rest. For the same
reason, it is essential to cut back
gradually rather than suddenly on
your total fat intake. Otherwise, you
will be treating HUGS™ as a diet
where changes are drastic and temporary.
If you do this the effect will be to lower your
metabolic rate as it responds to the sudden shock to

your system caused by being deprived of the usual number of calories.

Besides, you want permanent change, and your tastes can change only if you introduce new things gradually. This allows you to make healthy choices because of your new preferences, not because it is on your diet sheet. What a difference in thinking! Even if you have never dieted before, you may be partially in the diet mentality because of being influenced by society's preoccupation with food and weight. "I'll have it but I really shouldn't. I'll diet tomorrow." Slimmer people may not be necessarily healthy. Many starve and binge to maintain the desired figure or they are constantly on and off diets.

Change in thinking is crucial to long-term success. Eating in a healthy manner because you "have to" or are on a diet offers only a temporary solution because you are not in control. When you are not in control the changes won't be permanent. Making gradual changes allows you to acquire a taste for less fattening foods. In this way your preferences change, causing your choices to change. *Food choices are based on cultivated preferences rather than rigid self-control.*

Giving yourself permission to eat, using guidelines to help you retrieve more energy from foods will allow sweets to lose their appeal. When you realize that you don't have to give up sweets but can have them when you want, then eating only a bite or two to get the satisfaction from the food becomes easier. *You need to trust yourself to take charge, to make choices, to enjoy your life.*

If you believe you are in charge you will be.

Your nondiet thinking will allow you to have a chocolate bar if you really want it. By tasting and savoring the bar and eating it *without guilt,* you will probably be satisfied with less.

However, because of the high caffeine and sugar content of a chocolate bar, it may send your blood sugar for a roller coaster ride. Your blood sugar goes up quickly, causing your pancreas to oversecrete insulin, which causes your blood sugar to drop.

164

That's why you can't stop at one chocolate bar.

To help minimize this effect, when you have an urge for sweets and you have an empty stomach, ask yourself if you really want the chocolate bar or if your blood sugar is low because you are hungry. Have something to eat, then if you still want the chocolate bar, have it at that time. Remember that eating sweets and desserts after a meal prevents sugar highs and lows, because on a full stomach it takes longer for the sugar to hit your bloodstream. Continue this process of self-discovery.

For many individuals eating sweets on an empty stomach sends their blood sugar on a roller coaster ride causing their blood sugar to rise quickly and then plummet to a lower level coinciding with a feeling of immediate energy followed by a feeling of being very tired.

It is natural to want sweets when your blood sugar level is low and you are physically hungry. In order for you to remain in charge of the situation try this method of thinking and action.

• Eat regularly to prevent your blood sugar level from dipping too low.

• Eat a balance of carbohydrates and protein to allow a slower release of blood sugar into your bloodstream.

• If you have not eaten for 3 to 4 hours, have a more substantial snack such as bread, yogurt, bun, low-fat crackers, or fruit with low-fat cheese, glass of milk, etc.

Promise yourself that if you still want the cake or cookies, you can have them later on. In this way you are not denying yourself. You are better understanding your body signals and helping to distinguish between a craving and a physiological (physical) reason for the craving. You are dealing with the physiological reason first (i.e. low blood sugar). After that the psychological reason may seem less prominent.

CONFRONTATION IS A LIFETIME SKILL

In a confrontation situation dieters would say that you shouldn't have a chocolate bar because it is illegal. It is not on your diet sheet. The fact that it is forbidden causes you to think about it more and want it more. When you confront this urge and don't give in, this act of denial is termed willpower.

If someone is successful in losing weight, the person is said to have more willpower. A better term is "won't power." You think that denying the chocolate bar and not responding to the external cue will make it easier to remain in control.

Do you really want the sweet or do you think you want it simply because it is there and it is habit? *Confronting the urge to eat the sweet will give you the confidence to tune into your natural body signals. Believe in yourself.* Listen to your body with regard to physical and psychological hunger. *This will help you to distinguish between what you really want versus what you think you want due to habit.*

Confrontation is meeting the situation head on, and dealing with the cause of the problem. It is a positive skill. Learning to change damaging, self-defeating thoughts that lead to overeating by confronting them is a powerful tool.

What are your reasons for overeating? In order to be in charge, you must deal with the reasons for putting on extra weight. To end the constant struggle of dieting for the rest of your life, deal with the cause and find a permanent cure. Masking the cause only gives you temporary relief. Dealing with the cause however, may result in uncovering some information about yourself that may cause initial pain. HUGS™ will teach you the skills to deal with the problems and allow you to lead a fuller and happier life.

Let's go back to the scenario with the chocolate bar. Dieters see the chocolate on the table and ask: "Do I really need it?" or "Should I really have it?" The nondieter asks: "Am I really hungry?" or "Do I really want it?" Nondiet thinking empowers you to make the choice and puts you in charge.

Dieters are not using a technique; they are using

166

denial to deal with the situation. Nondieters tune into their hunger signals to check for actual hunger. If the blood sugar is low, nondieters may choose to have a snack first, knowing that the chocolate bar is available later on. Otherwise, eating chocolate on an empty stomach when your blood sugar is low, may lower it even further after the initial high. This could cause you to be unable to stop at one chocolate bar.

Eating the cookie dough because you believe that you cannot have the cookies or shouldn't have the cookies is also part of the denial process that occurs with dieting. With the HUGS™ philosophy, you know that you can have the cookies when they are baked so why eat the cookie dough. Rather, have a cookie after supper. The unexpected surprise may be that you feel satisfied with your supper and no longer desire the cookie since you know that you can have the cookie later on if you want it. In other words, you are not denying yourself, you are allowing yourself to have the cookie. The fact that you can *savor it without guilt* and enjoy it whenever you want, decreases your desire to want it.

Take that "pause" to decide if you really want the cookie and are physically hungry.

Confrontation decreases the incidence of automatic eating, that is, eating simply because it is there. If you do have the cookie after supper, it will have less effect on your blood sugar because it will take longer for the effect of the sugar to reach your bloodstream. And you will probably eat much less.

Test yourself. When you haven't eaten for a few hours and your blood sugar level is low, walk into a restaurant. You see a nice assortment of cakes that you want. Recognizing why you want the cakes is important. First sit down and have a meal. Taste and savor the meal and you will feel satisfied. The desire for the cake decreases. The waiter comes up to show you assorted cakes on the dessert tray but do you really want the sweet?

Calories are wasted if you are not having what you want, when you want it.

Here's the time to use confrontation. Are you really hungry or just curious to know how it tastes? If you can't resist, try sharing the cake with a friend and practise the confrontation technique to combat automatic eating. Or perhaps recall the many times the dessert looked better than it actually tasted. If you order and can't eat it all, there's nothing wrong with taking the rest home or leaving it on your plate. After all, if it is no longer satisfying to you, then it will only go to your waist.

Dieters react differently. They see the dessert and want it. They may start to eat it simply because of the external cue of sight. Dieters may even choose to eat less food in order to have the dessert. This counting calories could lead to trouble. If dieters didn't eat foods with enough substance, the sweet will ultimately create low blood sugar and the craving for sweets will continue. The only gain is a few more pounds. A sense of failure is felt for losing control and cheating on the diet. On the other hand, if the dieter wants the sweet and denies herself physically, this can lead to a binge or preoccupation with the denied food.

SEE
A
CAKE

CRAVE
A
CAKE

EAT
A
CAKE

*Monkey see,
monkey do.*

Confrontation does not mean total denial. It means that you will be satisfied with a small handful of chips rather than the whole bag. Confrontation means tuning into your needs at the moment.

Janet baked some great chocolate brownies for Saturday dinner dessert. She wondered what to do with the leftover brownies. How will the brownies fit this HUGS™ way of thinking? Taking them to work or giving them away is the "out of sight, out of mind" mentality of dieters. Why should she give them away? The rest of the family likes them. Once the new way of thinking is established, the brownies stay in the fridge. But since a small piece satisfies both Janet and her husband, the brownies may get stale. Instead of gobbling them all up, Janet now freezes her baking and takes out a small portion that satisfies everyone.

Confrontation can apply to any aspect of life, not just food. People often eat for other reasons that are not food related. Loneliness, anxiety, depression, anger,

168

stress may be temporarily relieved by food. This is using food as a comforter to make everything seem all right. Accept that it is normal to feel depressed sometimes. If you allow yourself to experience these feelings you may discover why you are distressed and be able to work through the feelings so they won't seem so severe next time.

When you eat for reasons other than physical hunger, you are eating to satisfy your psychological hunger. Your physical hunger may be on "full" when your psychological hunger is on "empty." That means that you are not focusing on the food but using it as a crutch to help you deal with the situation. In this state you can eat a box of cookies without even realizing what you are doing since you are pre-occupied with the psychological problem. To help you get more psychological enjoyment from food, try tasting and savoring it when eating it.

The end result of eating less on HUGS™ may be the same as if you were on a diet. However, the HUGS™ reason for eating less is very different. It's not because you have to. If you taste and savor your food, you are satisfied with less quantity.

If you are not getting psychological enjoyment from the food by tasting and savoring the experience, then you require more food to satisfy you. This goes against the principles of HUGS™. The problem that caused you to eat in the first place is still there. Confront your problems and deal with them. This will satisfy your inner self and you won't have to eat as a substitute.

> **If you hide your problems, you are not dealing with the inside so the outside will reflect on what's going on inside. You can change what you are by changing what goes on in your mind.**

Another point. If you eat because you are physically tired and are using the food for energy, perhaps you need to go to bed early. Otherwise, you are eating to stay awake rather than addressing your true need of sleep.

If you are lonely and eat to keep yourself company or

169

for entertainment, maybe you don't value your own company enough. You can be with someone and be lonely or you can be alone and not be lonely. It's all a matter of attitude. As you start to feel better about yourself, you will begin to find interests that keep you occupied and allow you to be constructive. You are worth the effort to make a nice meal for yourself and enjoy it. Falling into the tea-and-toast syndrome when you are alone becomes boring. Because you no longer enjoy or look forward to eating, you may actually end up eating more food, trying to get your psychological satisfaction.

Pamper yourself. You are worth it. Proper nutrition is the fuel for your body. Regular activity helps you to extract more energy to invigorate you in order to reach your potential. Notice your positive qualities. Don't always be down on yourself. Your negative attitude drains your energy. Focus on the positive, and on life-style changes. Find the reasons behind your eating, confront them, and deal with them.

See the skeleton in the closet.

Dieters eat when under stress. Nondieters do not. Switch your thinking to that of a nondieter, and you will be less likely to eat under stress. In fact, when dieting, stressful situations cause you to go off your diet. Why does this happen? It happens because dieting in itself puts a stress on your body as well as your mind. Using the principles of HUGS™, stressful situations can be handled with more confidence and authority. HUGS™ helps you get through the stressful situation with confidence.

Audrey, a person with diabetes, enrolled in our HUGS™ program. She related her present health problems to the dieting she had done in the past. She was undergoing very stressful situations at work which would normally cause her to eat and gain weight. HUGS™ has given her new focus, new thinking, and a positive attitude to stress. To her surprise, when she stepped on the scale, Audrey had lost weight. By not dieting, Audrey was no longer preoccupied with food. She learned to listen to her body and allow her hunger levels to control her food intake naturally.

170

"I can't be on a diet when I'm on holidays. My friend will expect me to eat her home baking." Does this sound familiar? You're not on a diet now but if your tastes are changing to healthier foods, why do you have to eat those high-fat/high-sugar foods that no longer satisfy you?

Eating to please others can be stressful. It puts the control in the hands of the host or hostess. When you are offered some food, you have a choice to take it or refuse it. If you really want the particular food item, then have it. If you don't want it because you don't particularly care for the food or you aren't hungry, say something such as, "Thank you, I'm full right now, maybe later." In this way you are leaving the door open to have the food later when you may actually want it or perhaps you may not want it at all.

Asking for a small piece as the cake is being cut can satisfy your curiosity as well as your host or hostess while allowing you to practise the principles of the most enjoyment coming from the first and last few bites of whatever you eat. You can always have more if you want it. This also takes a lot of pressure off the hostess who won't feel she has to prepare so much food for her guest.

Do you feel you have to bake up a storm before company comes to make an impression? Remember true friends and family come to visit because they value your company. Food does not have to be the center of attraction.

When you visit friends or family, reassure them that you have come mainly to see them. They will realize that they do not have to go to as much trouble when you come over.

Discuss your change of eating style with your host or hostess. You may be surprised that they are eating differently and only bake when company comes. Some hostesses realize that people are eating less sweets and they pre-cut smaller pieces of cake, laying them on a platter for company to sample. Often alternative healthier snacks are being provided. After all, the health wave is catching on.

171

Observe nondieters in social situations. Food is usually not the center of attention for them, only a pleasant accent.

The coffee klatch crowd is replacing their coffee and cake with a healthful walk or enjoying a visit and pleasant conversation in a stimulating environment. This decreases the preparation necessary for a hostess when she invites someone over. You don't need to eat coffee and cake. The skill of confrontation allows you to refuse these in a tactful manner so that others' feelings are not hurt.

If your meal will be later than usual, it's a good idea to have a snack prior to going out. This will prevent you from feeling famished, which may result in quicker eating without tasting your food or eating too much.

Distraction is another useful skill that can be used in situations where you have an urge to eat brought on by psychological hunger. Jim was used to finishing his meal everyday with dessert. Is this urge for a sweet due to physical hunger or to habit? In his case, it was simply habit. Remembering that urges gradually peak and then disappear, he temporarily distracted himself and the urge went away.

If having a dessert is simply a habit, then distracting yourself for a few minutes after the meal will cause the urge to go away. If there is some other underlying reason for wanting dessert, then it needs to be confronted.

Try distracting yourself with an activity that you enjoy that uses your hands or physically or mentally takes you away from the food situation. This skill is useful in situations where you are trying to break a habit. This form of replacement is only effective on a temporary basis before using confrontation. It can help you to collect your thoughts but it doesn't get to the root cause of the problem.

Doing activities that you enjoy could include going for a walk, having a bubble bath, doing a puzzle, sewing, dancing, listening to classical music, or deep breathing. If the urge for a sweet was due to an external cue such as smelling muffins baked in a bakery, then walking on by may allow the urge to go away. The reason this will work is that you distracted

172

yourself for the first few minutes when the urge was at its peak. By distracting yourself at this time, the urge will gradually diminish.

However, if there is a greater underlying cause than the external cues of sight or smell or habit, the urge will recur once the activity is finished. The activity is merely a "cop-out" from your desire for the food. It's a temporary substitute rather than a skill. You will still have to confront these feelings to minimize the chances of them causing you to eat.

Suppose you had a fight with your spouse that makes you angry enough to want to devour tons of calories to help make you feel better. In this way, you are trying to mask your feelings instead of dealing with them directly. Screaming at your spouse won't solve the problem either, no matter how angry you are. You may decide to go for a walk to allow yourself to calm down, think things over, and plan a strategy for when you come back. This temporary distraction could be helpful in allowing you to think and assess the situation. However, you will still have to confront the situation when you get back. If you don't, in go the cookies.

When you are using distraction techniques, it is important to find an activity that you enjoy. Doesn't it make sense that you can acquire a taste for enjoyable activities just as you can acquire a taste for less fattening food? My husband enjoys classical music. By going with the flow, I have learned to appreciate it and use it as a form of distraction to mentally take myself away from the situation or the day's cares.

On the other hand, if you do not enjoy the activity, using it as distraction will not work to alleviate the problem at hand. For example, you might do ironing as a form of distraction even though you do not like ironing. This is using the diet mentality of substitut-

> **Here's a new way of viewing distraction. Ask yourself what's happening in your life that is annoying or painful. Are you avoiding facing it or thinking about it by the distraction of eating?**

173

ing something inferior rather than finding excitement in a new hobby. You may feel deprived and still turn to food when you are finished. If you are not getting your psychological enjoyment from other activities, then you may turn to food to find that release. Look within and you may discover hidden talents that you would like to explore that can help you fulfill yourself more positively.

In order to confront your hunger and your inner feelings, it is important to understand what "hunger" feels like. For many who have been on so many diets, they are so out of tune with their bodies, that they are no longer able to know what it means to feel hungry. If you are still not in tune with your hunger signals, review Chapter 6. This is the key to helping you succeed.

Remember that anything worth doing is worth doing until you learn to do it well! So practise, practise, practise.

Diets show you how to ignore your hunger signals. If you are hungry and the diet sheet says not to eat, then you do not eat. You may drink something that temporarily makes you feel satisfied, only to be famished later on. Babies know when they are hungry. Adults ignore the signals because they are influenced by society's obsession with weight. Children too are subjected to parental restraint. Parents don't want their children to be large and this causes restrained eating. Statements such as "Don't you think you've had enough?" can worry the child and cause secretive eating. A child's or teenager's food needs are much greater than those of an adult. There is the danger that growing bodies will get insufficient calories or nutrients for proper growth. Another danger is instilling the "diet mentality" into young people.

Dealing with the cause rather than restricting eating is a more positive approach. Reinforce this by putting a family focus on active living, and fill in leisure time with life-style activities rather than centering activity around food.

Accept your body shape and that of your child's.
174

*Unrealistic expectations are the very seedbed of depression.
Breaking free of them unleashes the power to break free of
the diet mentality.*

CLEANING YOUR PLATE – HABIT OR NEED

Back in the days when you were growing up,
finishing everything on your plate may have been
from necessity. During the Depression, you never
knew when or if you were going to get another meal.
Eating everything just in case you would have to go
hungry for a while was accepted.

This philosophy of wasting nothing may have been
passed on to the children of the next generation. How
often have you heard, "Eat everything. The children
in Biafra are starving," or "I'll give you dessert if you
finish your meal." This condition placed on dessert
may have caused you to overeat so that you could
have the dessert.

This may have been the beginning of putting you out
of tune with your internal body signals. You were
responding to external cues, not internal ones. You
were moving away from your internal instincts and
depending on other people's ideas and reactions. No
doubt some parents still rely on this method of
getting children to eat everything from their plates.

Today's generation of weight watchers seems to be
trying to impose food restrictions on the child out of
fear that the child will become large like the parent.
This instills feelings of deprivation in the child, which
leads to binging. Many children today are out of tune
with their bodies and rather than stuffing themselves
may be undereating to comply with the parents'
wishes. This can result in inadequate growth,
deficiencies, and insufficient calories, causing
cravings and secretive eating. Eating disorders will
certainly emerge.

In fact, there is an increase in eating disorders in
North America. With teenagers, poor body image
and society's view of the "perfect body," stemming
from the "perfect child with designer clothes" may
cause teenagers to inflict periods of starvation on
themselves to attain this ideal body image. In pursuit
of thinness, their health suffers. Perhaps adults are

175

being poor role models because they are never satisfied with their own bodies, and constantly going on and off a diet.

Understanding the reasons why a habit has become entrenched allows this newly found insight to help you find the solution. Use the skill of confrontation to help you break the long-lasting habit. The attitude of "that's just the way I am" will not allow you to succeed in breaking the habit.

Automatically cleaning your plate after each meal is responding to an ingrained habit. You are not in charge, the chef or waitress is.

> **Eating until you are satisfied, and not exceeding that point, may mean leaving something on your plate. If finishing everything from your plate is simply a habit, then you are not denying yourself if you leave something on your plate. After all, you didn't really want it, you simply ate it because it was there.**

Stop partway through your meal to consciously decide if you want more. Putting a "pause" or "time out" into your meal may surprise you. You'll find you will be full sooner. Remember, it takes roughly 20 minutes for your stomach to tell your brain that you are full.

Ann commented that she had been taught not to waste food. However, if your body does not want any more food, then the extra food is just going to your waist. Out goes the notch on your belt. You are probably not tasting your food at this point, simply eating because everyone else is eating, because it's the thing to do, especially at social gatherings. Enjoy the event itself, its surroundings, the people, and the entertainment. These will take the main focus away from food. The food need not be the main reason why you attend the event.

At home, automatic eating occurs more easily when the food is served European style. You help yourself and the platters are left on the table. Second and third helpings may be eaten simply because the food is there and it tastes good, rather than because of physical hungry. Even when you're aware of the

176

situation, it's easy to sometimes get caught up in the social event of "dining" and to continue eating and talking.

Make an attempt to focus on eating while you are eating, and on conversation when you are talking or listening. Tune into your body and ask yourself if you really want any more or if your eyes were bigger than your stomach and you took too much. In that case, try not to eat for the sake of eating. Eat until you feel comfortably full. If you don't want it all, leave the rest for tomorrow, give it to your dog, or throw it out.

> **Eat for energy, not exhaustion. If you overeat, you feel overly full and tired. Eat until you feel comfortably satisfied. That means not undoing the notch on your belt to make it looser.**

Getting psychological satisfaction from food — taste, savor, and enjoy your food to the fullest.

As you begin to get tuned into your body, you will be better able to judge how much you really want and there will be less waste. It takes time to reach this point.

The English style of the cook serving you from the stove takes the control away from you. You may be given too much and feel obliged to finish it so that you do not hurt anyone's feelings. Don't feel that you have to stuff yourself in order to prove that you like something. "It's really good but I'm full. Maybe I'll have some later," works well to notify the cook that your stomach is signaling you to stop eating. If you say "no" and mean it, people will respect your wishes.

The most preferred method of service is for people to get their own plate and help themselves. In this way, you are in control of the quantity and type of food that you want. You can be selective, having more of what you like, and less of what you do not like. Chris liked this approach because she would no longer get blamed for putting too much on her husband's plate. Hubby is in control of the total quantity of food that he wants to eat. The bonus is less hassle for the cook, and of course, fewer dishes.

Using this method, family members take respons-

177

ibility for themselves. Those who want seconds can choose to get up and get some more. Leaving the food in pots also keeps it hot longer. No need to hurry through the food when you know the second portion will still be hot.

For those of you who are still having trouble leaving something on your plate when you really don't want to eat it, try to consciously leave something small on your plate such as a small scoop of potatoes or a few peas, just to break that cycle of having to eat everything. Keep in mind that the purpose of this exercise is to empower you, put you back in the driver's seat where you are in charge of your body and its needs. Eating past the point of satisfaction just for the sake of cleaning your plate does not allow you to listen to your body. Being aware that you do not have to eat everything on your plate can help you to eat only until you are satisfied.

"So what is wrong with taking a little less and still cleaning my plate?" asked Betty. Nothing, provided you really know at this point what your body needs and you are completely tuned into those needs. The danger of doing this is that many people reflect on what quantity they feel they should be eating according to one of the diets that they have been on. Rather than taking what they want and what their body desires, they may choose what they believe their body should have according to previous experiences. As you learn to tune into your signals of hunger and fullness, you will begin to take the amount that will satisfy you. In this case, you may finish everything on your plate.

The other danger is that there will always be social occasions where you may not be in control. Without practising this skill of consciously being aware of when you have had enough to eat, it is the social events that may cause you to overeat. Learning to leave something on your plate may help you to be more conscious of your body's needs.

Practise the skill of leaving something on your plate so that you are prepared for the social event. For many, the ingrained habit of cleaning the plate is

178

difficult to overcome, but it can be done. With time, you will be better able to assess what your body wants rather than eat with your eyes and overfill your plate. You will be in charge.

Observe nondieters. Do they actually eat more food or does it seem that they are eating more because they load up on the carbohydrates (potatoes, rice, pasta, grains, vegetables, bread, etc.)?

Nondieters may also leave more on their plates. For example, I eat what I like until I am satisfied, not until my plate is empty. If I have control of what I put on my plate by serving myself, then I take only what I like. However, I do experiment with different kinds of foods and give them a chance to be added to my food repertoire.

Eat till you are satisfied, not overly full.

You may feel at this time that you are in control and that the practice of consciously leaving something on your plate is no longer necessary. You may leave something on your plate only if you are no longer hungry. This is your goal. The conscious effort of leaving something on your plate is merely to break the habit of constantly finishing everything from your plate and ignoring your true inner hunger signals. Practising the skill will ensure that it becomes second nature more readily.

8

How Far Have You Come?

Focus on the internal rewards of energy and well-being

RATING YOUR PROGRESS

In order to successfully apply the principles of
HUGS™ and remain focused on this concept, you can
step back to assess what life-style changes you have
made. This gives you an opportunity to see where
you have come from, what you have accomplished,
and where you are going. It also gives you a chance
to set some goals, making you aware of where you
can put more time and effort towards practising
certain skills.

Evaluate your success in functional terms rather than
focusing on how many pounds you have lost. Has
your quality of life improved? Allow yourself the
time to enjoy the process of self-evaluation. An open-
minded attitude towards these new skills and ideas
can help make the breakthrough you need to make
HUGS™ work for you.

Here is how some HUGS™ clients talk about their
life-style changes.

"I am eating regularly and no longer starving and binging."
This is an accomplishment because, as you are now
aware, starving and binging can lead to lowering
your metabolic rate. Each time you starve, your body
compensates by storing more of those calories as fat
when you finally do eat. It conserves the calories
because your body is afraid that you will starve
yourself again.

*"I am beginning to understand when and why I'm hungry
because I tune into my natural hunger signals. I know I can
eat when I want to, based on my hunger."* This process of
self-discovery allows you to find out why you
overate in the first place; it deals with the causes and
lets you tune into why you are hungry. This process
of self awareness deals with the causes of eating in a
more positive manner.

"I am no longer punishing myself when I eat." Eating
food *without guilt* and the act of celebrating food can
allow you to taste, savor, and enjoy your food to the
fullest. It also allows you to be satisfied with less
quantity because you derive not only physical
benefit, but psychological satisfaction as well from
the food.

181

"I am eating differently because I want to and it tastes good. I don't get as tired as fast. I am able to complete my housework without sitting down to rest." The gradual change in taste for lower fat types of foods and increasing activity will build up your endurance so that you feel better and can do more in less time.

"I accept myself the way I am. I like myself." Self-acceptance allows you to believe in yourself and your ability to be able to listen to your body with regard to its food and activity needs. It channels your energy so that you can make positive life-style changes and gives you the confidence that you need. Otherwise, if you are always negative about yourself, this causes an energy drain where little to nothing is accomplished.

"I am really thinking about how different foods affect my body (metabolic rate and blood sugar). I am eating a balance of carbohydrates and proteins at meals, and feeling more satisfied." Cutting calories affects your metabolic rate, causing you to plateau after the initial weight loss. Accepting that diets don't work and that rather than cutting calories, the real answer is shifting the type of calories that you take into your body. Eating more carbohydrates gives you the energy to run your body. The balance of protein that is right for you gives you the sustaining energy, stabilizing your blood sugar. In this way, you will not have the highs and lows common to diets. This can help to stabilize your mood and general feeling of well-being.

By eating more carbohydrates, you are eating more of those calories that burn more energy in the process of their digestion and are less efficient in converting into fat. Simply by eating more carbohydrates you have automatically decreased the total fat content of your meals. By listening to your body, you are allowing your body to determine the energy level that you need on a daily basis. It will be different all the time. Some days you may need more food to make you feel satisfied, and some days you will need less. Some days you may prefer to have a dessert, and other days you will not. Listening to your body's needs and desires will allow you to get the most "punch" from your meal.

182

> Food choices are
> built on cultivated
> preference rather
> than rigid self-
> control.

"I've started to alter cooking habits to reduce fat. I am eating more fruits and vegetables, not restricting myself to the non-starchy vegetables." As fat content of meals is gradually being decreased a taste for less fattening foods is being acquired. For example, the comment, "I now prefer french fries prepared in the oven rather than in the deep fryer," demonstrates this point. Deanna was surprised to notice that after a number of months of gradually cutting back the fat content of her meals, she found fried chicken to be too greasy. She no longer enjoyed this meal and no longer chose to order it. Remember that food choices are built on cultivated preference rather than rigid self-control.

The gradual process of cutting back on your total fat intake in cooking, food choices, and baking is crucial in order to actually change your preference to foods that are lower in fat content.

Going straight from cheddar cheese to cottage cheese is a sudden drop in fat content. It can be a shock to your system causing you to shift back to the higher fat cheese. If you eat cottage cheese simply because it is good for you rather than because you like it, then you are in the diet mentality and your change in eating will not be permanent. In fact, if you can't acquire a taste for the low-fat food, this can prevent you from enjoying your meal, and you may find yourself looking in the cupboards for something that you really enjoy. "Gradual" implies going from cheddar cheese to skim mozzarella cheese, possibly combining the two and eventually going down to skim mozzarella cheese. Try other low-fat cheeses such as quark, ricotta, and skyr, but make them tasty by adding canned fruit in its own juice or some jam.

"I am understanding physical hunger and eating when physically hungry." Using food to fuel your energy needs feeds the body not the mind. Only then will your clothes begin to get looser.

"I am confronting my psychological hunger." This is an important skill not only to deal with hunger and foods but also to help you with all aspects of life so that you can face them in a more positive way. Dealing with the causes of hunger in an assertive manner can reduce the incidence of those feelings.

183

"I don't like that chocolate because it is not dark and bittersweet."

"I am asking myself if I am really hungry? Do I really want the food?" This is a form of *pausing,* where you are confronting yourself to determine your real desires rather than succumbing to eating automatically simply because the food is there. Take the time to check on what you really want.

"I am trying to combat my automatic eating. I am eating the first few bites and the last few bites and leaving the ones in the middle." Becoming aware of your eating, enjoying the act of eating, and eating only what you want allows you to be selective in your eating. Using the above technique can allow you to discover the enjoyment of tasting food, noting the quantity that you need to satisfy you.

"I am more aware of when and why I am eating and I am dealing with it in a more positive fashion." Getting to know yourself and becoming more conscious of the reasons behind your compulsive eating can allow you to deal with the causes. Once the reasons are resolved, the psychological eating decreases.

"I am beginning to be more active and actually enjoy it." Fun and enjoyment are the keys to life-style change. A gradual increase in physical activity is important. Your body and mind adapts to the change. You learn to enjoy physical activity, actually missing it when you do without it. Physical activity becomes part of you and your routine. The dieter will say, "Let's go for a walk to the donut shop. We'll wear off the calories by walking so let's have the donut as our reward for doing the exercise." The nondieter will say, "Boy, I went for a walk and I feel great." The walk becomes the reward in itself. It is an intrinsic reward, coming from within. Action creates motivation. If you wait until you are motivated, action may never take place. External motivation, such as walking to the donut shop for a reward, is only temporary motivation.

"I am more in charge of food." By empowering yourself and giving yourself the tools (skills and techniques) to make the choices, you become in charge of food and your life. These skills can last a lifetime and be used in any aspect of your life.

REWARDS THAT REALLY WORK

"If you want dessert, you'd better make sure that you eat

**STEPS TO CHECK IF YOU ARE INCORPORATING HUGS™
INTO YOUR LIFE-STYLE.**

• Am I eating regularly and no longer starving and binging?

• Am I beginning to understand when and why I am hungry and actually starting to tune into my hunger signals?

• By gradually decreasing fat content over the past few weeks, am I beginning to acquire a taste for less fattening foods?

• Am I eating a balance of carbohydrates and proteins at meals, putting more emphasis on increasing the carbohydrate content without feeling guilty?

• Am I enjoying the full experience of eating and am I eating until I feel satisfied in order to fuel my energy needs rather than my psychological needs?

• Am I tuning into how I feel and how my body feels, no longer relying on the scales to determine how my day will go?

• Am I feeling more energetic and more content with myself?

• Am I starting to use skills to combat automatic eating and confrontation to deal with those urges that make me want to eat even though I am physically satisfied?

• Am I beginning to participate in more physical activity and actually enjoying it?

• Am I more aware of what I am eating?

Master new ways
of thinking.

everything on your plate, Ellen." The mother who says this makes the dessert the reward for a job well done whether it was finishing your plate of food or transferring the food reward idea to other tasks such as doing your homework, etc. Why couldn't the act of eating or accomplishing something be the internal reward in itself? Why do we always feel that we need an external reward to finish the task or finalize the moment? Enjoy the meal itself and if you want dessert, have it but not because it is your reward for finishing the meal. *Revel in your accomplishments and experience the feeling of exhilaration without needing a food item to provide the finishing touch.*

Paul comes home from school and practises guitar. When he is finished, he goes to watch television as a reward. Why can't the enjoyment extracted from playing the guitar be the immediate reward? This is a healthier way of thinking that will instill positive life-

185

time habits. Enjoy the new skills that you are learning; focus on the intrinsic reward of the moment.

In the past, rewards may have been essential to keep you on track with your diet. Starving yourself before you weighed in at diet class resulted in a weight loss that you rewarded by some type of food after the weigh-in. After all, you have been faithful in depriving yourself. And because you are so hungry, something high in fat such as donuts is tempting. So off to the donut shop you go.

You equated the result with the weight loss and the natural reward is the thing you have been doing without—food. Are you really making a life-style change? No! What you are doing is only temporary, a means to an end. You may constantly repeat this cycle over and over again. Losing the weight, resuming old eating habits, regaining the weight, another diet. Your sense of well-being and self-esteem also goes down with the weight gain and you have a feeling of powerlessness.

Realize that *you count* by allowing the way you feel about yourself and your improved health to be your rewards. These are internal rewards and more likely to last. A positive feeling in itself allows you to keep on the road to life-style changes. Look at your accomplishments and remember that lapses from time to time are part of progress.

Unrealistic expectations can cause depression about your weight. The weight you lose cannot be the goal or the focus of your actions. Rather, improvement in health is the key to your long-term success. Applying some of the HUGS™ skills and techniques will allow you to experience mini successes and reduce the number of setbacks that occur. Focus on these gradual changes. They are progress and they can help keep your goals realistic and in focus.

Attempt to normalize your eating habits. The scale doesn't rule your life and should not be ruling how you feel each day. Take a look inside yourself for the clues. Soon the outside will begin to reflect your renewed confidence. You may be walking straighter, taller. You'll be in charge.

BEFORE

AFTER

AFTER THE
AFTER

Never mind what others say and think. Jealousy because you are in charge of your food and your life may cause others to try to sabotage your best efforts. Don't be fooled into thinking that another diet will get the weight off quicker. Quick weight loss results in quick weight gain.

Start living for the present instead of always focusing on the future. Enjoy and savor the moment. *The more psychological benefit that you can extract from life, the less need for food to fill this void and the greater will be your inner rewards.* Being desperate for a weight loss prevents it from happening naturally. Focusing on life-style changes allows you to master new ways of thinking. Practice will allow you to internalize them.

As these life-style changes become second nature, you will feel more energetic and confident that you are able to steer your life onto a path of health and vigor. With time your body will adjust naturally to the weight that you were predetermined to be. Keep in mind that these outward effects will happen more quickly only in those that allow it to happen naturally. Forcing makes these changes temporary. It doesn't allow you to "feel" and "experience" them. Life-style changes require effort to become established. Practice makes them easier.

Diets are initially easy because you operate within a prescribed regimen. However, they soon become boring and monotonous. Life-style changes require a change in thinking that motivates you. If you enjoy the process and heed the lifetime skills, time will not be a factor. Stress the positive, go with the flow, allow it to happen. It is a self-fulfilling prophecy. Believe in yourself, and have the confidence that you can make those changes. You will be successful because you have learned from past failures and allowed yourself to grow. You will move forward.

We all operate on a conscious or unconscious reward system. The most effective rewards are the ones you reap from your own individual value system. The achievement of meeting your own standard is a euphoric experience. Your own opinion about yourself is what counts; the opinions of others are

187

not as important.

If you live for others' comments and compliments, consider what happens after you have lost weight. The praise, encouragement, and compliments will stop after people have become accustomed to your new physical appearance. Will you then feel there is no more purpose in trying to keep the weight off? Or will you put the weight back on to gain attention? Or maybe you have realized that changing the outside self alone does not make you instantly happy or allow your problems to disappear. You are still the same person, the same individual. Your attitude or the way you think, feel, or act towards yourself or others has not changed. Your attitude towards food or life has not changed. It remains the same and so you will set yourself up for gaining the weight back.

Work on discovering yourself and what makes you eat. Deal with the causes and forces, and allow yourself to develop skills to improve your inner self. These can channel your energies into being the best that you can be! The inner strength that you gain will begin to reflect outwards.

KEY FOCUS POINTS TO MOVE YOU FORWARD

Use the following phrases as affirmations to be repeated frequently. They will help you to set your mind onto a positive track.

- I like myself. I feel good about myself. I'm a worthwhile person no matter what anybody says or does. I'm going to have a great day.
- I believe in myself and have the confidence that I can listen to my body. I know what to eat and when my body is hungry. I know the level of activity that is suited to me to allow physical activity to give me energy, not exhaustion.
- When I feel like eating as a result of feelings, I will first stop, meet the situation head-on, and attempt to deal with the reason for my eating. I will work at preventing the reason from happening again. I will look at ways of dealing with these feelings in those cases where the cause cannot be prevented or eliminated.
- I realize that eating only until I am satisfied may mean leaving something on my plate. In order for me to break the automatic habit of finishing everything on my plate, I will give myself permission to eat only until I am satisfied, and not feel compelled to eat all the food on my plate, even if it means leaving something.

Use the above affirmations regularly to help move you forward on the road to healthy living.

9
Maximum Satisfaction from Food

Use skills of confrontation to cope with bursts of psychological hunger. Stop: taste, savor, and enjoy your food to the fullest.

If you are eating only to feed your psychological hunger, then these calories are wasted. Take the time to taste and savor your food and you'll notice that you will be actually satisfied with less. Why? Because you took the time to satisfy your psychological hunger from the food.

FOCUS ON FOOD—PAYING ATTENTION

When you don't pay attention to what you are eating, you literally cheat yourself from getting satisfaction and pleasure from the food. Then, in searching for the sense of well-being that you denied yourself, you eat more than you need or want. Perhaps the tendency to avoid paying full attention when you are eating comes from the belief that you don't deserve to be good to yourself. If you actually sit down and enjoy your food, you have to acknowledge that you're giving something to yourself. This is very difficult for many people to do—especially women. Also, many people pride themselves on being able to do many things at a time. They say, "I work all the time; in fact, I don't even take time out for lunch." They think it's efficient to eat while they are doing 10 other things, rather than wasting time on eating without doing anything else. *Do these people really taste their food or are they eating it only because it's there?*

Experience the different taste sensations, textures, and aromas. The outcome of not tasting your food can be

- eating more food to satisfy your cravings,
- overeating due to unconscious eating and being out of tune with your body, or
- nibbling throughout the evening because you don't remember eating anything.

Any bite of food that goes into your mouth deserves attention. When you eat, do nothing but eat. Even if you're eating only a handful of raisins, sit down, take a deep breath, relax, and focus on the raisins. If you are doing anything else while you are eating, you are not concentrating on the subtleties of the tastes and flavors of the food. In this way, you not only deprive yourself of the enjoyment of the food, but you may form an association between eating and some other activity (see Chapter 12).

190

When you are eating by yourself it is easy to pay attention only to your food. When you are with another person it is more difficult to concentrate only on your food. Here's a tip. When eating with others, spend about 30 seconds focused on your food, then put your fork down and focus your attention on the other person and the conversation. You cheat the person you're with if you eat while conversing, and you deprive yourself of the pleasure of the food if you talk while eating. So alternate eating and talking. This will allow you to receive optimum pleasure from the food and your relationships.

OTHER FRAMES OF MIND THAT CAN LEAD TO ABSENT-MINDED EATING.

THE JUGGLER You're a person who always juggles 20 things at a time, and one of the 20 is eating. Have you finished all the kids' lunch leftovers during the half hour you spent putting away the laundry and listening to your neighbor on the telephone?

These people often feel that taking time out to eat is not productive. Yet focusing on eating allows you to put the "pause" into your day and gives your stomach time to signal your brain that you are full. The result is that it translates to decreased nibbling and increased energy and productivity later on.

THE ABSENTEE OWNER
These lost souls are dreamy, unconscious eaters who often don't even notice they're eating. While they're licking an ice cream cone, they're also day-dreaming, reading, shopping, or watching television. Suddenly, they realize with a shock that the ice-cream cone has mysteriously disappeared.

THE GIVER Givers try to be all things to all people and to perform many functions at a time. These people, often mothers, spread themselves too thin in their workloads, while their waistlines, not so ironically, often become considerably thicker. They telephone committee members, wash dishes, referee family squabbles, cook dinner, and write a report for work while at the same time picking away at food.

191

Make it a routine to eat only when you are sitting. There is no joy in eating on the run. Such eating is not satisfying and it encourages nibbling. It's interesting how, when you eat on the run, the mind erases the meal but the body doesn't. If you sit down at the table every time you eat, you will naturally pay more attention to your food. You will then enjoy conscious eating and you will remember that you ate.

THE TIME TRAVELER To get the most satisfaction from your food, your focus must be in the present. Time travelers either dwell in the past (feeling guilty about what they've done) or the future (worrying about bad things before they happen). John Curtis, founder and director of the University of Wisconsin Stress Management Institute believes that 90 percent of stress is brought on by not living in the present moment and worrying about what's already happened, what's going to happen, or what could happen.

Accept responsibility for the past, face the future with confidence, and focus on today, learning to taste, savor, and enjoy. It seems obvious, doesn't it, to taste and enjoy each bite? Why then is it so rarely practised?

Experiment with this theory. Try eating the same breakfast (one day in a hurry and the next day relaxed) at the table and actually tasting the food. Do you notice a difference in how long it keeps you satisfied?

Eating on the run or while focusing on what you have to do next rather than on the moment at hand deprives you of the psychological pleasure of the present. Constantly living for the future deprives you of the enjoyment of what is going on now. Take the time to savor the enjoyment of discovering your inner being as you begin to realize that you are important enough to pamper yourself with the time to taste and savor your meal. After all, *you count*! Experience HUGS™ and allow it to work for you.

George, a member of the HUGS™ group, came to class one day and told us that he had had second helpings because the food tasted so good. On further probing, he noted that he was rushed to get to class and he had hurried through his meal. He pointed out that normally he would have been amply satisfied with the first helping. Make sure you try this exercise. It will give you new insight into the true meaning of tasting and savoring your food.

As well, it is important to ensure that you are eating

192

the foods that you love. HUGS™ gives you permission to choose anything you want to eat. There are no good foods or bad foods, no "do's" or "don'ts." You can eat anything your body loves to eat. *Listen to your body.* At first you may hear your body say it wants all those "forbidden" foods you never allowed yourself when you were dieting. But as long as you eat only when you're hungry and stop when you're full, your body will soon crave the foods that it needs for your health and well-being. *Care enough to listen.* Be creative. Savor all the flavors of your food and drink, and when you eat, enjoy the food without washing it down with liquids.

VARIETY IS THE SPICE OF LIFE

Ann felt that she was doomed to suffer on a medically prescribed low-fat diet. She ate the same thing everyday for breakfast and lunch. There was a little more variety in her dinners but there was certainly no surprise or anything out of the ordinary to perk up her taste buds. She was bored, bored, bored with her food plan. No wonder she was prone to nibbling and feelings of deprivation.

It is so important to have something different to eat that is enjoyable so that your mind and attention are drawn back to the eating experience. New recipes, a variety of different breads and cereals, brightly colored vegetables, a new way of presenting an old favorite meal, or any number of other "attention grabbers" can be used so that they will register psychologically and you will know you have eaten.

Presentation of the meal can add to the enjoyment. It's fun emphasizing different colors and textures. Try not to fall into the trap during the winter season of the humdrum vegetables and fruits that are far from exciting when you see them over and over again. Carrots, apples, and oranges are great, but if you don't think of different ways to serve them they become monotonous.

When the fancier vegetables and fruits are out of season they are more expensive. But if you are unsatisfied with the meal due to its lack of "oomph" you will follow it by a rich dessert or chocolate bar to

193

satisfy your psychological craving.

Switching over to the HUGS™ way of eating may involve eating a greater proportion of vegetables and fruits that are more costly when out of season. However, clients tell me that overall, their food bills are less because of less consumption of convenience foods. Finding more satisfaction from the regular meal reduces the tendency to want more later on. Compare the difference for yourself and you may be pleasantly surprised!

LEARNING TO TASTE, SAVOR, AND ENJOY

Eating slowly can maximize your enjoyment of food and provide an earlier feeling of fullness for a given quantity of food consumed. It will also slow down the release of sugar into the bloodstream. Eating quickly can minimize your enjoyment of food and fool your body's appetite control mechanism into wanting more.

Listening to classical music while you eat may decrease your appetite and benefit digestion. A recent study performed by the Health and Stress Clinic at Johns Hopkins University shows that people who listened to classical music while eating took longer to finish the meal, took fewer bites per minute, and were satisfied with one helping. Those who listened to rock music and marching tunes ate faster, ate more per forkful, and asked for second helpings.[1]

Does focusing on your eating mean putting your fork down between bites? Think about it. Isn't this an external cue? It may work for a while, but it's not natural and may be difficult to internalize as a new way of eating.

Is filling up on water before a meal the answer? You will feel bloated and will not be able to eat as much. Is this dealing with your physical hunger or temporarily trying to avoid it? Will it not lead to greater hunger later on?

Naturally slow eaters do not put their forks down between bites. Start observing slow eaters. They are often slimmer but not because of dieting. Nondieters naturally focus on eating, while they are eating. On
194

the other hand, while talking, they may put their forks down and focus on the conversation. For them eating is not automatic, it is conscious and they are tasting every morsel and enjoying their food.

In order to slow your eating rate, be patient and practise the following techniques until the old patterns are replaced by new ones. The purpose of these techniques is
- to interrupt the process of automatic eating,
- to give your stomach a chance to register to your brain that you are full, and
- to slow down the release of sugar into the bloodstream.

These methods and techniques can put you on the road to slower eating.

TECHNIQUES TO INTERRUPT AUTOMATIC EATING

• Create a relaxed atmosphere prior to eating so that the mood is set to enjoy the meal. Classical music in the background may help create the mood. Dine, don't simply eat.

• Focus on what you are eating (taste, flavor, texture, and aroma) while you are eating. Don't smother your food with too many condiments that can mask the flavor. As you gradually cut back on the fats and enhance the flavor with herbs and spices, you will begin to enjoy the natural flavor of food.

• Build in a "pause" partway through your meal. Pause during your meal: start with 30 seconds. Gradually increase time to 1, 2, and 3 minutes. Initially, this may be a conscious effort to interrupt the process of automatic eating. This "pause" will help to put you in touch with your feelings of hunger and fullness.

• Focus on the food and the eating of it while you are eating. When you are talking to others, place your fork down and focus on the conversation. Otherwise, you end up talking with your mouth full of food and deprive yourself of the true enjoyment of either activity. Practising this technique is more natural than the artificial method of putting your fork down between bites.

• Come to the meal pleasantly hungry, but not famished. This will help to regulate your speed of eating. Build in snacks if you anticipate that your meal is going to be delayed.

• Be less efficient when eating. For example, when you are having a soup or salad and sandwich, don't be so organized that you eat the soup while holding the sandwich in the other hand. Then you will finish the meal in no time. Instead try making the soup piping hot and finish it first prior to starting the sandwich. Then you are fully enjoying the soup

195

and extending the time frame of your meal. Or eat a salad prior to the meal. Its texture will get you into the habit of chewing food more and will help to slow you down. After all, it's your special time. Enjoy it!

• Focus on the attitude that goes along with eating slowly rather than simply the behavior. In other words, if you sit down for a few minutes when you get home, it gives you a chance to break the "rush-rush" momentum that might have been built up all day. It allows you a chance to reflect on the day's activities. Plan for the meal, and maybe include a snack before dinner to avoid nibbling everything in sight. When you are pleasantly hungry it creates the right mood to help you eat more slowly and naturally.

VISUALIZATION: MAKING IT HAPPEN

Eating slowly is not simply a change in behavior; it's a state of mind that in turn will motivate you to fully experience on a regular basis the tastes, textures, aromas, and flavors of dining. Visualizing or imagining yourself as being relaxed before you begin the meal, and tasting and savoring your food as you eat will help. Stop at times, put your fork down, and engage in conversation. Your speed of eating will slow down more readily.

To demonstrate how effective this technique can be, say the following scenario to yourself while soft music is playing in the background. This creates a relaxed atmosphere.

"I have just come home from work. I do some deep breathing and a few stretches for a couple of minutes. Feeling relaxed but hungry, I go to the fridge, get myself a snack (i.e crackers and milk or whatever I find to be appropriate as a snack). I sit down at the table and enjoy the snack. I get up after 5 or 10 minutes, prepare the meal, and feel less anxious at mealtime. I am able to enjoy the meal and actually feel less hurried. My appetite is pleasantly stimulated for this meal. I'm glad I stopped to have a snack before I ate dinner. Now I can taste and enjoy the food. I am enjoying talking to my family. I stop eating at times to talk to my family about some of the pleasant events of the day's activities. I find myself tasting my food so I am eating more slowly. I realize that whenever I'm hungry, I can get myself something to eat so there is no need to clean off everything on my plate. I am satisfied now. I leave the table

196

feeling satisfied, but not overly full."

Now close your eyes and picture yourself eating in this manner. Visualize it. See yourself as this new person in charge of your eating, simply because you are enjoying the food, the moment, the company, and the event. Do this at least once a day until it begins to happen naturally and what you visualize becomes reality. No matter what the occasion you will find a way to enjoy it. Your fork still goes down once in a while which puts the "pause" in your eating, allowing you to decide if you really want more. It breaks the automatic eating and gives you a chance to feel if you are still hungry or are simply eating because the food is there.

Eating quickly may result from allowing yourself to get too hungry. Or you may eat too quickly to prevent the food from getting cold. Think about it. Are you actually allowing yourself to taste and savor the food when you eat quickly? Eating the food more slowly, even if it is cooler, allows you to extract more flavor and tune into the texture and get the enjoyment from the experience of eating. You are learning to view food in a different way.

If you are still concerned that this slower way of eating will allow your food to get cold, try heating the plates beforehand. Some people put them in the heat cycle in the dishwasher or in the oven on low heat. Actually, I find the food still tastes great even though it may be lukewarm. The flavors are more pronounced at this temperature. The extremes of temperature, whether it is very cold or very hot, do not allow you to experience the most flavor.

This total enjoyment of the food and the event will eventually allow you to be satisfied with less to eat. The end result of eating smaller portions may be the same as diet programs but the reason for arriving there is different. It is now *your choice.* Learning, practising, and enjoying add up to health benefits. You have different preferences which help regulate your feeling of fullness. You eat less for different reasons. You are in charge and you make the choices. The valuable skill of visualization can be used with

197

any type of activity or change that you would like to implement more quickly into your life-style. Athletes often use it prior to a big event, when they focus on their style, to gain poise and concentration.

You can imagine yourself more active. For example, if you close your eyes and see yourself walking and enjoying it, then you are more apt to want to walk. In this way, you have instilled a positive message in your mind about walking.

When trying this method to help internalize different skills or gain confidence, focus on the action involved. Imagine yourself being positive and making the life-style changes that will help you achieve a healthier body rather than focusing on looking thin or seeing yourself as slim. *Focus on the enjoyment of the process, not the end result.*

REASONS FOR LOSING CONTROL OVER FOOD

As long as you continue to avoid your favorite foods (ones that may be high calorie or high fat) without confronting the reasons behind your continued cravings, you will continue to deprive yourself psychologically. This sets you up for overeating these foods when you are finally exposed to them.

You want to eat but it isn't because you are physically hungry. You are upset and haven't confronted the situation. You are afraid to confront it so you continue to eat to make yourself feel better temporarily. Feelings of anger, frustration, or loneliness seem to be relieved through eating. However, you are still faced with the situation at hand.

If you continue to ignore your problem or deal with it in an ineffective manner, you will never resolve it and this cycle of eating may lead to gaining more weight. This will further lower your self-esteem. You won't have a good feeling about yourself and you will never be able to take control of the problem and of the food.

During your childhood you may have learned to keep your emotions to yourself. Pent-up feelings of anger can be very bad for your health. Displaying

198

anger in a negative way is called aggression. Displaying anger in a positive, controlled manner, is confrontation which is a form of assertiveness.

Initially, you may want to use distraction to relieve some of your anger. Try going for a walk or going away from the situation to give yourself a chance to gain perspective. This may give you the opportunity to sort things out and better understand what is really troubling you and what you really want to say.

Think before you talk; otherwise, you may say things in anger that you do not really mean. Voicing your feelings in a constructive way can set you free from those pent-up emotions and keep you from feeling the need to eat to fill this emotional void with food. State your request or your complaint clearly and in a positive manner. Think it through and deal with the situation rationally. You will never know the outcome unless you try to deal with the problem. Spouses or friends cannot read your mind.

It is essential to go back and discover the reasons for your eating and the reasons why you are eating compulsively. Treating your overeating by going on a diet is only a temporary solution. Awareness of the reasons for your overeating is the first step to permanent success.

Congratulate yourself for every success and every new awareness. Change is stressful, so introduce changes gradually, taking it one step at a time. If you introduce just one new life-style change this week and repeat it at every opportunity, it will take root and you will take a major step forward. Your aim is to make one small and concrete change and to really enjoy the way it makes you feel. One can derive much satisfaction from the awareness that you are on the right path, one that you alone have chosen to take.

This awareness can lead to action. It allows you to continue to practise the skill of confrontation with regard to the situations themselves, not only with food. After all, it may be the situations that are causing you to eat. If you can make the effort to deal with them, the need for food as a crutch or comforter will no longer be necessary. It will be much easier to eat only when you are actually physically hungry.

Compulsive behavior can be expressed in many ways. The workaholic has compulsive behavior that is accepted by society. Yet it can endanger health by putting both physical and mental stress on the body. The resulting burnout affects eating and activity habits. The person becomes stressed out and may compensate by eating too much.

EXAMPLES TO HELP YOU WORK THROUGH YOUR NEW SKILLS AND HELP YOU DISTINGUISH PHYSICAL FROM PSYCHOLOGICAL HUNGER.

Example 1
Jane walks by a bakery, smells muffins, and wants to have one. This is an example of psychological hunger where Jane is responding to an external cue. She smells it, she wants it. Does she really want it because of hunger or is she just used to responding to the external cue?

What kind of learned skills can she use? An urge to eat builds gradually like a wave, peaks, and gradually reduces. If Jane keeps on walking, the urge may go away if it was elicited simply by the smell of the muffins and she wasn't physically hungry.

If there is a psychological reason for feeling hungry, she may try to confront the urge. If, as Jane keeps walking, she still desires the muffin, there may be another reason for wanting it. She could find out the reason and deal with it using confrontation skills.

If Jane walks into the bakery and really wants a muffin because it is her favorite chocolate chip type, should she have one? Yes. If she doesn't, she may think about it for the rest of the day, then raid the fridge when she gets home because she feels deprived.

Jane orders the muffin she wants. She is selective and orders only what she wants. She remembers that most of the satisfaction comes from the first and last few bites of what she is eating. So she tastes and savors the muffin but notices that it doesn't taste as good as it did in her mind. She packs up the rest for her dog. Her other option is to leave whatever is left once she has satisfied her urge.

On the other hand, if Jane was really hungry, a muffin may not be the best choice. Many muffins are high in fat and sugar which may send her blood sugar for a roller coaster ride, especially on an empty stomach. And what about all that fat that will just go to body fat? She could try not to let herself get too hungry.

Example 2
It's 4 o'clock and you are usually hungry at this time. What type of hunger is this? It may be either physical or psychological.

What kind of learned skills can you use? If you haven't eaten for about 4 hours you are simply physically hungry. In that case, have a snack. If you try to hold off until supper, you may end up famished by that time. This is no way to go to a meal. It does not allow you the opportunity to taste and savor your food.

However, if you had a snack at 3 o'clock, but you always come home from work hungry, this may be caused by the let down of the day, by loneliness, or habit. You are the only one who can determine what kind of hunger it is and use the appropriate skills to handle it. Confront the urge and deal with the cause.

Check with yourself on the role that food plays for you and your family at different times of the day. Do your children need a snack before supper? Are you concerned about them spoiling their supper, so they remain hungry and cranky until supper time? The idea of a snack is simply to dampen hunger, not to spoil the next meal. Arrive at the table pleasantly hungry, not starved.

YOU ARE WORKING AGAINST YOUR BODY WHEN

- you ignore your natural hunger signals and undereat at the expense of health,
- you overeat to find emotional satisfaction from food rather than from other parts of your life,
- you undereat to try to change your body shape to what you feel is accepted by society,
- you overeat because you are not paying attention to food to derive both physical and psychological satisfaction from it.

Learn to work with your body. Tune into the enjoyment of your life in balance. Meet the situation head on, and delight in your progress.

10

Reading What It's All About

Exercise your choice in the purchase of products suited to your new taste

Now it's time to learn how to make the most use of food labels so that you are able to exercise your choice in the purchase of products suited to your new taste for food.

The food label is the manufacturer's way of communicating with the consumer. In order to best utilize this handy tool, it is important to understand how to read the label so that you get the information you need to make your decisions.

A BLUEPRINT FOR LABEL READING

The ingredients on the label are listed according to the proportion by weight of the ingredients in the product. The main ingredient in a recipe is first on the list. Check the list for the first 5 ingredients. If any of them are a source of fat or sugar, then the product is probably high in calories.

Reading only the front of the label can be confusing and even misleading. Take the example of the sugarless chocolate bar. The information on the front of the chocolate bar label makes it sound enticing to the person with diabetes and maybe even to the individual who is concerned about sugar or weight. It is important to note that the words "sugarless milk" are on the front of the label in large print while the message to individuals with diabetes is in small print and hardly noticeable. The chocolate bar was bought at a store where the owner had a large sign advertising the fact that the chocolate bar was sugarless.

The small print on the back of the label is more revealing. The ingredients are listed as cocoa butter, sorbitol, milk, mannitol, cocoa, ground hazelnuts, skim milk, emulsifier, saccharin, vanillin.

The main ingredient is cocoa butter, a fat that will

203

convert into fat in your body very efficiently. Further reading reveals that the bar contains 80 calories. You need to read it carefully, in order to realize that it means 80 calories per serving size of 4 squares and not 80 calories for the large chocolate bar. With 6 servings per bar, this equals 480 calories per bar. Most of the calories come from fat. Why does the chocolate bar have so much fat (56 percent of the calories come from fat)? One of the functions of sugar is a tenderizer. Taking out the sugar requires the addition of fat to bring back that smooth texture. With more sugar, the quantity of fat could be reduced.

Since this product does not contain any granulated sugar necessary for the smooth texture that is part of a good quality chocolate bar, does that mean that it does not contain any sugar at all? Not so. Sorbitol and mannitol are sugar alcohols that eventually break down into sugar in your system. Saccharin is an artificial sweetener. Combining these 3 sweeteners may simulate the taste of sugar but they do nothing for the texture. More fat is needed. The result is a chocolate bar that would not satisfy the chocolate connoisseur. Yet it contains the same number of calories (maybe more) than your old reliable chocolate bar!

The moral here is that if you really want a chocolate bar, don't settle for a substitute that leaves you wanting the real thing. Acquiring a taste for less sweetening and fattening foods requires gradual changes, not sudden disappointments. Inferior substitutions can lead to feelings of deprivation, eventually leading to binging on the real food.

Tasting, savoring, and enjoying your real chocolate bar may allow you to be satisfied with less than the whole bar. After all, if you know that you can eat it without guilt and enjoy it and have it at any time, you may eat only what you really want at the time. As you begin to think more like a nondieter, you may become more selective in the type of chocolate bar you like (i.e. not as sweet due to taste for less sweetening foods).

SUGAR, WHERE DO YOU FIND IT?

Anything ending in "ose" — sucrose, maltose, lactose, glucose, etc.

Anything ending in "ol" — sugar alcohols such as mannitol, xylitol, and sorbitol

Sugar from natural sources such as fruit (i.e. an orange contains natural sugar equivalent to 2 to 3 tsp (10 to 15 mL) of sugar)

Honey, molasses, corn syrup solids, etc.

See list at end of chapter for more complete version.

FACTS ABOUT HEALTH FOODS REVEALED

Many foods lead you to think they are nourishing, but they are not. Don't be lulled into a false sense of security by a healthy-sounding name. *Always read labels.* Some foods pretend to be health foods but are they really healthy?

Frozen Vegetarian Pasta Even though pasta on its own is fat free, prepared pasta products that omit meat may contain whole-milk cheeses that are high in fat. A 10.5-ounce (298-g) serving of one popular frozen vegetable lasagna contains only 225 calories; however, 50 percent of those calories come from the 12.5 grams of fat, which is largely saturated. The dish contains 3 cheeses and bread-crumb topping moistened with partially hydrogenated oils. In contrast, the percentage of fat calories in one regular meat lasagna, another frozen dinner, is only 32 percent.

Packaged Pasta Salad Packed in the same way as instant soups, you boil up dried pasta and dehydrated vegetables from one packet. Another packet contains seasonings (including lots of sodium) which you blend with oil for a dressing. Unfortunately, 38 percent of the 190 calories in a 1/2 cup (125 mL) serving on one well-known brand of pasta salad come from 8 grams of fat (7 of which you added yourself). *Question whether adding all this fat is necessary.* Another option would be to cook your own pasta (just as quick) and add your own mix of any of the following seasonings by itself or combined with nonfat yogurt: unsalted herbs, Dijon mustard, chili powder, Worcestershire sauce.

Bran Muffins If the muffins contain bran, they will certainly contain fiber, but it may be very little. Most store-bought muffins have far more hydrogenated oils, sugar, and eggs in them than oat or wheat bran. Check the ingredients list. If bran is close to the bottom, you're being deceived. Look for whole wheat flour as the main ingredient, not wheat flour (refined white flour).

Carrot Cake If it is dense and moist this indicates a high-fat content. A typical cake may contain more than a cup (250 mL) of oil which has nearly 2000 calories by itself (about 200 calories per slice before

TIP If muffin weighs heavily in your hand (some are 5 oz or 140 g or more) and has a sticky surface, it is likely to have as many calories and fat as any cupcake. If it leaves a grease ring on the napkin or leaves your hands with an oily feeling, it probably is high in fat.

adding the other ingredients). *Note* These are all fat calories. Nearly all store-bought carrot cakes also contain a variety of sugars, refined flour, eggs, and shortening, plus cream cheese and more sugar in the frosting. From the point of health, you'll almost always be better off with apple pie, even though it may be loaded with sugar (does not apply to persons with diabetes).

Banana Cake and Banana Bread These are not much different than chocolate cake. One widely sold banana cake begins with sugar, continues with partially hydrogenated vegetable shortening and then flour. After that come the bananas. Just as carrot cakes do, banana cakes usually get 40 to 50 percent of their calories from fat. Store-bought banana breads may be as full of fat as the banana cakes. To avoid this, make sure that flour is first on the ingredients list and shortening toward the bottom. Less fat and sugar are required in making your own banana bread.

> **Many low- or no-fat food products contain so much extra carbohydrate, in the form of sugars, that they provide virtually the same number of calories as the full-fat version.**

Frozen Tofu Desserts These are widely advertised as healthful stand-ins for ice cream. Cholesterol and lactose-free they are, but their calorie and fat content may actually be higher than that of ice cream. *Note* They may also be nearly tofu-free. Half the 230 calories in a 4-ounce (113-g) serving of one well-known frozen tofu product comes from sugars (high-fructose corn sweeteners, corn syrup, and honey) and the other half from fat (partially hydrogenated). Tofu is ranked fifth on the ingredients list. If the dessert has a chocolate or carob coating this will add more fat and calories.

Popcorn This is a no-fat, low-calorie snack when popped with little or no oil or salt and left unbuttered. *Note* A hot-air popper requires no oil. Microwave popcorn and pre-popped corn usually contain twice as many calories as conventional popcorn, a hefty dose of salt, and more fat per ounce or gram than most cookies. The fat comes from vegetable oils that are usually hydrogenated (saturated) and sometimes cheese is added as well.

Vegetarian Paté Some of these patés mimic the fatty texture of traditional liver paté by the addition of fat.

206

One brand lists palm kernel oil (more highly saturated than animal fat) second among its ingredients after water. Peanut oil is listed a little farther down the list. *Note* In this case the predominant vegetable ingredient is potato starch.[1]

Peanut Butter Most commercial brands of peanut butter contain salt and sugar as well as added hydrogenated oil (which keeps it from separating), as well as salt and sugar. The kind made solely from peanuts has about 15 percent less fat and almost no salt. Even though this peanut butter that is made straight from peanuts derives nearly 80 percent of its calories from fat, the fat is mostly unsaturated. It's an inexpensive protein source with no cholesterol and could fit into a heart-healthy diet for adults. One tbs (15mL) contains 5 grams of protein, some niacin, potassium, and magnesium, 95 calories and 8 grams of fat. If the natural peanut butter is still too greasy for your taste, try spooning off some of the fat layer that rises to the top at room temperature. Add this lower fat peanut butter to whole grain toast with jam for a combination that provides moisture with less fat.

Crackers Some crackers have as much fat as potato chips. Read the label and watch for hydrogenated vegetable oil. If they leave a wring on your napkin or feel greasy to the touch, they probably will taste greasy and be high in fat. Gradually introduce some high-fiber crackers that are lower in fat. *Concentrate on the crunch and taste of these crackers.*

Cheese Check the label for M.F. (milk fat) or B.F. (butter fat) to guide you on the amount of fat in the product. You will note that some of the higher fat cheeses that contain more than 20 percent M.F. leave a sheen of grease on the surface when melted. As you begin to experiment with some of the lower fat cheeses, you will note that they have a stringier texture and are great for holding the ingredients of a pizza in place.

Most cheeses labeled "slender," "lite," "low-fat," or "part-skim" contain only slightly less fat than regular varieties. Even if a cheese has 50 percent less fat, as some labels promise, an ounce or gram of it may still contain about 5 grams of fat which is mostly saturated. This can account for 60 percent of its total calories. A popular cheese that claims to be 25 percent less fat than a regular brand contains 6.3 grams per serving rather than the 8.4 grams per serving in the regular version. This translates to 60 percent of the calories coming from fat rather than the 68 percent in the regular brand. This is certainly not 25 percent less fat.

> Health and Welfare Canada's new nutrition labeling regulations define low fat as not more than 3 grams fat per serving and a maximum of 15 percent fat on a dry matter basis. The proposed definition for lean meat or poultry is no more than 8 grams of fat per serving.

This doesn't mean that you should be eating only low-fat foods. The idea is to increase your carbohydrate foods and gradually cut back on the fat used in food preparation. As your tastes begin to change, it will be more natural to choose prepared foods and meats with lower total fat content.

Remember, a healthful diet is all a matter of balance. Be careful not to totally avoid those foods that do not fit into the low-fat definition. If you approach label reading in this way you are right back into the diet thinking. As one of my client's put it, "I didn't need self-control, I just needed to think normally. I have gained the ability to look at my eating as part of my life, not as an all time-consuming hobby."

> Read the labels so that you will be aware of high-fat foods to continue guiding your preferences towards low-fat foods.

HOW TO APPLY THIS KNOWLEDGE
Contrast this muffin recipe with the following recipe.

No Egg, No Sugar, No Fat Bran Muffins
Makes 12 muffins

Mix the following dry ingredients together.

2 cups	whole wheat flour	500 mL
1-1/2 cups	natural wheat bran	375 mL
1 tsp	cinnamon	5mL

Add

1-1/2 cups	buttermilk	375 mL
1-1/4 tsp	soda	6 mL
1/2 cup	honey	125 mL
1 tsp	vanilla	5 mL
1 cup	apple chopped (unpeeled)	250 ml
1/2 cup	raisins	125 mL
	Juice from 1 orange	
	Grated peel from 1 orange	

Mix all ingredients together. Lightly grease muffin tins, or line with paper muffin cups. Fill muffin tins. Bake at 350°F (180°C) for 20 to 25 minutes.

These muffins taste good and contain no fat. But do they really contain no sugar? There is no white granulated sugar in the recipe, but they do contain honey and sugar from natural sources such as apple, orange, and raisins. These are very nutritious, no-fat muffins that are moist and tasty. As you begin to acquire a taste for less sweet foods, you may even find these muffins too sweet. Cut back on the "sweet" ingredients slightly and re-evaluate the taste.

Raisin Oat Bran Muffin
Makes 12 muffins

1 cup	all-purpose flour	250 mL
2/3 cup	oat bran	150 mL
1 1/2 tbs	sugar	22 mL
2 tsp	baking powder	10 mL
1/2 tsp	baking soda	2 mL
1/2 tsp	cinnamon	2 mL
1/2 tsp	salt	2 mL
3/4 cup	buttermilk or sour skim milk	175mL

(to sour skim milk, add 1 tsp (5 mL) lemon juice or vinegar to 3/4 cup (175 mL) skim milk. Let stand for 5 to10 minutes at room temperature, then use.)

	1 egg, lightly beaten	
1 tbs	corn oil	15 mL
1 tbs	molasses	15 mL
2 tsp	vanilla	10 mL
1/4 cup	raisins, finely chopped.	50 mL

Lightly grease muffin tins, or line with paper muffin cups.

209

In a bowl, combine flour, oat bran, sugar, baking powder, baking soda, cinnamon, and salt. In a separate small mixing bowl, combine buttermilk, egg, corn oil, molasses, and vanilla. Make a well in dry ingredients, pour in buttermilk mixture and add raisins. Mix just until dry ingredients are moistened.

Fill muffin cups 2/3 full. Bake in a 400°F (200°C) oven for 20 minutes or until lightly browned.

These muffins fall more into the category of the bread group and they are a little dry. Going from store-bought or restaurant-made muffins (which are 300 to 500 calorie cakes in a muffin tin) to these muffins may be too drastic a change. If these muffins are not sweet enough or moist enough, try noticing the difference in the 2 recipes. Adding fruit can give moisture and sweetness to a recipe. Also popping it in the microwave may moisten the baked muffins. A little jam or jelly can also add moisture and sweetness. Try cutting the muffin up in pieces, adding some ice cream, and having it as a dessert. Do not feel restricted. You can modify this recipe to suit your taste.

The latter recipe offered the option of using an artificial sweetener to take the place of the sugar. What does this indicate to you? Is replacing the 45 calories in a tablespoon (15 mL) of sugar, with an artificial sweetener really going to make a difference? It can be compared to eating a large meal and then ordering coffee and using artificial sweetener. Use your judgment and modify the recipes where necessary. Try adding different spices to the muffins to suit your taste. Mace and cardamom or lemon or orange peel are other seasonings that you may want to try. Let your creativity run wild. Vanilla is the extract in this recipe. However, there are a multitude of other flavorings on the market such as almond extract, lemon, coconut, rum, etc. that can give a new flavor sensation.

The baking powder and baking soda were increased in this recipe to allow the muffins to rise. These compensate for the low amount of sugar which is necessary for the egg to coagulate at a higher temperature. It is important to sift the baking powder and baking soda with the dry ingredients; otherwise, pieces of powder or soda will be found in your finished baked product. If the taste of the baking soda or baking powder is undesirable, you may choose to slightly decrease these ingredients while increasing the content of sugar to 1/4 cup (50 mL) and adding some fruit.

Some guidelines to help you along in your process of experimentation.

• Cut down fat and sugar *gradually* so that you still enjoy eating the end product. For example, cutting the fat in half in your regular pie crust recipe and rolling the dough thinner with lattice crust on top (another option would be to use cookie cutters to cut out some of the top crust) results in a lighter pie crust that accents rather than detracts from the taste of the pie filling. Another tip would be to make the fruit filling thicker.

• To enhance the flavor, try other seasonings and flavorings. When cutting back on fat or sugar, adding more vanilla (i.e. doubling it) can bring out the flavor.

• To help moisten the recipe, try the addition of fruit or juice. Juice contains natural sugar, but the addition of liquid can also incorporate more moisture into the product.

In the United States, there is legislation for the word "light or lite". It is defined as 1/3 fewer calories or 50% less fat. If more than half the calories are from fat, fat content must be reduced by 50% or more.

• Sometimes words on labels may be misleading. For example, "Light." There is no legislation to govern the use of this word. It may refer to the product being "lighter" tasting, such as certain kinds of olive oil. It may refer to the product being "lighter" in color, such as certain kinds of soya sauce. Or it may refer to the product being lower in fat content such as certain kinds of mayonnaise.

"Light" yogurt, in spite of its name, is not low calorie. It is a regular product at 260 calories per 8 ounces (225 g) and it is sweetened with sugar. Ingredients read: low-fat milk, sugar, skim milk, strawberries, water, bananas, food starch (modified), yogurt culture, natural flavor, gelatin, citric acid, with sorbic acid and ascorbic acid (to ensure freshness), artificial color.

211

Read the entire label carefully to determine its meaning.

• Today there is overuse of the words "contains no cholesterol." Here is an example.

> The product may contain no cholesterol (for example, there may be no eggs in the product) but it may be high in saturated fat which has a greater affect on blood cholesterol levels as well as weight. As more consumers are catching on to the fact that the words "no cholesterol" may be misleading, many manufacturers are attempting to lower the amount of saturated fat in the products. But we're still not getting the whole story. The product may in fact be low in cholesterol and saturated fat but high in total fat.
> CONSUMER BEWARE.

Reading this front label leads you to believe that these cookies are good for your heart and are healthy to eat. A closer look at the nutrition information per

Ingredients enriched wheat flour (wheat flour, niacin, reduced iron, thiamine mononitrate, riboflavin), sugar, vegetable shortening (partially hydrogenated soybean and/or cottonseed oil), rolled oats, chocolate chips, bran, raisins, corn syrup, honey, leavening (baking soda), salt, cinnamon, natural butter flavor, caramel color.

serving gives other information. One serving of 1 cookie contains 34 calories (these cookies are very small). The cookie has no cholesterol but it does contain 2 grams of fat. We know that there are 9 calories/gram of fat so this equals 2 x 9 calories = 18 calories of the total 34 calories coming from fat (18 divided by 34 = .529 x 100 = 53 percent of calories in this cookie comes from fat). So these cookies are high in fat which is going to affect both weight and cholesterol level.

Check the ingredients list. *Note* Even though the cookies do not contain tropical oils (palm, coconut oils that are saturated), the third ingredient is vegetable shortening, a saturated fat that will affect blood cholesterol levels. The word hydrogenated in a product indicates hardened fat which makes the fat saturated. Even though the type of fat is from a

212

vegetable source, it has been chemically altered through the process of adding hydrogen to the product which is called "hydrogenation." This process allows the product a longer shelf life and makes the fat hard at room temperature. Any positive effect of oat fiber on cholesterol levels is negated by the high amount of fat in the product.

Misleading labels and information can be confusing. The food manufacturer in order to sell his product has to make you want to buy it. *Highlighting trendy information that will grab your attention is what he will aim to do.*

Read the fine print as well and note where the different ways of saying "fat" and "sugar" appear on the label. Make it a learning and fun experience! Get the children involved. They may actually enjoy helping you. However, ensure that you don't get caught up with being preoccupied with the label. The product has to taste good and satisfy you.

THESE WORDS ALL MEAN "SUGAR"

Brown sugar   A soft sugar whose crystals are covered by a film of refined dark syrup.

Carbohydrate   Sugars and starches.

Corn sugar   Sugar made by the breakdown of cornstarch.

Corn syrup   A syrup containing several different sugars that are obtained by the partial breakdown of cornstarch.

Dextrin   A sugar formed by the partial breakdown of starch.

Dextrose   Another name for sugar.

Fructose   The sweet sugar found in fruit, juices, and honey.

Glucose   The type of simple sugar found in the blood, formed from food and used by the body for heat and energy.

Honey   A sweet thick material made in the honey sac of various bees; sweeter than sugar.

Invert sugar   A combination of sugars found in fruits.

Lactose   The sugar found in milk.

Levulose   Another name for fruit sugar.

Maltose   A crystalline sugar formed by the breakdown of starch.

Mannitol   A sugar alcohol.

Maple sugar   A syrup made by concentrating the sap of the sugar maple.

Molasses   The thick, dark to light brown syrup that is separated from raw sugar in sugar manufacture.

Sorbitol   A sugar alcohol.

Sorghum   Syrup from the juice of the sorghum grain (sorgo) grown mainly for its sweet juice.

Starch   A powdery complex sugar (carbohydrate), i.e. cornstarch.

Sucrose   Another name for sugar.

Sugar   A sweet carbohydrate.

11

Fluids— How Much Is Enough?

Are you really hungry or are you merely thirsty?

What kind of fluids could you be drinking and are they necessary for your health and well-being? Up to this point the discussion has centered on the technique needed to tune into our internal body signals to regulate hunger and the quantity of food your body needs. The act of tasting and savoring your food was also stressed because it allows you to be satisfied with less. Pausing during your meal allows you to stop and focus on your eating and consciously decide if you would like more, also allowing you to be satisfied with less.

Many individuals in the diet mentality fill up with water, coffee, or soup to lessen their hunger pangs temporarily. They are avoiding their natural hunger signals. Filling up with liquids instead of a meal makes them feel bloated and temporarily full. However, by the following meal, they may be famished and eat anything and everything.

LATER...

Filling up on water prior to the meal is the diet method of dealing with hunger pangs. This makes you artificially full and you eat less at the meal. In other words, the bloating effect of the water causes you to eat less. This is not dealing with your physical hunger; it is avoiding the hunger or trying to dampen it artificially.

HUGS™ philosophy is to eat when you are hungry and drink fluids when you are thirsty. If you try to trick your body by filling it up with fluids when you are actually hungry, it may work temporarily, but will lead to uncontrollable hunger later on.

Adequate fluid intake is important for your health and well-being. Using the technique of tuning into your body to determine when you are thirsty is not as effective as it was for regulating hunger. Scientists don't yet fully understand how the thirst mechanism works. However, they do know that if you wait until you are thirsty, then you are partially dehydrated.

If you avoid your thirst signals you will eat more. All foods contain a certain amount of fluid. If you are not obtaining enough fluids from water or juices to rehydrate your body's proper functioning, your body will signal you to eat more to obtain these fluids.

215

If you go for a walk, and your natural cooling mechanism causes you to lose some water through perspiration, you need to rehydrate yourself when you come back.

Suppose you come back from your walk and see some watermelon in the fridge which contains 92 percent water. You are thirsty and it sure looks good. You eat 4 slices to quench your thirst when really what your body wanted was water. Your fluids are replenished from food rather than from fluids. Unfortunately, you may be even more thirsty due to the high-sugar content of the fruit.

The HUGS™ strategy would be to drink a sufficient amount of fluids, namely water, to rehydrate your body. If you still want the watermelon, have it after the fluid replacement, and you may actually be satisfied with less watermelon. Filling up on ice cream, popsicles, or a milkshake to cool you off and replace fluids does not address the real problem. These items are cold and they do not effectively replenish the fluids in your body. You may still be thirsty and feel unsatisfied.

SIGNS OF DEHYDRATION
How do you know if you are not consuming enough fluids? Watching for the signs of dehydration can give you the answer. Water is as critical to the body as oil is to a car's engine. The body needs fluids to function properly. Fluids allow reactions to take place in the body processes that keep you going.

Blood consists mostly of water and it carries oxygen and nutrients to your brain. Without enough water, you get a headache. This pain in your head is caused by insufficient oxygen, carried by water, to your brain. Dizziness and lack of concentration can also result if less nutrients and oxygen are carried to the brain.

Water is also the main ingredient in urine which carries wastes away from the body. Water is also needed to keep food moving through the intestinal tract and to help prevent constipation which may occur if you're eating high-fiber foods.

Without water we would die in a few days, yet we

216

> A dark-colored urine where only small amounts are eliminated is an indication of dehydration. If your body is not taking in sufficient fluids, it keeps you from further becoming dehydrated by releasing less water.

can live for weeks without food. A dark-colored urine where only small amounts are eliminated is an indication of dehydration. If your body is not taking in sufficient fluids, it keeps you from further becoming dehydrated by releasing less water. Your urine is darker as it becomes more concentrated. Fluid retention may be another indication that our body is not taking in enough fluids. When the body gets less water, it perceives this as a threat to survival and begins to hold onto every drop. If you are taking vitamin pills, and you take in more than your body needs, the water-soluble vitamins B and C are passed through the urine, making it a darker color. In this situation, color would not be a good indicator of a state of hydration.

A weak fluttering pulse may be another sign of dehydration. A lower intake of water means that you will have less volume of blood. This will cause your heart to race or beat faster in order to pump the diminished supply of blood to your muscles.

Some water is produced as a by-product of metabolism. Six to 8 glasses of liquid per day are usually needed to make up the balance. For example, under stressful situations, your blood becomes thicker once the reflex responses have kicked in. Drinking 6 to 8 glasses of water per day can offer a protective effect since it dilutes your blood.

> For weight loss, water is particularly important because it is necessary to help the body metabolize or break down fat. In short, water is necessary for your health and well-being. You know when you are dehydrated and consuming insufficient fluids; however, your thirst mechanism is not very sensitive in telling you when to drink fluids.

QUENCHING YOUR THIRST

Going from soda pop or diet drinks to water is quite a drastic change. The more enticing fluids attract you because of their appeal to your senses of color, flavor, and taste. You may shift to drinking water because you feel you should drink it, rather than because you enjoy water and like the taste of it. If you change to water gradually you will get used to it.

Let's take a look at the different types of liquids and

217

their relationship to rehydrating you and quenching your thirst. Fluids listed as diuretic do not rehydrate you due to their effect of ridding the body of fluids by increasing urine production.

FLUIDS AND THEIR FUNCTIONS

Type of Beverage	Rehydration	Quenches Thirst
Coffee	No, it's a diuretic	Yes
Tea	No, it's a diuretic	Yes

Coffee and tea cause the blood vessels to dilate as the result of the xanthine content. Although caffeine is the strongest stimulant in coffee, tea, and cocoa, these drinks also contain other related xanthine compounds such as theophylline and theobromine that have similar, though less potent, effects. Caffeine is the main xanthine in coffee; but theophylline predominates in tea, and cocoa contains large amounts of theobromine. These chemicals contribute significantly to the stimulant effects of tea and cocoa.

Decaffeinated coffee	No, it's a diuretic	Yes

Note that decaffeinated coffee still contains 2 other stimulants called theophylline and theobromine. Cutting out coffee and tea can cause caffeine withdrawal symptoms such as headaches, so taper off coffee and tea consumption gradually. Switching from coffee to tea can lead to a gradual decrease in caffeine content. A 5-oz (150 mL) cup of strong tea brewed for 5 minutes contains 45 mg caffeine while a 5-oz (150 mL) cup of percolated coffee contains 110 mg caffeine. Use the substitution of tea for coffee only if you enjoy the taste of tea; otherwise, you may feel psychologically deprived by using what you would classify to be an inferior substitute.

Milk	No, net effect is dehydration due to high calcium and protein content	Yes
Soft drinks	Partially	No, due to high concentration of sugar, which makes you more thirsty.
Diet drinks	Yes	Somewhat

These drinks are artificially sweetened and have a sweet taste. Substituting these for regular drinks does not allow you to acquire a taste for less sweet foods. The increased consumption of artificially sweetened products has not decreased society's craving for sweets or the incidence of obesity. However, diet drinks do have their place. If you particularly like certain diet drinks, try adding a little water to them. Gradually increase the amount of water you add. This will allow you to achieve the goal of learning to acquire a taste for less sweet foods.

Juices	Partially	No, high concentration of natural sugar, makes you more thirsty.

Usually drinking pop or juices leaves you with the feeling of wanting more.

Alcohol	No	No

Even though alcoholic beverages are not diuretics, they do have a diuretic effect in that they increase urine production.[1] Alcohol inhibits the secretion of the antidiuretic hormone. During an alcoholic bout, lack of this hormone combined with the dilating of the vessels of the kidney add to this effect. The diuretic effect of alcoholic beverages can cause a state of dehydration commonly known as a hangover.

No more than 2 to 3 cups of coffee per day is recommended. Large amounts of coffee can cause diarrhea while the tannins in tea may help stop simple diarrhea.[2] Adding milk to the tea can bind the tannins and partly reduce their effect.

Drinking tea with meals can inhibit the absorption of iron from non-heme sources such as cereals and vegetables. One study showed that drinking tea with a meal decreases iron absorption by 62 percent.[3]

A mechanism by which tea is thought to influence iron absorption is by the formation of insoluble iron tannates. When milk is added to tea, the protein in milk reacts with the tannin in the tea and prevents the body from absorbing tannin. Adding milk to the tea binds the tannin, therefore improving the absorption of iron. Tannin in tea also slows the release of its caffeine and makes it a less immediate shock to the nervous system than the caffeine in coffee.

It was found that coffee may also decrease iron absorption, but not as much as tea. In a study done by Morck, Lynch, and Cook,[4] a cup of coffee (250 mL) reduced iron absorption from a hamburger meal by 39 percent as compared to a 64 percent decrease with tea. This study suggests that reduced absorption was most marked when the coffee was taken with the meal or up to one hour later. A significant fraction of the meal would still be in the stomach after one hour and therefore the coffee would still decrease iron absorption.

> **Drinking coffee or tea prior to a meal or at least one hour after you finish eating, will not interfere with iron absorption. Drinking fluids high in vitamin C such as juice spritzers (see p229) can enhance the absorption of iron from cereals and vegetables. (Refer to Chapter 4 p107 for list of foods high in vitamin C.)**

Switching from coffee to tea provides a gradual drop in caffeine content. Since tea has about half as much caffeine as does coffee; withdrawal symptoms would be minimized. One way to test how addicted you are to caffeine is to try to stop using it for a day or two. Withdrawal symptoms are common. The first one to occur is usually a headache, which may develop as soon as 18 hours after the last dose of caffeine.

The headache typically begins with a sensation of fullness in the head and progresses to a painful throbbing that is made worse by bending over and by exercise. It is relieved by caffeine, or painkillers that contain caffeine such as Anacin or Excedrin. Caffeine is included in headache remedies to constrict blood vessels in the brain, since dilated blood vessels contribute to migraine-type headaches. Regular coffee drinkers who abstain from caffeine in the evening may wake up with a headache the next morning.

Caffeine is one of the nonprescription mood-altering drugs. Abrupt withdrawal may mimic the symptoms of consuming too much caffeine.

In a study done at Johns Hopkins University, it was found that withdrawal symptoms began 18 hours after caffeine intake, peaked at 24 hours, and then gradually decreased. Withdrawal symptoms included headache, fatigue, muscle stiffness and soreness (flu-like symptoms), and significant deterioration of mood and behavior.

> **SYMPTOMS OF CAFFEINE WITHDRAWAL OR OVERDOSE**
> • headache
> • drowsiness
> • lethargy
> • yawning
> • runny nose
> • irritability
> • disinterest in work
> • nervousness
> • mental depression
> • nausea
> • vomiting

Wean yourself off coffee gradually by decreasing the number of cups of coffee by one or two a day until you're down to a safe level of 2 to 3 cups (500 to 750 mL) a day. Switching to tea is a gradual reduction of caffeine. Eventually steep the bag for less time for less total caffeine content. Start switching to tea only if you enjoy the taste. Otherwise, you will be using it as a poor substitute for something you really like. The end result may be a feeling of deprivation, which is something you are striving to avoid. Another method would be to gradually mix more decaffeinated coffee into the pot brewed each morning.

Further insight revealed that overnight abstinence of caffeine caused low-grade withdrawal symptoms. For this reason, taking coffee in the morning may give you a lift because it suppresses withdrawal symptoms. Caffeine drinkers are more lethargic and irritable in the morning before drinking coffee than are caffeine abstainers.

Heavy consumption of caffeine is considered to be about 8 cups (2 L) of coffee per day. Moderate consumption is 4 cups (1 L) of coffee or less per day.

220

Even though chocolate contains cocoa which contains caffeine, you would have to consume about half a pound (225 g) of dark chocolate and a pound or more

CAFFEINE CONTENT OF FOODS		
SOURCE	AMOUNT	CAFFEINE
Brewed coffee	6 oz (175 mL)	66-180mg
Instant coffee	6 oz (175 mL)	60-100mg
Decaffeinated coffee	6 oz (175 mL)	2-5mg
Tea (5-minute brew)	6 oz (175 mL)	79-110mg
Tea (1-minute brew)	6 oz (175 mL)	20-45mg
Colas	10 oz (300 mL)	22-50mg
Chocolate milk	8 oz (250 mL)	2-7mg
Hot cocoa from Mix	6 oz (175 mL)	6-30mg
Milk chocolate	1 oz (28 g)	1-15mg
Dark chocolate	6 oz (175 g)	5-35mg
Baker's chocolate	1 oz (28 g)	26mg

(±450 g) of milk chocolate to get the stimulant effect of 1 or 2 cups (250 to 500 mL) of brewed coffee.[5] Coffee is the main source of caffeine.

When a healthy human adult consumes caffeine, about 99 percent of it is absorbed, with peak blood levels reached within 15 to 45 minutes. The half-life of caffeine, or the time it takes for the body to eliminate 50 percent of the caffeine consumed, varies from 3 to 7.5 hours.[6]

When you drink a cup of coffee, the caffeine enters your bloodstream, and you feel alert. Within 3 to 7.5 hours you reach for another cup of coffee to get the same feeling back again. However, this effect can be achieved naturally through a healthy life-style. Because caffeine stimulates the body to release more glucose into the bloodstream, it can artificially give you that mental lift to keep your energy level high. The sudden rise in your blood glucose causes your pancreas to over secrete insulin which causes blood glucose levels to quickly drop. This is what makes you want another cup of coffee shortly after the first cup—to bring the blood glucose levels back up.

Are you "jump starting" your body with caffeine instead of food? Needing that first cup of coffee to get you going signals a physical dependence on an unnatural stimulant. Natural stimulants such as physical activity and healthy eating decrease the dependence on these artificial stimulants.

221

Try eating a more substantial breakfast, followed by a single cup of coffee. This uses the beverage more for enjoyment than for a lift. Using coffee in the right way will allow you to enjoy it. Using it in place of food will not benefit your health.

If you can't live without that cup of coffee first thing in the morning and use the stimulants in coffee to get you going, you are likely addicted.

TEA/HERBAL TEA

While many herbal teas are perfectly safe, others contain potent drugs that could prove more hazardous than caffeine. Herbal teas are popular because their range of claims are said to pick you up, calm you down, speed up or slow down the bowels, and even improve your sex life.

Treat herbs as drugs. They may have ingredients that affect the system in the same way that caffeine and alcohol do. These biologically active ingredients are usually present in low concentration so that drinking a little presents no noticeable problem. However, some teas are combinations of herbs that may increase or decrease the effect of a drug you are taking.

> Currently in Canada, there are no government regulations controlling the sale of herbal teas. Some ingredients are safe, some are not. Knowledge is your best protection.

Some Rules of Thumb to Consider

- *Read labels* If the herbal tea package doesn't list ingredients, don't buy it!
- *Not all herbal teas are caffeine-free.* Herb or spice blends that contain black tea, green tea, or mate have caffeine.
- *Introduce a new tea slowly* Brew weak tea at first. Allow the tea to steep for a few minutes then remove the herbs. Drink only in moderation until the tea's effect on you is known to be safe.
- Brew fresh tea each time, since active chemicals are slowly leached from the plant as it steeps.
- Use the HUGS™ philosophy of listening to your body. Try half a cup (125 mL) of weak tea the first time, and if it has no ill effect, you might try a full cup the next time.
- Know your herbs and how to use them.

Putting the Zip in Tea: A Safer Alternative

Tea is a sensible alternative to soft drinks and coffee. After water, it is the most reasonably priced

TEA INGREDIENTS CONSIDERED SAFE

Peppermint
Spearmint
Mellissa or Balm
Dandelion
Red and Black Raspberry
Cayenne
Slippery Elm
Ginger
Rose hips (high in vitamin C) and hibiscus

None of these teas have been known to cause birth defects. Both rose hips and hibiscus have mild laxative and diuretic effects. There is no reason not to use them.

INGREDIENTS TO BE AVOIDED - DEADLY

St. John's Wort
Golden Seal
Calamus Root
Sassafras or safrole

Sassafras tea is a mild stimulant that contains a potent cancer-causing compound known as safrole. Prior to 1960, it had been widely available. It is available today in health food stores.

SEVERE DIURETICS OR STRONG LAXATIVES

Juniper Berries
Shave Grass (Horsetail)
Buckthorn Bark
Senna Leaves, Flowers
Dock (Burdock)
Aloe Leaves and Bark
Alfalfa Tea (in excess)

MIND-ALTERING

Hyssop
Juniper
Catnip
Hydrangea
Kavabava
Lobelia
Jimsonweed
Wormwood
Nutmeg in high doses

These teas affect the central nervous system. Typical symptoms are blurred vision, dry mouth, inability to urinate, bizarre speech and behavior including hallucinations.

ALLERGIC REACTIONS

Yarrow
German and
Roman Camomile
Goldenrod
Marigold

These teas should be avoided by sensitive persons such as those allergic to ragweed. For all persons they should be consumed in moderation only, not more than 2 cups (500 mL) per day and not on a daily basis.

OTHERS TEAS TO AVOID

Ginseng*
Fennel*
Licorice Root***

*These have hormone-like affects such as painful or swollen breasts even in men. Prolonged use (over 6 months) may cause insomnia, diarrhea, and depression.
***In large amounts, tea may cause water and sodium retention, possible high blood presure, and even cardiac arrest.

beverage, costing just a few cents a cup.

Note For weaker tea with less caffeine, brew for less time. Adding juices to the tea adds some flavor, dilutes the caffeine in the tea, and decreases the diuretic effect of the tea.

DIRECTIONS FOR A NICE CUP OF TEA
Bring fresh, cold water to a full rolling boil. Warm teapot by filling it with hot tap water. Use 1 tea bag or 2 tsp (10 mL) of loose tea for every 2 cups (500 mL) water. Pour the warm water out of the teapot, add the tea and then pour boiling water over the tea. Cover and brew for 3 to 5 minutes, stir, remove tea bags or strain loose tea, and serve.

Adding more variety and interest to your beverages allows you to get more psychological benefit from fluids. Here are some ideas to use tea as a more exotic beverage.

• Combine equal amounts of freshly brewed tea and warm apple juice. Sprinkle with cinnamon and nutmeg or include a cinnamon stick. This is especially good for those trips in winter when you take along a hot thermos of your favorite drink. The flavor from the cinnamon stick will leach into the water.

• Hot tea plus a few teaspoons (mL) each of lemon and honey is a favored remedy for sore throats any time of year. To make it extra special, top it off with a twist of lemon peel.

• Freshly brewed cup of tea plus 1 tsp (5 mL) grated orange peel and a cinnamon stick to garnish.

• Freshly brewed cup of tea plus 1/4 tsp (1 mL) each of vanilla and almond extract.

• Freshly brewed tea plus fruit juices. Try pineapple, grapefruit, or orange juice, half and half, with hot tea. Garnish with lemon or orange slice.

• For a hot vegetable sipper, combine 1/2 cup (125mL) freshly brewed tea with 1/2 cup (125mL) warm vegetable cocktail juice. Season with 1 tsp (5 mL) Worcestershire sauce.

• Equal portions of hot tea plus warm pineapple juice plus a few lightly crushed cardamon pods. The aroma is wonderful; the taste is sensational.

The juices provide some of the natural sweetness.

Add sugar or honey to sweeten, if desired. Keep in mind that you gradually want to acquire a taste for less sweet foods. The juices provide sweet calories from the natural sugar, so check carefully. Do you really want that extra sugar or is it purely habit?

CAFFEINE AND WEIGHT

Can drinking more coffee burn fat? This question is asked from time to time in the HUGS™ class.

Here's the answer you've been waiting for. Caffeine raises the metabolic rate which means that you will burn more calories at rest. Caffeine is also known to burn more fat during exercise. It does this by sparing glycogen, your carbohydrate stores, and using fat as a fuel source. The down side of caffeine consumption is that it triggers the release of insulin which causes blood sugar to drop, as discussed on p221.

As you know, when your blood sugar is low, you are hungry. You eat more, replacing the fat that you lost. Increasing your caffeine content does not give you any overall weight loss benefit. As for increased endurance that occurs by sparing glycogen and using fat as a fuel source, this will be offset if too much caffeine is consumed. It is known that athletes who drink 3 to 4 large mugs of coffee before competition become so hyper they perform poorly.

Normally when on a diet, a person switches from regular drinks to diet drinks. But is this learning to acquire a taste for less sweet foods? You still crave sweet foods even though you substitute a diet item for the regular one. Studies have shown that switching to diet products is not decreasing the incidence of obesity.

Diet thinking suggests that you are allowed to eat more if the product contains less calories. "I'll eat a big supper and finish off with an artificial sweetener in my coffee." This all-or-nothing thinking is pre-

Our society used to be concerned with sugar. Now sugar is no longer bad; it is fat that is the culprit. Yet there is no such thing as a perfect way of eating and no food is good or bad. It is the food balance that is important so that you minimize the starve/binge cycle.

dominant in our society.

Carol used to drink diet drinks all the time and she relies on diet products. She couldn't understand why she always craved sweets when she saw them and she binged on them at social occasions. Possibly it was because the artificially sweetened foods still allowed her to like the sweet taste.

However, by gradually adding water to her beverages, Carol learned to acquire a taste for less sweet foods. She still likes chocolate cake but now a few bites will satisfy her. She actually finds the cake too sweet. The goal is to change your taste rather than simply reduce the calorie intake which does not address the real problem. If you have a sweet tooth you can gradually learn to like less sweet foods.

If you can't live without that cup of coffee first thing in the morning and use the stimulants in coffee to get you going, you are likely addicted.

***This scenario is typical of many people
in our society.***

John stayed up late last night and felt rushed this morning. He ate chips while watching the late movie.

He had no time for breakfast and didn't feel hungry anyway. He grabbed a cup of coffee and a donut at work. Then he felt better and ready for a day's work.

By 10 o'clock he was feeling tired and hungry. John thought he shouldn't eat any more so had another cup of coffee. That kept him going until lunch.

226

When blood sugar is low, you are hungry, tired, lack energy, and feel irritable. This lowers your level of productivity, decreasing your ability to concentrate. You may turn to these foods or beverages that lessen these symptoms temporarily (coffee and donuts) but end up sending your blood sugar on a roller coaster ride. This scenario is part of the "office syndrome." Can you relate to it? Now you understand why it happens.

ENJOYING THE TASTE OF WATER

People do not drink simply to quench their thirst; they respond to a need that's as much in the mind as in the body. Psychological satisfaction is the reason they drink (often something other than water) even if they're not really thirsty. They may simply want to enjoy the taste of the beverage. Presentation of drinks and flavor combinations that excite the eye as well as the palate go a long way towards giving a person psychological satisfaction from drinks. Serving drinks in tall, fancy glasses or using a carafe full of a

At lunch he felt starved and had a headache. He gulped his food so fast that there was little consciousness of what he ate and he neither tasted nor savored the food. He had room for dessert so ate it, rationalizing that he hadn't eaten much earlier on so deserved it.
He ended the meal with 2 cups (500 mL) of coffee to get him going for the afternoon.

By midafternoon he felt sluggish. Since he overate at lunch he felt he shouldn't eat anymore. He compensated for overeating by having only a cup of coffee to give him a boost. The coffee gave him an immediate surge of energy but then he felt wiped. His head was pounding.

By supper time, John was too tired to prepare a decent supper. He ate some cookies and plunked himself in front of television. He was tired of fighting the overpowering cravings and dealing with his wildly erratic energy levels.

Why was this happening to John? Poor eating habits caused him to depend on caffeine rather than food for energy. The choice of donuts provided an immediate burst of energy from the carbohydrates but 50 percent of these calories came from fat. Combined with caffeine which also resulted in a sudden increase in blood sugar, the foods gave a surge of insulin, resulting in a sudden drop in blood sugar.

227

colorful drink on ice is appealing to the eye. Try making your drink special. You are worth it.

Just as you gradually decrease the fat content of foods you choose, you can gradually add water to beverages to learn to acquire a taste for less sweet drinks. Diet drinks do not help you to resist the inevitable binge on sweets at a social function if you have not conquered your craving for sweets.

Nondieters are more selective and eat only what they really like. If you learn to acquire a taste for less sweet foods, then you may choose to omit some sweet foods or have only a few bites since the food will taste too sweet to you. The end result is less quantity eaten because you choose to eat less, not because you feel you should stop eating sweets but because you do not crave them. You will eat only what you really want.

Eating more carbohydrates that break down into natural sugar will allow you to crave less sweets. Restricting carbohydrates causes your body's natural defense mechanism to kick in to cause you to crave the sweets so that you obtain the energy source from these foods.

Gradually add water to any juices, drinks, or diet drinks that you are now using as part of your fluid intake. This can also apply to coffee or tea. Eventually you will end up with colored water that will taste refreshing and will rehydrate you more effectively as well as quench your thirst.

Mary didn't like orange juice because she found it too

FLAVORED SELTZERS, JUICE SPRITZERS, OR REFRESHERS
These creations quench thirst as well as appeal to the eye and taste buds.
Start with 2/3 cup (150 mL) beverage or juice and 1/3 cup (75 mL) water,
then go to 1/2 cup (125 mL) beverage or juice and 1/2 cup (125 mL) water
a week or 2 later, followed by 1/4 cup (50 mL) juice or beverage and
3/4 cup (175 mL) water a few weeks later,
until you reach the level that works for your taste buds
and psychological satisfaction.
By doing this you don't add substantial "sugar" calories to your waist,
and you quench your thirst besides.

acidic. By adding more water than the directions specified, she made a taller drink, cut the acidity, got vitamin C, and at the same time quenched her thirst. She also began to enjoy foods that were not as sweet tasting.

FRUIT SPRITZERS & REFRESHERS

• Combine different juices and add ice cubes and spring water. Add slices of lemon or lime or a squirt of lemon or lime concentrate. Diluting lime cordial is another option.

• Spring water on ice with a squirt of lemon or lime is refreshing.

• Start with different cranberry versions of cocktail juices. Cranapple, cranraspberry, and crangrape add color and flavor to your drinks. Gradually add more water. Blackcurrant or raspberry cocktail can also make a refreshing drink.

• Invent your own flavored drinks. For example, mix a few drops of grenadine or blackcurrant syrup with water, and serve with fruit slices.

• Fruit juice spritzers are delicious. Try grape spritzer. Use 1/4 cup (50 mL) unsweetened white grape juice; 3/4 (175 mL) cup bottled spring water alone or with some diet 7- up. The bottled water will dilute the sweet taste of the diet 7-up so you are still learning to acquire a taste for less sweet foods by using the diet drinks in this way.

• Lemonade spritzer can be made from bottled water or ice and regular water added to lemonade. Water will cut the strong concentrated flavor of the lemon but leave the punch and appeal.

• Wine spritzers or light beers or diluted liqueurs are enjoyable.

• Try a shandy. Mix half beer and half ginger ale or lemonade. Add a little lime juice or lemon juice if you like. Try your shandy with light beer.

• Sangria is made from red or white wine on ice. Add spring water and fruit such as strawberries, lemon, lime, or orange pieces, some root beer, coke, or 7-up.

• Effervescent drinks (soda pops or diet drinks) can add bubbles to your juice spritzers instead of using bottled water and save you money at the same time.

• Squeeze an orange or lemon on ice water and add some slices or slivers of orange or lemon for a fast drink.

• Add celery sticks to water. The flavor will leach into the water with time, leaving a refreshing taste.

WINTER SEASON DRINK SUGGESTIONS

• Add water to apple juice with a cinnamon stick or a dash of cinnamon. Heat it up in the microwave.

• Any of the refreshers on p229 can be heated up for a warmer drink for the winter.

• Try various fruit combinations of tea. The less time you allow the tea to steep in the water, the lower the caffeine content. Add fruit spritzer to regular tea for another version of a hot drink.

• Hot milk with a dash of instant coffee or a squirt of liqueur can be used for a special occasion. If you would like the alcoholic content to go, add liqueur to milk, and then heat it up. In this way, you get the benefit of the flavor without the alcohol.

• Heat milk for 1 minute in the microwave or on the stove, add 1/2 tsp (2 mL) of your favorite flavor of instant international coffee. Stir. This gives the hot milk an added punch with very little extra calories. Note that the first ingredient on these coffees is normally hydrogenated coconut oil to give them that rich taste. A little goes a long way.

• Eggnog, HUGS™ style: Add milk to purchased eggnog to taste. Sprinkle with cinnamon and nutmeg. Heat and serve.

Another idea is to try beverages, including water, at different temperatures. For some people, having a beverage too cold or too hot may not allow them to extract the true taste and enjoyment from the liquid. This is true even with water.

Water doesn't have to be boring. By creating some excitement with beverages, you will drink more fluids and eat because of physical hunger, rather than because your body needs to replenish the fluids.

Use your imagination with drinks. Fine-tune your fluid concoctions just as you did your present recipes.

Drinking plenty of water to rehydrate your body after exercising is important; otherwise you may feel dizzy because your body is pumping a diminished supply of blood to the brain. Use the technique of confrontation to determine whether you are really hungry or simply thirsty. Tuning into your signals for thirst may not be as effective as tuning into your hunger signals. When you drink, your thirst will feel quenched long before your fluid loss is replenished. This is especially pronounced during physical activity when you may become significantly dehydrated before you feel thirsty. It's possible to lose up to 2 quarts (2.3 L) of water before you notice your fluid loss. This is why it is important to drink water before, during, and after exercise in cold weather and in hot. Increase your fluid intake between meals and during meals and determine whether it helps you to actually eat less.

Dieters tend to drink fluids prior to meals hoping this will cause them to fill up on liquids. This in turn may make them eat less simply because they are temporarily more bloated. It leads to increased hunger later on once this feeling subsides.

When increasing the fiber content of your meals, water is essential because high-fiber foods absorb water. In order for foods such as whole grains to allow you to relieve constipation, enough water must be consumed. Increased intake of water in itself will help to improve your bowel movements.

Finding new excitement in fluids can allow you to derive psychological satisfaction from them, allowing you to better tune into your body's true needs.

12
Life-style Strategies

Take time for yourself and relax. You are special too!

BUILDING RELAXATION INTO YOUR LIFE

"I do not have any time for myself. I have a career, family, and husband. Taking care of their needs absorbs all my time. It leaves nothing for me." This situation is common with today's working mothers. Although many women work outside the home, to a great degree the responsibility of family and household care may still be theirs. The result is burnout, a deprivation of time for themselves. They become both physically and emotionally drained and have no way to renew their energies. As these women try to be all things to all people at work and at home, their desire for perfection adds to their problems.

For example, Liz has an obsession to provide clean towels for her family. She had instilled the habit of a clean towel for each person every day. After work her evenings were spent doing laundry and folding towels. She was overwhelmed and her resentment grew because she felt deprived of any time for herself. Without this time, she could not restore a sense of balance to her life.

When Liz realized and accepted the effects of her perfectionist attitude she formed new rules for herself and her family. Three towels a week per individual. Did the family miss the towels? Not really. They were delighted with a more flexible and happier Mom, which was the result of modifying her schedule to include a little "free time" to renew her self-esteem.

> Special time for yourself should focus on an activity that you enjoy. What do you really want to do?
> * go for a walk, some quiet time to close your eyes and daydream or take yourself away to a place you would like to be (visualization),
> * read a book or newspaper,
> * have a snack to take care of your hunger when you come home from work,
> * have a bubble bath,
> * do a crossword puzzle,
> * listen to classical music,
> * do stretching exercises, and/or deep breathing.

How can you create time for yourself? There are

demands on your time as soon as you walk in the door. You must plan carefully to reserve some time to attend to your own needs.

Lisa said, "Everybody is hungry when I come home and they want to eat right away so they can get on with their activities." You are worn out trying to attend to everyone. And if you are constantly running on low energy, tired, and irritable, your quality of life and that of your family suffers. Some of the proposed solutions would be to make it known that you need a half hour to yourself when you get home from work. Or perhaps you are a victim of the arsenic hour, that hour before supper when the kids are dogging your footsteps, they're cranky, and they don't stop pestering you. Perhaps they are simply experiencing low blood sugar. They are probably hungry. Putting the meal in front of them immediately seems the easiest solution, but to do that you must forfeit your special time for your own well-being. Does it sound like a dilemma?

Perhaps there is a solution. A handy snack to dampen immediate hunger pangs will allow the children to be in a state of "pleasant hunger" so they will more likely taste and savor their meal. The added bonus is that they will be in a better frame of mind to enjoy supper. This will also eliminate that "Mom, I'm hungry," an hour after supper is over.

The snack could consist of celery sticks with quark cheese, low-fat muffins, fruit, milk, crackers and cheese, toast with peanut butter and jam, or any other of their favorite foods. Snacks can even be prepared after supper for the next day while you are still working in the kitchen. To make this process even simpler, have easy ready-made purchased snacks handy. Try seasoned bread sticks, melba toast, cheese and crackers, yogurt, milk, bread, rolls, or fruit.

As the children get older, they can take responsibility for the snacks themselves. The former years that you prepared the snacks could serve as an example for them to follow. This creates independence and further frees more time for Mom.

234

While you are resting let the oldest child be in charge for the first half hour and make the others aware that they are to sit quietly and color or watch television. Once a routine is established they will accept it.

Your special time is for you and you alone. In order to avoid noise and distraction you may want to go for a walk to collect your thoughts, regain your composure, and put the sanity back into your life. The real benefit of building a daily relaxation period into your life is that you are not exhausted by the time your holiday time comes around, and vacations can be a pleasure and not a necessity for a person suffering from exhaustion.

Often people go to extremes. They work too hard and play too hard as well. If they dine out they overeat, and tend to eat and drink too much at parties. The balance is gone from life.

By building in a daily "time off" period, you can regain the relaxed composure necessary to enjoy the moment so that you can eat your meal or listen to your children. You can give them your interested attention. You become more focused and a better listener. You also become more efficient because you focus on the situation and enjoy it.

If you don't take the time out to renew your energy you sap your reserves by continuing to overwork your body and mind. You feel overwhelmed most of the time and this causes further energy drain. It's time to take charge and do something positive rather than continue to complain about your situation.

Don't wait until you are burned out and your body forces you to stop working. Listen to your body so that before burnout you can pull back and recharge to keep your balance of health and vigor.

Society's demands, pressures of the job, your own high expectations create a high-stress level for you. Your own attitude towards a situation, the necessity of doing everything right the first time, and unrealistic goals and aspirations can aggravate the stress level.

235

Of course, you want to strive to be the best that you can be. Your inner strength comes only from acknowledgement of your own self-worth. So be nice to yourself. Don't use failures to whip yourself. Rather use them as stepping stones to something better. You can do this if you retain a balance in life. So do not compromise your relaxation time. If you do it will drain your energy reserves and cause you to be less efficient and productive.

Taking time out allows you to focus more on the event as you are doing it. Do you find you are absent-minded? If you are concentrating on supper when you put your wallet down, you may spend a lot of time looking for it the next time you want it. Why? Because you were living for the future, instead of the present. You were not thinking of where you were putting your wallet when you put it down and so when it comes time to find it, you don't know where it is.

You, not outside events, control how extensively stress affects your life. Stress is your *response* to the situation, not the situation itself. For example, if you get stuck in traffic, an event that is out of your control, you can choose to get annoyed and yell at anyone who beeps his horn. Or you can view the time you're sitting there as the only uninterrupted 15 minutes you'll have all day, a time to reflect, a time to turn on some classical music. It's all a matter of attitude and how you handle the situation.

Building in time for yourself helps to stop that rushed feeling and allows you to do things more systematically, thinking of what you are doing while you are doing it. It puts you in a more relaxed frame of mind for mealtime. You can enjoy the meal rather than feel "let's get it over with so that I can finally relax."

The rushed way of thinking involves doing things to extremes, getting everything done, so you can relax. This approach is unhealthy, unbalanced, and self defeating. By the time you rush in order to relax you're too tired or too edgy to relax. You are living for the future when you will have "time off" rather than enjoying each moment and living it comfortably

236

at a level that you are able to handle. Living in any other time than the present produces stress. Work on finding ways to let this renewed energy and feeling of being in charge work for you daily, not only on vacations.

Waiting until vacation time to relax can leave you burned out during the year. To prevent this, build in daily mini-relaxation breaks and short weekend getaways for that circuit-breaker when you simply need a little re-energizing. Then your longer vacations will be a pleasure not a necessity. They will get you away from work and home and allow you to relax completely. All of these rechargers can restore the balance in your life.

Allow spontaneity and adventure a place in your life. A last-minute spontaneous weekend getaway that allows you to explore new territory, get some fresh air, and be active can sometimes be an effective pick-up and do you as much good as a month-long holiday. Make the most of what is available to you!

Observe those around you who have the ability to relax naturally. Peter relaxes by going downstairs and listening to classical music. After a while he feels regenerated. Interestingly enough, even though he frequently consumes high-fat foods, his cholesterol level is normal. He knows how to "let go" of daily problems. He puts them on hold and his attitude towards life is upbeat and positive.

His wife, Louise, also lives a healthy life-style, eats in a healthy manner, and has become a nonsmoker. However, her preoccupation with eating perfectly and making the right choices along with a difficulty in scheduling time out for herself may be an indicator in determining a higher risk for heart disease. Acquiring a taste for new interests such as learning how to listen to music and appreciate it could help her relax. Or she could build in some other form of activity that she enjoys to regenerate herself and give her more energy.

If you find it difficult to relax, take time to eat, breathe deeply, or have a nap and you find these

237

activities unproductive and a waste of time, try to make yourself do them. Introduce them gradually. Taking the time to relax can serve to recharge your battery. Individuals who exhibit the "hurry-up" behavior, called Type A personality, are 7 to 10 times more likely to develop heart disease than are their more relaxed counterparts.

In a study done in England, 200 participants were divided into 2 groups. One hundred participants were the control group and the other 100 were asked to have a half-hour nap sometime during the day. The latter group decreased their risk for heart disease by 30 percent. A little *pause* during the day can go a long way for health. Next time you feel you'd like to lie down for a nap, don't feel guilty. It may help you to regenerate yourself.

Tim works hard and enjoys his hobby. Taking time out for crossword puzzles and jigsaw puzzles allows him to acquire new concentration skills and extended vocabulary while relieving some of the pressure of everyday life. The relaxed disposition of people like Tim is apparent in their ability to handle stressful situations. So, as you've observed and learned from nondieters, try to observe those who have the ability to relax naturally and learn how they do it. These people seem to be able to react positively even in negative situations. You can benefit from them.

You can make eating a positive experience. By learning to focus on eating, you will be celebrating food, and you will derive both psychological and physical satisfaction from the activity. If you've been eating in a rushed manner for years, you might ask, "How do I go about tasting my food? How can I take time to spend time eating?"

Wait a minute. Are you feeling that you are not worth the time? Do you ever consider that by focusing on what you are doing while you are doing it you will actually free more quality time for you and your family? Taking time to enjoy your meal and making it a pleasurable dining experience can make your meals "special."

238

Tasting and savoring your food allows you to focus on your eating while you are eating and therefore you feel as if you actually ate a meal when you are finished. When you do this it disrupts the automatic eating that leads to taking in more than your body needs or wants. It also prevents constant nibbling throughout the day and evening. You will have more time as your new focus on food will transfer to other activities so that you begin to do all things more systematically. For example, concentrating on where you put your keys when you put them down will allow you to find them again when you want them without wasting time.

> **These preparations and skills will help you focus on eating while you are eating.**
>
> • Adopt a new attitude towards eating. Attitude can be defined as the way you think, feel, and act. For example, if you are dreading eating, or simply eating to consume food and get it over with, you are not deriving physical or psychological benefit from food. You may be focusing on what you will be doing after eating, rather than celebrating the act of eating itself. Enjoy the act of eating your food.
>
> • Create a more relaxed atmosphere in which to eat your food. Do this by breaking the constant rush of the day's activities. If you are pressured all day and come home only to hurry to feed yourself and your family, the enjoyment of the meal is gone. Everybody feels tense. Relax when you come home prior to your meal, then actually enjoy the meal together as a family.

With more rest time, you will be a happier, more energetic mother and wife. This is a bonus to your family. By building in that time-off for yourself, you are allowing yourself to be "special." You will no longer feel controlled by the whims of your family. As you relax, you will give your family more of your time because you want to, not simply because of duty or necessity.

The bonus for you is that you broke the rushing syndrome and created a more relaxed atmosphere to enjoy eating at mealtime. Allowing yourself to have a snack between lunch and supper if you are actually hungry prevents you from coming to the table

239

famished and eating out of control.

> **Focus on your food while you are eating.**
> This means to focus on the event of the moment and savor the moment
> instead of allowing future events to rob you of the moment itself.
> By creating a more relaxed atmosphere and celebrating food,
> it will be easier to focus on the actual meal. In fact, this new way of
> approaching a meal will allow you to eat more slowly.

Color, texture, and aroma can highlight the experience of eating.

Many things can help you celebrate food. Present the food in an attractive way. Color, texture, and aroma can highlight the experience of eating. Make every meal an event to enjoy, an occasion to anticipate. Special dishes, tablecloths, candles help to create a special atmosphere and need not be restricted only to holidays. Create more special days throughout the year by adding in these trimmings.

COMPARING DIETER'S AND NONDIETER'S APPROACH TO MEALS
The Dieter's Approach
Not hungry in the morning. Gotta run so you dash out the door with no breakfast. Your system is used to it. The day is busy, packed full of work and decisions to be made. Can't stop for lunch; otherwise you won't be able to complete the work. You work through lunch. You will be having a big supper so you better not overdo it by eating a big lunch. You grab a chocolate bar on the way home for quick energy in order to cope with the excitement at home. You feel edgy and when your kids are hungry, tired, and irritable and make demands on you, you feel drained. Somehow you manage to find the energy to make supper. It's one more job to be done before you can actually relax. You live for 7 o'clock. You rush through supper so that you can get the dishes done and finally relax. You plunk on the couch at 7:30. You turn on the television, feel hungry again since you ate so quickly, and go to the kitchen to fix yourself a snack. Peace at last.

Analyzing the Situation
Nibbling in the evening can dampen your hunger for breakfast. You could try to eat in such a way that you are hungry at breakfast time. That may mean trying

240

to forgo your evening snack or to make it smaller. Eating a breakfast, essentially "breaks" the "fast" and gets your system revved up to begin the day.

Since you seem to focus on total time rather than efficient time you have skipped lunch because you were busy. Thinking more clearly about making your time more valuable and more productive through healthy eating and activity can improve your focus and productivity. *It is not the total amount of time that counts, but what you accomplish with the time available.*

Nibbling or not eating through the day to compensate for a larger meal at supper causes your battery to run low all day. This is the diet mentality. The chocolate bar that you eat for a pick up gives you an immediate caffeine and sugar boost. The effects are almost immediate because you consume it on an empty stomach. However, the boost doesn't last long. The caffeine in the cocoa and sugar in the bar result in an immediate quick increase in blood sugar that sends your blood sugar tumbling again due to over-secretion of insulin by the pancreas.

The result is that you are "wiped out" (fatigue, irritability), as you wait for the day to end. You are definitely not equipped to handle the situation at home. You have low energy, little tolerance, and extreme hunger. You may grab anything in sight or end up nibbling as you prepare supper. Since you are focusing on the needs of your family, you deprive yourself of the proper nourishment of mind and body that could restore your balance. You may actually resent the fact that you have to spend the time to prepare a meal and you may resort to convenience foods. High fat and little taste and flavor may cause you to feel that you missed out on the enjoyment of the meal that you were looking forward to all day. Then eat sweets to compensate for your disappointment.

The entire day has been out of balance and this leads to the final let down at the end of the day. You may continue in this manner day after day and miss out on the pleasure of living.

A healthier version of the same scenario puts you in

241

control of your life by putting the balance back into it.

The Nondieter's Approach

Using a nondieter's approach, this scenario could occur more frequently.

You know that tomorrow will be an extremely busy day. Getting up a few minutes earlier seems impossible so you pack yourself a breakfast the night before. Depending on the time, you may decide to eat it before you leave for work, in the cafeteria at work if you arrive a little early, or at your first coffee break. Even though your day is busy, you make sure you take time for lunch. The pause in your busy schedule plus the lunch helped you to refocus for the decision-making in the afternoon. Because you felt regenerated you accomplished more productive work the rest of the day.

Feeling hungry on your way home, you ate some crackers stored in the glove compartment of your car. This helped dampen the feelings of hunger that you usually experience at this time.

When you arrive home, your kids have eaten the snacks you left for them. You have established a half hour for yourself and the kids do not bother you. You relax and leave behind the rushed feelings you had at work. You are entitled to this.

You remember that your father took time before supper to read the paper or lie down and your mother made sure that you did not bother him for at least a half hour to an hour after he came home from work. The difference then was that your mother was working in the home and helped build this balance into your home life. Now with women working outside the home, they also need this transitional time to unwind; otherwise they will become burned out.

Depending on how you feel, you may choose to have another small snack, go for a walk and reflect on the day's activities, read a magazine, or lie down. You close the book on your work life activities and plan for family activities. You may decide to put supper in the oven while you relax in your free time. If the children are old enough they can be responsible for supper or your husband can take a turn.

Rather than dreading supper, with this scenario you look forward to it and enjoy the occasion. You value this family time and treasure mealtime to review family activities.

The above scenario allows you to put the balance back in your life. It allows you to be happier and more productive, a bonus to both the employer and the family.

REVIEW

☐ You had a snack to dampen your hunger before supper (that is, if you were hungry between meals).

☐ You built in some time for yourself to create the proper atmosphere for eating.

☐ You are learning to focus on your eating while you are eating.

PUT RELAXATION INTO YOUR LIFE-STYLE

A rushed life-style leads to rushed eating. Taking a few moments to relax prior to eating can put you in a more relaxed frame of mind to enjoy your meal. If you don't take the time to enjoy and savor your food, it can cause automatic "nibbling" later on because you will still be looking for satisfaction from food.

• Use the breathing technique (see p245) if you feel anxious or as a way of building in the pause to relax.

• Sit down for a few minutes prior to preparing supper to read the paper, daydream, have a snack, go over the day's activities, go for a short walk (while supper is cooking).

• Leaving relaxation time only until the end of the day is the all-or-nothing thinking of dieters comparable to having a reward, probably food, at the end of the day. Building in relaxation more regularly in the form of short breaks, for example, will allow you to focus on your work and be more productive.

Pamper yourself. You're worth it and you'll feel better for it.

EATING AND ITS ASSOCIATIONS

Jean had a good business meeting and accomplished many things. She felt wonderful and on her way home stopped at the convenience store to pick up a bag of chips. As she turned off the ignition, she realized that she usually rewarded herself with food whenever she felt she had accomplished something. She confronted the situation and realized that the accomplishment itself was the reward. It was an internal reward.

Many people reward themselves with food when they feel either happy or sad and rob themselves of the experience of the emotion itself. It's normal to feel depressed when something goes wrong. Many people try to see the positive in the situation by allowing themselves to feel the emotion and work it through. Talking to others about it helps you to see the situation in a more objective framework.

Building in relaxation time for yourself can help you to focus on becoming more aware of activities that may be associated with eating. A quick form of relaxation is deep breathing. It is a skill that if practised when you are not stressed, can do wonders for you in stressful situations. Take a few minutes daily to practise it. It will help you to build the *pause* into situations naturally as you master the skill.

MAKING THE MOST OF DEEP BREATHING
The following technique is a skill that will help you to relax. It is very effective if you practise it regularly so that you are prepared to use the skill when you are under stress. It can help you when you feel anxious which may cause you to want something sweet to eat or smoke a cigarette to calm you.

Deep breathing is also a way of taking time for yourself. Don't feel guilty when you take time to practise this technique. The little time you are taking will help you to put the "pause" into your life-style and help you to refocus and re-energize.

In order to get the most out of the technique, it is essential to understand the purpose of the inhalation and exhalation phase.

INHALATION PHASE	EXHALATION PHASE
It is invigorating, tension-producing — used somewhat like a yawn, — used when ready to terminate an exercise: a deep breath or 2 will create tension and help bring you back to your normal level of alertness, — important in reversing the relaxed state and is used to come out of the relaxed state, — usually combined with the flexing and stretching of muscles (i.e. as if you are awakening from a state of sleep).	It is relaxing — promotes a feeling of sinking down, slowing down, and heaviness to a feeling of complete relaxation.

Technique
• Breathe normally and observe the natural breathing cycle.

• Inhale slowly and steadily through the nose, expanding your abdominal area rather than the rib cage. (Many people do this incorrectly by sucking in their stomachs when they breathe in). When you permit your body to inhale by itself without any conscious thought on your part, you will do it naturally and correctly.

• Focus your attention on the exhalation phase of the breathing cycle. Concentrate on it and think about it, exhaling slowly, and allowing the abdominal area to contract naturally. It is during this phase that you feel and experience the sensations described under "Exhalation phase" that will result in an overall state of relaxation.

• The key to this exercise is to feel the sensations as you exhale, and only on the exhalations.

Practising this technique will allow you with time to relax quickly at a moment's notice.

Sometimes associations can trigger a desire to eat. You may not be actually hungry but feel compelled to eat anyway. You may be eating and not be conscious that you are doing it. For example, you may be watching television and eat peanuts or chips compulsively, not even remembering tasting one. This is another form of automatic eating.

If you are not tasting the food, then it becomes wasted calories.

This form of eating is more a habit than a need or desire. You somehow associate television with eating. However, some of these associations may be so ingrained that you do not recognize what is happening. Ten pounds later your slacks no longer fit.

Earlier I spoke about eating as a temporary relief from stress, and I tried to deal with the reasons behind the eating using positive techniques to overcome the negative situation.

Some activities associated with eating are also automatic. These are triggers that lead to eating and the focus is on the activities rather than on the food.

Here is a list of possible activities:
• watching television
• reading a book, magazine, or newspaper
• social occasions where everyone else is eating
• associating certain individuals with certain foods
• using food as a comforter when you are feeling low to restore warm feelings.

As society moves from the industrial age to the information age, keeping abreast of news and recent happenings in your field becomes a greater priority. Reading the newspaper or watching television while eating may be timesaving to accomplish two things at once. Are you really enjoying either event to its fullest?

The other scenario may be that you are beat after work and have only enough energy to watch television. You sit in front of television in the evenings hoping to unwind. You may come home from work too tired to make supper and you use convenience foods to prepare a quick meal. However, your poor eating habits give you less energy. The high-fat content of convenience foods may weigh you down and make you more sluggish. Plus there is very little psychological satisfaction from this food. You feel too tired to move, so there is no energy or time to do any physical activity.

246

Time or lack of it seems to be used as an excuse for being sedentary. You may not even perceive activity to be important enough to make an effort. Yet the extra energy that you can retrieve from regular activity can give you more time by improving your efficiency during the day and evening. It is not the number of hours worked but the amount accomplished that counts. You can look busy without accomplishing very much. Productivity is what really matters.

What is the common factor in these two situations? In both instances, attention is on the television set, not the food. Over time these television/food associations become so strong that they may seem impossible to break. However, your new way of thinking will find these sedentary activities less enjoyable.

Bob's situation is an example. Bob came home from work feeling tired and he wanted to watch the news. The family sat down to supper and were not able to say a word because Bob was watching the news. Bob gulped down his food keeping time with the momentum of the news. He often didn't even know what he was eating. He ate because the food was placed in front of him and it was mealtime. Was he hungry? Or was he tuning into the clock as an external cue for time to eat? He seemed not to be paying attention to his internal clock of hunger to regulate the amount of food he ate.

After supper, Bob's wife did the dishes. Bob changed and sometimes helped her dry the dishes. When finished, he would turn on the television again to watch his series of evening programs. As soon as he turned on the television he was hungry again. The association was there between watching television and eating.

Bob had just finished supper. How could he be hungry again? The answer is that he wasn't. Bob never focused on his food while he was eating. He was not tasting and savoring his food. He didn't even remember eating or what he ate.

247

Perhaps you could exchange the television for the table as a trigger to eat. Try to eat in one place at the table and eat only when you are in that spot. This can help to narrow down one area of the table for eating. Do not play cards or do bookwork or any other activity in that spot. Otherwise, it may trigger you to eat and you will end up building in a new association.

Saving one spot at the table only for eating may be difficult to do and may not be necessary to continue. However, for a few weeks it may help you to discover what triggers you to eat. An awareness that there is an association and that you are wasting the calories if you are not tasting and savoring the food, may be all that is necessary to break the habit. After all, you are not depriving yourself when you choose not to eat simply because it is habit. This differs from denying yourself the food when you want it.

For those people living alone, television may provide company. Some people find that by placing a tray in front of the television set while eating, the tray becomes the signal to eat. When finished eating, the tray is removed, and the desire is gone. If you use a tray in front of the television set, be conscious of the fact that you are actually tasting your food and savor it slowly. Do not pick up the momentum of the television program, causing you to eat quickly.

The craving to eat that occurs while you are watching television may come about simply because you need to do something with your hands. If so, try working on a puzzle, do some knitting, or realize that it is all right to do nothing with your hands.

The above situations may cause you to change your behavior towards food by disassociating it with other activities. *However, behavior change is an external change and may not be natural.* A keen awareness of the things that trigger you to eat, and an understanding of the fact that you are not really concentrating on the food enough to eat at a certain time will help to change your attitude towards these activity/food associations. This internal change in the way that you view these associations can help you to change the way you act towards the food and the activity.

While discussing this in class, Elliot felt that people should have 2 places to eat, one at the table for the meal and another place specifically for snacks. He discovered that by associating a specific chair with snacks he had to take the trouble to ask the family if he could sit in the specific chair before he could eat.

The process of deciding whether he really wanted to ask them to move out of the specific chair, put a *pause* into his automatic eating. In many instances he decided that he really wasn't hungry and did not want the food after all. Just as confrontation allows you to put the *pause* into eating for the sake of eating or for other reasons by asking yourself if you are really hungry, confining your eating to only a few places allows you to do the same. It makes you more conscious of whether you are really hungry and allows you to decide if it is psychological or physical hunger. As you begin to develop these skills you eat less because you choose to. It is your decision and you have discovered it so it empowers you to act in a positive way.

When my mother visited from Montreal, she used to come loaded down with all sorts of goodies for our freezer. The association of Mom and home-baked treats came from my growing up in a European home. Cakes and cookies were plentiful in our home. It was my Mom's way of saying "I love you." This association was so strong that whenever I went back to Montreal or my parents came to Manitoba, I ate too much and I seemed to lose control.

I tried to analyze the situation. Did this occur because I hadn't had these foods for a while and felt deprived? Or was it simply because these foods conjured up nice warm protective feelings of home and Mom? Or was it the association of seeing Mom that made me feel I had to eat these sweets? It probably was a combination of all of these.

Today I am more aware that much of this eating was automatic. I wanted the food, but not the huge quantities I was eating. Tasting and savoring the food and focusing on the food while eating allowed me to be satisfied with less. I got my satisfaction from the first and last few bites.

Because of my life-style change, some of the foods Mom brings are too sweet or too rich for me now. So I am satisfied with a taste. My Mom and I had a discussion about this. I love her for herself, not because she bakes these goodies. She may still bring some cakes and cookies when she visits, but now they stay in the freezer longer and are not all devoured at once. The balance is there. I don't use them as comfort foods. My walks provide me with all the serenity I need to provide comfort and help me to pace myself better.

The act of eating can cause the release of endorphins which acts as a pain reliever and tranquilizer to give you a good feeling. However, the feeling may be only temporary because guilt feelings may occur later about eating the food. Laughter and exercise can also release endorphins that leave you with a good feeling. So go out there and enjoy yourself, and find the fun in physical activity as well.

Some people depend on food more than others do. Cathy could coax Billy to go to Uncle Joe's only by telling him there was food there. Yet his brother Christopher was so excited to go because of Uncle Joe's jokes and the fact that Uncle Joe played ball with him. Christopher was more active and slimmer than Billy who often stayed home with Mom and liked to eat. Because Billy was not as active, food became his source of entertainment. As he grew, so did his waist size. *Does food have to be the center of attention in order for you to have fun?*

Every time Jean went to get gas at a specific gas station, she craved a chocolate bar. A few months ago, she bought her favorite brand when she went to pay for the gas. She continued this a few more times. Had an association built up? What could she do?

She could change gas stations. The other option would be to recognize the association and to confront it to see if she really wanted the chocolate bar. If she is usually hungry at this time, maybe she could have a snack at afternoon coffee break. She discovered that

250

the chocolate bar didn't get tasted; rather it was gulped down quickly. The immediate rise in blood sugar followed by low blood sugar actually caused her to crave more.

Sherry ate a large meal but still wanted dessert. Was this because of psychological hunger or the fact that desserts trigger the end of the meal? If Sherry had been dieting recently, wanting dessert was a natural response to past feelings of deprivation. Try to get away from the diet mentality when you are ordering food in a restaurant. Do you order salad because you believe it is lower in calories and will compensate for the calories in the dessert?

Will salad and dessert hold you over? Depending on the type of salad, it may be high in fat (salad dressing) and contain very little substance in the form of carbohydrate or protein. Check how you feel a few hours later. If dessert triggers the end of the meal, try to find a more suitable replacement. Or is a replacement really necessary as your attitude changes about how to end the meal?

Where it is required, tea with milk serves as a warm ending to the meal. Eat the dessert if you really want it, but if it is simply habit, perhaps you could skip dessert until later and be satisfied with tea. By giving yourself the option to have it later, you are getting rid of the sense of deprivation if you choose not to have it. When you do have the dessert, eat it without guilt. In this way, you will derive more satisfaction from it which will allow you to taste and savor the food better.

By including variety and spontaneity in your day, your life will become less humdrum and excitement will take its place. Sometimes you may choose to have dessert to signify the end of the meal and sometimes you may choose to have nothing. There is no set rule or perfect way of eating: go with the flow.

EATING OUT HUGS™ STYLE

Approximately one-third of Canadian meals are eaten out and this rate is expected to go up to two-thirds by the turn of the century. Obviously, this is a preferred life-style choice for many people. An added

251

benefit to eating out is the opportunity to experiment with different flavors and textures. The excitement of making new discoveries can add zip and variety to mealtime.

Perhaps you can try a recipe at home. Be inquisitive. Ask the waiter what herb is in that white sauce to bring out the flavor and use your new findings to experiment with your own meal.

Many people binge when eating out. Marilyn used to be very strict with her diet during the week, and looked forward to the weekends when she allowed herself to go off the diet and eat out. Her ritual would be to have no breakfast and maybe no lunch to compensate for the extra calories she consumed at supper. This diet mentality caused her to be overly hungry by supper. She felt starved and therefore overate. She rationalized that it was socially acceptable to binge when eating out.

This starve/binge cycle led to a drop in her metabolic rate. This was her body's way of saying that when she finally did eat, it would "squirrel away" a little more fat just in case she did something silly again, such as not eating until supper. Marilyn realized that when she went to a restaurant starved, she actually was not even tasting her food. Marilyn's strategy changed. She ate regularly and went to the restaurant meal pleasantly hungry and enjoyed the food.

Many people eat one way at home and differently when visitors come or when they are at a restaurant. If you choose high-fat foods on these occasions it's no wonder you can't seem to stabilize your weight. There's nothing wrong with eating some foods higher in fat content. But switching back and forth between high-fat and low-fat content foods impedes your progress in changing your food preferences.

It's better to discover some low-fat entrées in restaurants that are both physically and psycho-logically satisfying. As you begin to cook low-fat versions of your meals in a tasty way, your company will love the food. Don't feel that you have to bring out the high-fat meals when visitors show up.

With the HUGS™ philosophy, you can go to any social occasion and be in charge. So keep the HUGS™ principles in mind when you eat out.

1–*Eat regularly* Eat regular meals during the day. Don't starve at breakfast and lunch to compensate for eating out at supper. This will allow you to feel more energetic throughout the day rather than feeling dragged out, waiting for that huge meal to devour at suppertime. You will arrive at the meal pleasantly hungry instead of famished. Being overly hungry leads to quick eating due to the insatiable hunger that you have built up. A pleasant hunger results in enjoying the meal thoroughly, allowing you to feel in charge.

2–*Order what you really want* One day, when I was in a restaurant for a meeting around 10:30 a.m., I wanted to eat something. I noticed the cinnamon bread and asked to have it toasted. Forgetting that toasting bread usually means loading it with butter, the result was soggy toast with little texture or cinnamon taste. The lesson learned was to be assertive. If unsure how a food is prepared, ask.

If you order what you really want in a restaurant, you feel satisfied. But first you have to tune into what you really desire. Rose went into the restaurant with her friend and wanted spaghetti and meatballs, which she ordered. She felt satisfied with the meal and it had sustaining power since she satisfied herself both physically and psychologically. By contrast, her friend did not know what she wanted and finally ended up ordering a sandwich. According to HUGS™, this in itself should have been physically satisfying, yet she wanted more. She had not satisfied the psychological part of her hunger and she craved something more.

You can have what you want in a restaurant so be assertive. One evening Mitchell and I went to a concert and arrived early. We wanted something to drink and went into the cafeteria. We took a juice, a glass of water, and another empty glass. At our seat, we added water to the juice to suit our tastes.

Here is another example. Allison was at the lake on the weekend and prepared a tasty supper. She ate until she was satisfied and wanted to finish with something chocolate. She and her family decided to go out for a snack. On the dessert menu was ice cream, chocolate brownies, and apple pie. Chocolate brownies were what Allison wanted and she and her friend Grace ordered them. The rest of the family ordered what they desired.

A few minutes later the waitress came back to say there were no more chocolate brownies. Allison settled for apple pie with ice cream and Grace, after some hesitation, ordered apple pie. But that is not what they really wanted, so why did they order it? Why settle for something that you don't want because you feel you must order something? While they were eating the apple pie, they were still thinking about the chocolate brownies and were still not satisfied so in fact, they wasted those calories.

When ordering, learn to be assertive, to have what you really want.

The next day, Grace, who had an even stronger built-up desire for chocolate ate several pieces of dark chocolate. Finally she was satisfied. The lesson learned was that refusing the apple pie would probably have yielded the same outcome. She could have bought a chocolate bar at a convenience store instead of having the pie. Decide what you really want and go for it.

**Don't settle for less.
Check if the special of the day is what you really want;
if not, why order it simply because it is on special.**

If the meal is not enjoyable, you will crave dessert to satisfy that unfulfilled need. For example, the sandwich and fries may be the special of the day. If you do not care for fries, order a salad instead, or order à la carte, perhaps soup and a sandwich.

Try this technique. Say to the waitress, "I know that the special comes with fries and I would prefer to have the soup so could you arrange this?"

The words have special meaning.

254

"I know," indicates that you understand the situation.

"And," states how you feel about the situation.

"So," is your request for their action.

You can use this form of confrontation anytime you are in a situation where you need to be direct in a polite manner. If nothing on the menu particulary suits your taste, why not order à la carte. An example of this would be breakfast of a scrambled egg with dry toast (whole wheat), orange juice, and water. Use the water to dilute the juice as regular juice is usually strong and too sweet. A substitute for the protein, in this case the egg, would be peanut butter and jam with the toast.

3–*Use nondiet thinking* "I'd better get my fill of the cheesecake now because when I go back on my diet tomorrow I won't be having cheesecake for a while."

"I feel full but I still have room for a big piece of pie. Afterwards, I'll go lie down."

This diet thinking can be replaced by a more positive attitude.

"I'll take a small piece of that cheesecake. It looks good and I wonder what it tastes like. If I don't try it, I'll be wondering what it tastes like and may end up feeling deprived. That will lead me to binge on whatever is in sight when I get home."

"I can always have more food later because I feel full now. I can ask the hostess if I can take a piece of pie home for another day when I will appreciate it more. That way I am not denying myself and I am not stuffing myself either."

> When refusing food it's easier to say "I'm on a diet" because society accepts this reason for denying yourself something you want. If you say you don't want it, it appears to be rude to the hostess. Try saying "I'm not hungry right now, maybe later." Later may or may not come.

Even slim people are often in the diet mentality. Observe different people at a social occasion. Non-dieters, those that are not starving and binging to remain slim, are more selective in their choices. They may eat what they want and may eat a little more than usual, but their regular eating habits prevent them from intentionally binging or overeating.

It is easier to resist food if you are feeling satisfied and realize that this is not the last time that you will see lemon pie for a while. After all, you can buy a pie or make one anytime or you can ask to take some home. Slightly undereating at mealtime to leave room for dessert may be done on special occasions if it is not carried to the extreme.

Eating very little at mealtime so that you can try all the desserts reverts to the diet mentality. "I'd better eat all I can now because it may not be there later on." In a society of plenty, running out of food is not a problem. Nondieters know this and are more selective in choosing the meal. They will eat desserts only when they truly desire them.

4–*Striving for a balance of carbohydrate and protein* Choose a balance of carbohydrates and protein in your food because you want to, not because you feel you should. You may not always feel like choosing the right balance to give yourself the maximum energy, but striving for this balance and its sustained energy value will result in a satisfying dining-out experience.

Eating in this manner will help you to focus your energy on the mealtime event rather than just the food. The company and entertainment are also part of the evening. Food is no longer the center of attention for you. You will be able to taste and savor your food and have enough energy reserve to enjoy the rest of the evening. Overeating makes us feel uncomfortable. You don't feel like being sociable and all you want to do is go home and go to bed.

Here are some examples of different restaurants and the kinds of choices that indicate the principle of balance.

ITALIAN   Pasta dishes are great but the "in thing" these days is pasta with various cream sauces. These are richer than the traditional tomato sauces and have a higher fat content. The protein content may be

256

minimal. A more balanced option that is lower in fat content is the traditional spaghetti with meat sauce or meatballs. You may choose to ask for a tossed salad instead of garlic bread.

Some restaurants skimp on the protein source and give you a hefty portion of noodles topping it off with garlic bread. It is cheaper for the restaurant and customers are usually satisfied since carbohydrates fill you up quickly. However, the insufficient protein content may necessitate a snack later on. Otherwise, insatiable hunger will strike, making you raid the refrigerator. Decide what you really want. Some cream sauces with sufficient protein content are not too heavy and could be your choice.

FRENCH   French cuisine usually involves a variety of sauces to add flavor to the meat portion of the meal. Try meals cooked in wine sauce rather than in a cream sauce. These meals are tasty and nicely flavored with herbs. A food doesn't have to be rich to be tasty. For lunch, quiche and salad may be loaded with fat, so take control and minimize the fat by asking for the salad dressing on the side.

CHINESE   The more traditional combination plates consist of an assortment of deep-fried foods (chicken balls, shrimp, etc.) and sweet and sour sauces (spare ribs). You eat a high-fat content as well as sugar and little meat. There are excellent stir-fried dishes that you can order instead. Examples are beef and broccoli, curried chicken, and a variety of other combinations. Ordering one of these with stir-fried chinese vegetables and the usual rice that comes with the meal presents a colorful and tasty balance. In many cases, you may want to ask for more rice. If you are going with someone else and you choose 2 different entrées plus the rice and vegetables, you can still have some variety to the meal. Acquiring a taste for less fattening foods means that you eventually prefer the latter choice to the higher fat foods.

Ask the waitress when you are unsure if the dish is deep-fried or stir-fried. In one instance, my husband and I ordered a couple of dishes and to our surprise, the chicken dish (lemon chicken) came to us in a deep-fried batter version. We both tried it and didn't care for it. Mitchell picked off the thick batter and ate the little piece of chicken inside. The batter was too greasy for his taste. He shared the rest of my dish and the rice and vegetables and asked the waitress to wrap the rest up for our dog. Our dog is extremely active and lives by the HUGS™ philosophy so she could handle the higher fat meal.

GREEK   A variety of kabob dishes (chicken, beef, lamb) served with rice and vegetables offers a nice balance for a meal, lunch or evening.

SALAD BARS   These are often the dieter's choice. Salads certainly fill you up quickly because of the high water content of vegetables, yet salads do not provide the balance you are looking for. Most important of all, is it really what you want to eat or are you eating it simply because you feel it is lower in calories?

Lettuce is relatively low in fiber content but many of the vegetables have a higher fiber content. You get water, vitamins, and minerals but little else. Besides, because of the mayonnaise and cream-based mixtures in salad dishes as well as the dressing itself, the total fat content of a salad can be quite high.

The salad bar choice for a meal can be misleading. Some estimates suggest that selections from a salad bar result in total caloric intake from 250 to 1000 with 60 to 70 percent of these calories coming from fat. It seems to be a healthy selection, but it can lack substance, leading to a binge later because of feelings of deprivation. Bread could accompany this meal to boost the carbohydrate content. Pasta salads may add carbohydrates but may also add to the total fat content.

Eating salad so that you can have dessert is deceiving. In the first place, you may not have saved any calories and certainly not fat content. Furthermore, this thinking puts you right back into the diet mentality. "I'm having less at lunch so I can have the chocolate mousse." When you make these kinds of choices, you still end up with very little "holding-over power" in your meal and this can lead to a binge later on. This may occur because of your lower blood sugar level a few hours later. You are not any farther ahead in this situation.

FAST FOODS AND PIZZAS   Ordering a hamburger on an unbuttered bun with a salad can be a nice combination. Try to frequent the restaurants that broil or barbecue rather than fry their hamburgers.

Pizzas can give you carbohydrates from the crust and protein from the cheese and toppings. Go with the thicker crust to increase the carbohydrate content of the meal. Vegetables are often part of the topping. Adding a salad can round out the meal nicely. Some restaurants use the higher fat cheese which you can notice by the greasy sheen on the pizza not to mention the greasy feel that it leaves in your mouth. Try different pizza places and food combinations to find the ones that are right for you.

5–Eating until satisfied — the "doggy bag" option
When eating out you have the option to ask for a doggy bag if you cannot finish your meal. The leftover food may be a treat for lunch the next day. You may also choose to leave what you cannot eat on your plate if you are feeling satisfied and pleasantly full. If supper time is planned to be later, and you know you will be hungry, schedule a snack for yourself. Stuffing yourself on bread while waiting for your dinner and then forcing the whole dinner down because you paid for it is not truly enjoying the meal.

The snack you ate prior to the restaurant meal and a little bread at the restaurant will allow you to create the right atmosphere of relaxation so that you are able to eat the meal slowly and fully enjoy it. If you fill up on bread, then you may not have enough room for the meal itself which is really what you are paying for.

Enjoy, taste, and savor the meal. Dine, don't simply eat. If you anticipate that the meal will be too much food, you may make some arrangements with your partner beforehand. In my case, my husband can eat more than I can, so I ask him to eat very little bread beforehand so that I can give him some of my meat portion (the expensive part of the meal). Otherwise, we ask for a "doggy bag" and take it home for the next day or feed it to our dog. A meal for 2 ends up being a meal for 3.

Some restaurants serve smaller, more reasonably sized portions that most people can eat. Tasty options in some restaurants involve an item with a heart beside it that indicates it meets the Heart Foundation's criteria and is lower in fat. This allows you to experience these lower fat versions firsthand before attempting to make them yourself. Here are some other suggestions that will help to make the restaurant meal what you want it to be.

• Ask for the salad dressing on the side. The house dressing usually contains a nice blend of herbs and may be lower in fat (vinaigrette-based rather than cream-based). If the house dressing is thicker, try dipping salad into dressing. You will end up using less.

• Ask for gravy to be served on the side or ask for a small amount of gravy. If your plate is served with too much gravy you can always scrape off what you do not want.

• Ask for butter or sour cream on the side. This allows you to be in control of the quantity that you want. Some potatoes taste so good by themselves that they hardly need any addition of fat to mask or hide the flavor. It's the same for hamburger that is ordered with so many condiments that you do not even taste the hamburger. Or the cob of corn that is seasoned and loaded with butter and salt. Are you really tasting the corn? You might as well take a bit of butter on the edge of your knife and eat it straight up. The idea of the fat is to enhance not mask the flavor of the food. Decide what you really want using condiments such as butter, salt, sauces, and gravies tastefully.

• Share your dessert. This will satisfy your curiosity about how it tastes without overstuffing yourself. Be selective and order only what you really want. Substitutions in restaurants are often possible, as long as it isn't the rush hour.

6–*Tune into what it feels like to overeat* So you overate. Experience and remember this uncomfortable, heavy feeling and decide whether you like this feeling. Is it allowing you to enjoy the occasion or are you too tired to care? A big meal takes a lot of energy to digest, so the scenario of eating and lying down on the couch is a common one. Not wanting to repeat this feeling can lead to more instances where you will enjoy the food as well as the event but eat for the enjoyment of it. Eating past the point of satisfaction is often no longer enjoyable.

HOW TO ELIMINATE SWINGING ON THE FRIDGE DOOR

• **Eat regularly, every 3 to 6 hours when physically hungry.**
Purpose Keeps blood sugar from going too low, that could result in insatiable hunger, and frees you from cycles of starvation and binging.

• **Eat "balanced" meals that include carbohydrate and protein at all meals.**
Purpose Stabilizes blood sugar, sustains energy, keeps your body in the "drive" mode.

• **Be in charge of food and situations. Use skills of confrontation and distraction, techniques to combat "automatic eating."**
Purpose Empowers you, freeing you from the obsession of food, recognizing that much of your eating is emotional.

• **Understand how food affects your body. This allows you to postpone eating certain high-sugar foods on an empty stomach.**
Purpose Prevents your blood sugar from going up quickly, leading to a drop in blood sugar that will make you lose control. Eating a snack if hungry and adding in those "extras" when your body is better equipped to handle it, puts you back in the driver's seat.

• **Eat only until satisfied. Learn to tune into feelings of hunger and feelings of fullness. Allow yourself to be more relaxed with eating. Not feeling guilty allows you to extract more enjoyment from eating. It's permissable to leave something on your plate if you are full.**
Purpose Satisfies your needs by allowing you to eat what you want and at the same time providing you with the skills to realize when your

261

body is saying "Stop. I'll have more later if I really want it."

• Put in the "pause" prior to eating.

  1) By using confrontation and asking yourself if you are really hungry;

  2) By stopping half-way through a meal to consciously reassess if you want more;

  3) By focusing on eating while you are eating, and confining your eating to a minimum number of places so you will think before grabbing something to eat;

  4) By eating in a relaxed manner, tasting and savoring your food.
Purpose   Helps you find different ways of being more conscious of what you are eating, rather than resorting to "I see it, I want it" or "Everyone else is eating, so I'll join the crowd." You realize that you can participate in the fun and enjoyment without mimicking their every action.

Go with the flow. Gain confidence in your ability. Most of all enjoy the process of discovering or rediscovering yourself.

13

Gauging Your Progress a Day at a Time

Treat setbacks as a learning experience, a necessary detour towards being the best that you can be!

Make a small change today for a better you tomorrow!

STRESS REDUCTION

Energy comes from a balance in food, activity, and attitude. Too much stress can drain your energy level. Just as you eat and exercise for energy, you can find the stress level that is comfortable and stimulating for you without the feeling of being overwhelmed. Find the balance in your life so that stress can work for you to make you feel alive and vital.

> **Stress for energy and stimulation, not exhaustion. Tune into your body. Know when to pull back.**

Through the process of self-discovery you can learn how to pull back when the stress level gets above your comfort zone. Here's how to do it.

1. By *not dieting*, you reduce both physical and mental stress.

2. By setting yourself *free from perfectionism*, the "all-or-nothing" way of thinking that can transfer from food to other areas. If something does not go quite the way you planned, ask yourself what is the worst possible thing that could happen. Could you live with the outcome? This usually puts things in perspective.

Often when the events in your life go wrong another opportunity presents itself. When one door closes, another opens. Be responsive to new ideas. In order to grow, some pain may be involved, yet you will gain a sense of freedom and wisdom, and you will know yourself better. Growth can be inspirational.

Consider these points in your daily routine. Enjoy activity as a release valve so that you exercise for fun. Even if it's hard to get going, if you tune into your body's needs the benefits of vitality and feeling good about yourself gained from physical activity will keep you going.

ACTION CREATES MOMENTUM

Build in time for yourself. When you put that *pause* into your day you have time to catch your breath and enjoy life, rather than let it pass you by. Assess and evaluate your own situation.

Practise some relaxation techniques such as deep breathing. This helps you to unwind.

auging Your
rogress a Day
t a Time

Incorporate some exercises that can be done at the desk during the day (semi-circles, shoulder shrugs /rolls, biceps and triceps curls, calf stretch, lunge, hamstring stretch, ankle rotations, etc.) Refer to the warm-up and cool-down section in Chapter 3 for more examples.

Like yourself and accept yourself the way you are. This does not mean that you won't do anything to try to improve yourself. It means that you care enough about yourself to nurture yourself and take care of your body and mind. Be the best that you can be!

> **Too much stress can drain energy even if you are eating in a healthy manner and exercising regularly.**

Allow yourself to be YOU. Release yourself from attaching your self-worth to
- the number on the scale,
- your accomplishments,
- what others say about you,
- compliments or criticism.

Unlock the little child in you. As people grow older they tend to become more serious and are bogged down with a planned and organized life. Restore some spontaneity and fun in your routine to keep you interested and vital. *Lighten up! Relax! Learn to laugh at yourself.*

Believe in yourself and have the confidence in your own ability to accomplish goals by using skills such as confrontation in everyday life situations. By confronting situations and dealing with them you will not move past your stress level zone. Focus on your progress. The ability to take things calmly can diffuse a potentially difficult and explosive situation. *Be proactive rather than reactive.*

BELIEFS AND ATTITUDES AFFECT EXPECTATIONS

If you need praise to feel good about yourself you may feel badly if you do not receive it. Self-doubt may set in. Remember the affirmation: "I like myself. I am a worthwhile person, no matter what anyone says or does." Turn your negative feelings into something positive. Catch yourself when you put yourself down and praise yourself instead.

Rather than feel defeated, accept setbacks as part of the growing process.

If you feel that you can do it, you can. The inner strength you gain from a positive attitude will translate into

the ability to get things done. Accept that some things cannot be changed and stop trying to change them. Be satisfied with the things you can do.

Enjoy the journey instead of focusing only on the destination. *Focusing on the process rather than the end result reduces the stress level and you will, with time, reach your goal.*

A DAY AT A TIME

Small accomplishments in life-style changes can be compared to building a wall one brick at a time. Once you begin to make life-style changes the wall will begin to become stronger, making it more difficult to knock down. Don't be discouraged by temporary setbacks. They are part of the growth process. Don't forget that Edison had about 2000 temporary setbacks before the light bulb got invented!

Success is an ongoing process. It is the daily expression, acceptance, and appreciation of yourself. Each time you achieve a mini-goal and make a life-style change more permanent, you feel good and your self-esteem goes up. The life process itself is 95 percent of the fun and 100 percent of the reward. Using your energy to point your life in the right direction will help you to learn, practice, and enjoy your way to better health. This is your lifetime goal.

Building a wall one brick at a time lays a strong foundation

Earle and Imrie in their book, *Your Vitality Quotient,*[1] used the analogy of an archer to describe this life direction. You are not so much focusing on the end result of aiming at the target as you are becoming at one with the process of drawing the bow and releasing the arrow. You are the flight of the arrow. The bonus is that when you truly focus on the process, you inevitably hit the bull's-eye. The

auging Your
rogress a Day
t a Time

difference in this way of thinking is that your energy is focused on the process itself (i.e. life-style changes) rather than solely on the end result (i.e. numbers on the scale).

Redefining success in terms of life-style changes and health status rather than the tangible result of weight loss puts a new perspective on how you feel about your weight. What does success mean to you? In the past it may have been defined as weight loss visible on the scale. Chances are this success was not long term. Why not try for something more permanent.

Keep in mind that with rare exceptions, none of the available programs for treating obesity are based on current scientific knowledge. If they were, according to Wayne Callaway, Associate Clinical Professor of Medicine at George Washington University, these programs could not promise rapid weight loss.[2] It seems we have been using an inaccurate and ineffective measuring tool to judge long-term success.

**The 3 Ps to
Long-Term
Success**
• **Perspective**
• **Priority**
• **Perseverance**

THE THREE Ps TO LONG-TERM SUCCESS

A fresh new approach to health is that the internal changes made by life-style change motivate people to keep practising those life-style changes. The HUGS™ approach can be labeled as the three Ps to long-term success. Here they are.

Perspective With a positive perspective on life, you learn to be more flexible, accept life's highs and lows, and learn from them. You no longer isolate specific instances and blame others or yourself for shortcomings; you put the problem into proper perspective. This new lease on life gives you the opportunity to savor the precious moments and deal with the "downs" as a stepping stone to something better. It is part of the plan to mold you into reaching your full potential in health and in life. Breathing new excitement into life allows you to take on new challenges and strive to be the best that you can be in every aspect of life!

Priority With the new attitude that you have learned, you need to take time for yourself and make this a priority. We know that you have the choice to

267

keep your life in balance or to be overwhelmed with your unending list of duties and responses to external cues. Feeling better about yourself and having confidence in your ability minimizes the effect that comments from others have on you.

When you set your priorities and schedule "time off" for yourself, you leave some time for unexpected emergencies. Improving your self-esteem shows you that you do not have to answer to anyone else but yourself. There will always be those who try to sabotage your best efforts or make you feel insignificant. You have learned to put this in the proper perspective. The final decision is yours.

With an improved self-concept you no longer need as many compliments to prove yourself to others. It no longer matters to you what others think. You strive for excellence in the best way that you know and you realize that the struggle for perfection is not worth the effort. Perhaps it is superficial, artificial, and energy-draining rather than a constructive, meaningful experience contributing to your growth.

Perserverance "Hanging in there" is certainly worth the effort. The result is a new life-style that puts your life in balance and gives you an inner glow that radiates outward and brings with it health and vibrancy. You have a sense of accomplishment. This way of life is one of celebration and it is for a lifetime; it doesn't end when you attain a temporary goal.

The key to keeping life-style change going is to enjoy the process. Just as a flower buds, and only with time does it come into full bloom, so your process of growth will also be gradual.

You could take the time to note the more positive ways that you are dealing with situations, and savor freedom to live your life to the fullest.

SUCCESS REDEFINED
One source of stress in people's lives is that they don't feel good about themselves and they lack self-esteem. They have a lot of anxiety. They feel they're "losing it."

268

By redefining success as the process of improving your health and life-style your physical and mental stress is reduced. Consider these points.

- Feel "in charge."

- Feel good about yourself; improve your self-image and gain more confidence.

- Increase your activity gradually and enjoy it.

- Make gradual life-style changes because you want to.

- As your waist/hip ratio improves it indicates a lower risk for heart disease, high blood pressure, and diabetes.

- Simplify your life-style for healthier living.

- Celebrate food in its proper place. Food is no longer the center of life.

- Look forward to getting up in the morning.

- Feel free to eat.

Overall, the above points define an improved health status. Healthier individuals in both body and mind are more apt to reach their full potential that makes life fuller at every moment.

RATE YOUR PROGRESS IN THE PROCESS OF HEALTHY LIVING
Complete the Life-style Quiz again on p270 and compare this evaluation to the assessment you made at the beginning of the book (p19). Note where your greatest improvement in life-style behavior occurred. Use the checklist on p272 to pinpoint areas that need more focus to achieve your new life-style. Focus on your improvement in attitude and life-style change.

LIFE-STYLE QUIZ

1 Always
2 Very often
3 Often
4 Sometimes
5 Rarely
6 Never

☐ I am unhappy with myself the way I am.

☐ I am preoccupied with a desire to be thinner.

☐ I weigh myself several times a week.

☐ I am more concerned with the number on the scale than my overall sense of well-being.

☐ I think about burning up calories when I exercise.

☐ I am out of tune with my body for natural signals of hunger and fullness.

☐ I eat for other reasons than physical hunger.

☐ I eat too quickly, not taking time to focus on my meal and taste, savor, and enjoy my food.

☐ I fail to take time for activities for myself.

☐ I fluctuate between periods of sensible, nutritious eating and out-of-control eating.

☐ I give too much time and thought to food.

☐ I tend to skip meals, especially early in the day, so I can "save up" my food for one big feast.

☐ I engage in all-or-nothing thinking. I tend to feel that if I can't do it all, or do it well, what's the point?

☐ I try to be all things to all people.

☐ I strive for perfection in my life.

☐ I criticize myself for not achieving my goals.

☐ Total   Add 4 to the score to determine your percentage.

Please share your success with others

Now that you've discovered the true benefits of healthy living and size acceptance, you can help spread the message.

Your assistance is important. Our programs are fine-tuned through the research data that is requested in the life-style quizzes. Your response to these questions is the key to the process. Total professional confidentiality is assured, and your reward is the satisfaction of knowing that HUGS™ will be more effective and have broader appeal.

How to participate

1. Make a photocopy of your beginning quiz (p19).

2. Make a photocopy of the concluding quiz (p270).

3. Now that you have worked through the book and made adjustments to your life-style and attitude, there will undoubtedly be a change in your response to these same questions. Mentally celebrate your new score!

4. Complete the mailing address information below.

5. Send your photocopies and address to the HUGS™ office at
Hugs International Inc., Box 102A, RR#3
Portage la Prairie, Manitoba, Canada R1N 3A3.
or **FAX (204)428-5072**.

6. In appreciation of your participation we'll provide you with 2 complimentary issues of the HUGS™ newsletter— a biannual publication full of healthy living inspiration and ongoing practical help ideas.

NAME

ADDRESS

CITY   PROVINCE   POSTAL CODE

HOME PHONE   WORK PHONE

THE HUGS™ HEALTHY LIVING CYCLE
It begins with self-acceptance,
simply feeling good about yourself.

As you follow our healthy living steps, your physical and mental well-being will be constantly improving.

• Throw the scales away and focus on rebuilding health.
• Exercise regularly at your own level with an activity you enjoy.
• Balance your meals appropriately to fill your needs for fullness and energy.
• Eat regularly starting with a balanced breakfast.
• Be creative in food preparation using herbs and spices to replace fatty ingredients.
• Tune in to your natural hunger signals. Eat whatever you want whenever you want, as long as you are physically hungry.
• Eat until you are physically satisfied, and not overly full.
• Focus on the internal rewards of energy and well-being.
• Use skills of confrontation to cope with bursts of psychological hunger.
• STOP, TASTE, SAVOR and ENJOY your food to the fullest.
• Exercise your choice in the purchsse of products suited to your new taste.
• Ensure you are hungry, not merely thirsty.
• Take time for yourself and relax. You are special too!
• Treat setbacks as a learning experience, a necessary detour towards being the best that you can be!
• Make a small change today for a better you tomorrow!
• *You Count, Calories Don't.*

BE THE BEST THAT YOU CAN BE!

Can you identify with any of the comments from HUGS™ clients who were asked how the program helped them?

"I became more in touch with my body and mind as related to becoming a healthy individual."

"I have benefited in many ways, especially not feeling guilty about everything I eat. I feel happier with myself, which makes me feel more confident."

"Increased understanding of the role of carbohydrates in my diet has increased my awareness of factors affecting my eating behavior. I have gained a new guilt-free acceptance of myself."

"HUGS™ has helped me get off the diet roller

coaster. If I eat something that's fattening, so what? Nothing is blown. I'll eat healthier tomorrow. I also have more reasonable expectations about myself. I'll get healthier in time and have fun doing it!"

"HUGS™ has shown me a life without diets. Also it has shown me that by thinking of myself, I am becoming a better person, better meaning healthier."

"HUGS™ is a good program that has made me think more about myself, what I want, and the other things in my life that need to be managed."

"HUGS™ helps to put food in perspective. Instead of it being the focus, fitness and a healthy life-style are more important."

"You are taught to think about life-style changes in both nutrition and exercise. You don't feel the scale is number one. You learn to be motivated by gradual and positive change."

"The HUGS™ program was very informative and enjoyable. It helped me realize that people have the power to change their way of thinking and eating and their attitude about themselves through other methods than dieting."

"HUGS™ doesn't end when you achieve your goal. It incorporates life-style change and balance."

"HUGS™ got me to change my attitude. I didn't need self-control, I just needed to think normally. This program has given me the ability to look at my eating as part of my life, not as an all-consuming hobby. I still have lots to work on, but I now have the tools to deal with the problems as they arrive."

"My focus has changed. I am not afraid to eat certain foods. I am also more aware of what I am doing and eating."

"HUGS™ has given me a new outlook on food. I think differently than I did about food and nutrition. It's a great program."

"HUGS™ has taught me how to implement permanent life-style changes. Diets in the past were only temporary weight-loss practices which ultimately ended in weight gain."

"HUGS™ focuses on change in life-style and there

273

are no strict "can" and "cannot" guidelines on what to eat."

"HUGS™ is a different approach to food and eating. I have not lost weight but I do feel better. The effects may settle in on me later. HUGS™ is more insight-oriented than prescriptive."

"HUGS™ means well-balanced eating, to be easy on myself, to realize this is for life. Thanks for a great learning experience!"

"The other programs tell you what to do but don't attempt to address the reasons why you have weight to lose in the first place."

"HUGS™ helps to develop life-style changes and helps to tune into what your body is telling you. I have gained a better understanding of why my previous eating habits were so poor."

"HUGS™ is reasonable, I understand it. It has definitely helped me tune into myself. I don't feel guilty about food. Overall I am happier, no more diets."

"HUGS™ addresses reasons why others (diets/programs) fail, (i.e. deprivation, lack of self-esteem). It answers why and educates us on how our bodies work."

"HUGS™ is better than other programs because the philosophy is right and because dieting leads to obsessions with food and self-hate. I am sure I will look at dieting quite differently from now on. And I will be eating in a healthier way."

"HUGS™ concentrates on the positive rather than the negative. It looks at long term (i.e. life-style rather than immediate weight loss) and takes away the guilt."

"I really enjoyed the HUGS™ program. It was very enlightening to learn that a lot of my eating behaviors were part of the 'dieter's' thinking and not a result of 'psychosis' on my part. I'm not any thinner yet, but I feel thinner. I'm more positive about myself and believe in one-step-at-a-time life-style change! Great program!"

14

A New Concept of Cooking

You count, calories don't

Most of us have a repertoire of a dozen recipes that we tend to use over and over again. Do you realize that by making small changes, (changing one of your usual meals to a tasty lower fat version each month) you will have a new way of eating? Rather than relying solely on new recipes, the HUGS™ philosophy allows you to fine-tune your present food preparation methods. Experiment with herbs and spices to add flavor where fat was once the sole source of flavor. The talented cook is the individual who can make a tasty meal without depending on fat as the only flavor source. Herbs and spices can add a new taste sensation to a meal. Try them out. It's fun to experiment.

CREATIVE COOKING TIPS

- Start with 1/4 tsp (1 mL) dry herbs or 3/4 tsp (3 mL) fresh herbs for a dish that serves 4 people. Fresh herbs contain more moisture with a milder flavor. You will need 3 to 4 times more fresh herbs than dried herbs. For example, 1 tbs (15 mL) fresh herbs equals 1 tsp (5 mL) dried herbs.
- Crumble the herbs between your fingers to release the flavor prior to adding to the dish.
- Heat the herbs in a bit of oil to heighten and extend the flavor.
- With soups, stews, and large quantity dishes, add the herbs during the last hour of cooking so the flavor doesn't evaporate.
- Store the herbs in a cool place in an opaque container to retain their flavor. Do not store near the stove.
- Routinely replace your supply of herbs. Ground spices retain their flavor for about 6 months. Herbs dry out after 4 months.
- Rub herb mixture onto meats prior to cooking.
- Until you become experienced, use herbs singly and advance to blending herbs together later. In this way, you will pinpoint whether you like the flavor and aroma of the dish and which particular herbs enhance the flavor for you.
- When using seasoning packages, try using only 1/2 the package as the flavors are usually too concentrated, especially in salt. The remaining amount can be used for seasonings for home-made barbecue sauces or added to meats, etc. I will refer to these tips throughout this section as I discuss how to put some "oomph" into your meals. Refer to Chapters 4 and 5 for some other recipe ideas. Use the herb chart (p286) to help orient you to the taste of herbs.

You can use the foods you enjoy now and make slight changes to fit in with the HUGS™ philosophy rather than spend time gathering special ingredients and end up with a product you don't like. Here's your chance to try new ideas gradually. You may find that certain foods that did not appeal to you previously gain flavor and your approval with your new preparation methods. Examples of how to modify existing recipes have already been discussed. What follows are a few more examples of how to lighten a meal, without sacrificing flavor.

HOW TO ADD FLAVOR TO SOUPS

- Sauté vegetables in a little bit of oil with some herbs to extract the flavor.
- Cream soups with 1 percent or skim milk.
- Add a variety of grains (i.e. bulgur, couscous, wild rice, pastas) of different shapes. If you cook the grain in soup, it will help thicken it.
- Keep some fresh herbs handy in a pot on your windowsill. Snip and chop some fresh herbs into your soup, sauté them at the beginning and/or add during the last hour of cooking.
- Leftovers are great to add to soup (i.e. leftover hamburger, gravy, sauce, seasoning from rice, etc.). Let your creativity run free!

RECIPES TO GET YOU STARTED

If your first impulse is to scan the following recipes for information on portion sizes and calorie content, you won't find it! Keep in mind that you're eating to satisfy your taste and feelings of hunger, so whether a recipe yields 12 or 18 servings is irrelevant. As for calories, remember *you count, calories don't* in your new perspective about food.

SOUPS

QUICK & EASY TOMATO MUSHROOM SOUP

1 can	light cream of tomato soup
1 can	light mushroom soup
4 cans	water
2 cans	1 percent milk
	chopped vegetables as desired (e.g. chopped carrots)
	herbs to go with tomato (basil and oregano to taste)
	herbs to go with mushroom (sage and savory to taste)

Combine all ingredients and heat. Add noodles or some type of grain to thicken the mixture. Serve when hot.

Note that more water was added to dilute the salty flavor. Herbs and vegetables were added to pick up the flavor. Adding water also diluted the thickness so rice, noodles, or bulgur was added to thicken it again. Milk added some creaminess without the fat. Another option would be to add skim-milk mozzarella cheese to the soup to boost the protein content.

LEGUMES SOUP

3 cups	legumes	750 mL
12 cups	water	3 L
1	chicken breast	1
1	ham bone	1
2	bouillon cubes	2
	touch of sugar	
	dash of tabasco sauce	

Cook all the ingredients together for 1 to 1-1/2 hours or until thick. The protein comes from the legumes and chicken. Note that any leftovers in the fridge can help to complete the protein in the legumes or make it more useable for the body. Add some pasta or grains to the soup or serve with some bread and it becomes a meal in itself. Adding some tomatoes or white wine can give the soup heightened flavor. Using some vegetables on hand adds to the color and texture of the soup.

Cutting swiss chard

CHUNKY GARDEN BORSCHT

Here is an example of hubby putting his creativity to work!

4	medium-sized onions (coarsely chopped)	4
8	small beets (coarsely chopped)	8
6 med. (or 12 small)	carrots (coarsely chopped)	6
1/2 head	cabbage (coarsely chopped)	
2 handfuls	green string beans (coarsely chopped)	2
1 cup	green garden peas	250 mL
2 handfuls	swiss chard (enough to fill a large pot)	
2 tbs	vinegar	25 mL

Fill a large pot with 12 cups (3 L) of water until it is 2 in (5 cm) from top of pot. Bring to boil. Add beets for 2 minutes. Remove. Peel beets. Discard water.

Refill the large pot with water. Place over heat. Add chopped vegetables except swiss chard. Bring to boil. Stir. Fold swiss chard leaves in half and remove heart. Discard. Cut coarsely. Add swiss chard to top of pot. Turn heat down to medium-low. Simmer. Stir when swiss chard has sunk into soup. Prepare fresh chopped dill. Pack dill into tea strainer and immerse. Add 2 teaspoons (10 mL) each of salt, vinegar, and sugar or to taste. Simmer for 1-1/2 hours, stirring occasionally. Serve with low-fat condensed milk or light sour cream.

Variations For extra flavor, add ham bone, tomatoes, beef bones, or bouillon cube, 1 can kidney beans, or 1 to 2 tbs (15 to 25 mL) each ketchup, sugar, and vinegar to taste.

FRESH TOMATO SOUP

1 tbs	oil	15 mL
2	onions (chopped)	2
1	green pepper (chopped)	1
	basil and oregano to taste	
4	tomatoes (chopped)	4
8 to 16 oz	water (with a boullion cube)	250 to 500 mL
1	bay leaf	1
1 tsp	brown sugar	5 mL

Heat oil in large frying pan. Sauté onions and green pepper with basil and oregano. (This technique helps to extract the flavor from the herbs.) Add chopped tomatoes. Add water and bouillon cube. (Any leftovers such as chicken stock or ham bone can add flavor to this soup.) Add bay leaf and brown sugar to taste, cover and simmer until tomatoes are cooked. Taste and adjust seasonings. Thicken with instant thickener, adjust seasonings to taste, and add skim milk at the very end.

Option Add noodles, bulgur, or barley to thicken the soup.

When using legumes that are gas-forming such as beans, soak them in water overnight and discard the water. The component that causes flatulence dissolves in the water and will be discarded. If you are extra sensitive, it may be advisable to add fresh water, cook for 10 minutes, and discard this water as well.

LUNCH IDEAS

LAYERED SANDWICH WITH A TWIST

Slices of toast, covered with leftover meat or canned fish, add tomato or pepper slices, or chopped onion, and top with shredded cheese (skim) and herbs sprinkled on top (i.e. oregano or thyme). Heat in microwave until cheese is melted

LAZY MAN'S CABBAGE ROLLS

Brown extra lean ground beef in teflon frying pan (no oil necessary due to fat in beef) or cook beef in microwave and then drain off fat. Layer the ground beef in bottom of casserole dish. Add chopped cabbage, uncooked rice, and tomato soup. Add water if necessary. Sprinkle with basil and oregano. Cover and cook at 350°F (180°C) until done (about 1 to 1-1/2 hours). Serve with noodles.

FRUIT PANCAKES

Great for breakfast, brunch, or lunch!
Makes 12 pancakes

These pancakes are moist and satisfying due to the technique of folding the egg whites into the batter. Use of whole wheat flour adds to the fiber content. More fruit adds to the moisture and more cinnamon, a sweeter spice, adds to the flavor.

1 cup	sifted whole wheat flour	250 mL
1 cup	all-purpose flour	250 mL
2 tbs	sugar	25 mL
1 tbs plus 1 tsp	baking powder	20 mL
1 tsp	salt	5 mL
1 to 2 tbs	cinnamon (as desired)	15 to 25 mL
2	egg yolks (well-beaten)	2
2 cups	low-fat milk	500 mL
2 tbs	oil	25 mL
1 cup	fruit (chopped)	250 mL
2	egg whites (stiffly beaten)	2

Sift together dry ingredients. Combine egg yolks and milk; stir into dry ingredients. Add oil and fruit. Blend. Carefully fold in egg whites. Bake on hot griddle or seasoned non-stick frying pan using 1/3 cup batter for each pancake. Spread batter evenly with a spatula. When done, remove from pan and serve immediately. Spread on quark, skyr, or ricotta cheese to add protein and richness to your meal with less fat.

TASTY & QUICK SPAGHETTI MEAT SAUCE

Sauté onions and garlic. (For a shortcut, add onion powder and garlic powder to the lean ground beef.) Add lean ground beef to the sautéed mixture. Brown, drain fat with turkey baster. Add seasonings. For 2 pounds (1 kg) of beef, add

1–5-1/2 oz can	tomato paste PLUS 1 can of water	156 mL
28-ounce can	tomatoes	795 mL
	Basil and oregano to taste	
1 tbs	brown sugar or honey	15 mL
	salt and pepper to taste	
1	bay leaf (to pull all the flavors together)	1

Simmer until flavors are mingled (about 1 hour). Adjust seasonings to taste.

Serve over whole wheat pasta or rainbow noodles. *Any leftovers can be used on toast as sloppy joes for lunch the next day. Add a salad and you have a tasty lunch that is pleasing to the eye.*

QUICK & TASTY PIZZA

Start with a frozen pizza crust (found in frozen section of super-market). Cover with grated mozzarella cheese. Initially you may want to mix the regular version of mozzarella cheese with the low-fat version if you haven't acquired a taste for the low-fat cheese. Otherwise, you may miss some of the flavor in the fat of the cheese. Eventually, you will like to use the lower fat version by itself.

Add any of the following toppings to the cheese:

Leftover meat

Cooked sausage (even though it is higher in hidden fat, the balance is there if you used low-fat cheese which offsets the higher fat in the sausage)

Canned tuna or other canned fish, drained

Ham (see instructions on p 283)

Cut-up vegetables such as red peppers, zucchini, cabbage, green peppers, or any other favorite vegetable.

Mild herbs such as oregano or thyme can be sprinkled on top.

Worcestershire sauce or other additional herbs can also perk up the flavor.

Note The flavor improves the next day due to the mingling of seasonings overnight. Leftover pizza made with low-fat cheese is tastier the day after.

Experiment with different methods of cooking for variety. For speed and convenience, the use of a slow cooker can work wonders in having a tasty meal on the table with little effort.

SOUP WITH THICK SANDWICHES

Use bagels or different kinds of whole wheat bread or try a pizza twist. Add leftover meat or canned fish or egg salad filling. Add lettuce and tomato if you like to give moisture and color without the fat. Serve with a piping hot soup pp 276-278 for a satisfying meal.

STIR-FRY

This is a terrific way of using up leftovers. Start with a teflon frying pan. Add meat, leftover rice, potatoes, or noodles, and serve with salad or add fresh or cooked vegetables. Cover when cooking to retain moisture.

Beans/Toast/Raw Vegetables or Salad

This is an old reliable when in a hurry. It is also a way of increasing your intake of vegetable protein. The toast or bread completes the protein in the meal.

NOODLES & CHEESE WITH SALAD

Use macaroni with cheese or noodles with quark, skyr, or cottage cheese. Serve with canned fruit in its own juice.

QUICK MACARONI WITH VEGETABLES & CHEESE

Use whatever vegetables you have on hand: in the spring, asparagus and mushrooms are nice; in the fall, try leeks and zucchini. Carrots add nice color any time of year.

1 cup	macaroni or	250 mL
4 oz	pasta	125 g
1	green onion (diagonally sliced)	1
2 cups	vegetables (thinly sliced) (carrots, celery, mushrooms, asparagus, broccoli)	500 mL
1	egg	1
2	egg whites	2
1/4 cup	milk	50 mL
1/4 tsp	dried basil	50 mL
	freshly ground pepper	
1/2 cup	part-skim mozzarella cheese	125 mL
2 tbs	grated parmesan cheese	25 mL

In a large pot of boiling water, cook macaroni or pasta until *al dente* (tender but firm). Steam green onion and vegetables until tender-crisp. Whisk egg and egg whites. Stir in milk, basil, and pepper. Drain macaroni and return to pot; add egg mixture and cheeses. Cook over low heat, stirring constantly for 1 to 2 minutes or until cheese has melted and sauce has thickened slightly. Stir in hot vegetables.

Courtesy "Eating Eggs to your Heart's Content" by the Canadian Egg Marketing Agency.

MACARONI SALAD

2 cups	macaroni (cooked)	500 mL
1/4 cup	plain yogurt	50 mL
2 tbs	light mayonnaise	25 mL
dash	lemon juice	dash
2 tbs	chopped onion	25 mL
2 stalks	celery, chopped	2
1 cup each	broccoli & sliced carrots (blanched)	250 mL
1/2 tsp (more, if desired)	dill	2 mL

Salmon, tuna, or chicken may be added to convert this dish from a side dish into a meal.

Note Adding different colored pasta gives a splash of color to the meal. Very appealing!

MEATS

HAM

Soak in water overnight to get rid of excess salt. If ham is large turn it and soak longer. Discard water. Add a bottle of beer or pineapple juice and boil until done. The result is a tender, flavorful ham that is not overly salty. It is great for lunches, especially when served with bread and pickled beets. It can also be used as a protein source at breakfast.

BACON

The procedure for ham can also apply to bacon. Since the surface area is smaller, it requires only a short time of soaking (30 minutes).

SAUSAGE

Prick sausages with fork and cook on rack in roaster. *Note* Sausage and luncheon meats contain hidden fat; therefore, fresh meats are a better option.

BEEF, CHICKEN, PORK, LAMB

Roast Lamb Often individuals do not like lamb because of the odor produced while it is cooking. However, this odor can be masked with the right combination of herbs and spices.

Cut garlic cloves in small pieces and insert into the lamb roast. Make a mixture of the following spices: onion powder, dill, mint, marjoram, basil. Rub over roast. Cook on a rack in a closed roaster to keep the meat moist.

When you remove the roast, throw ice cubes into the juices, and remove excess fat. Reheat juices and thicken. If you would like heightened flavor, add more of above spices or some salt and pepper to taste.

Refer to Chapters 4 and 5 for more ideas to bring out the flavor of foods that you are cooking. Remember that wine, sherry, rum, whisky, bouillon cubes, stock, leftover sauce, and juices can add a different taste to a meal.

Fruited Pork Chops Trim fat off pork chops. Sprinkle the chops with sweeter spices such as cinnamon and savory instead of using brown sugar. Add canned peaches for zesty natural flavor. Bake on rack in covered dish until brown and tender.

Fruited Chicken Sprinkle with thyme and rosemary. Add canned cherries and bake on rack in roasting pan.

MEAL ACCOMPANIMENT

The next time you make jello, try adding low-fat cottage cheese and some unsweetened crushed drained pineapple to the jello at the sloppy stage. Start with adding1/2 cup (125 mL) cottage cheese to a small package of lime or lemon jello. Increase the quantity of cottage cheese, if desired, the next time you try it. Serve the set jello on a lettuce leaf.

Cottage cheese seems to be a dieter's choice but is often left to go moldy in the fridge when the dieter goes back to normal eating habits. To put cottage cheese into your changed life-style find ways to dress it up and introduce it slowly so that it will become more appealing. After all, it is one of the cheeses that is lowest in fat content and it can add variety to a meal plan.

Other Ideas Whip cottage cheese in a blender, add favorite seasonings, and make into a spread for toast or add to noodles for a meal and serve with canned fruit in its own juice or in a salad for lunch.

Another good idea is to serve cottage cheese on waffles topped with fresh strawberries in season. It's a great snack, breakfast, brunch, or lunch idea.

SALAD DRESSINGS
OIL & VINEGAR
Makes 1/2 cup (125 mL)

2 tbs	oil	25 mL
2 tbs	water	25 mL
4 tbs	seasoned gourmet vinegar	60 mL
	(dill vinegar, tarragon, cider, or white wine vinegar)	
	favorite seasonings (thyme, oregano, chives, dill, garlic powder)	
1 tbs	sugar to taste	15 mL

Note that the oil is diluted with water so that the fat content is low and there are only 30 calories per tablespoon (15 mL). Seasoned vinegars and herbs add punch to the salad dressing.

Seasonings such as thyme or oregano can be rubbed between your hands to extract the flavor and then sprinkled over lettuce. Oil and vinegar dressing can then be added. Some of the flavor of the seasonings in the dressing will pick up the basic oil and vinegar flavor as the salad stands. Add some toasted sesame seeds if you like for extra crunch and flavor. Toss salad and serve.

If you use regular vinegar, you may replace the water with canned fruit in its own juice and a dash of garlic powder. Add chopped green onions with green leaf lettuce and mandarins, pineapple, or alfalfa sprouts for added color and flavor.

CREAMY DRESSING

	light sour cream or plain yogurt
	paprika
	dash onion powder
	sugar to taste

Thin out with a little bit of milk so that it spreads easily. Add to salad sparingly.

WILTED LETTUCE

2 slices	back bacon, crisp	2 slices
	chopped onions to taste	
1/4 cup	vinegar	50 mL
3/4 cup	water	175 mL
1 tbs	sugar	15 mL
dash	salt	dash
1 head	lettuce, cleaned, in pieces	1 head

Fry bacon crisp. Add chopped onions, if desired. Strain off excess fat. Add vinegar and water, mix with sugar and a dash of salt according to your taste. Boil. Pour over cleaned lettuce. If lettuce is not wilted enough, repeat the procedure.

CAESAR DRESSING

Makes 1 cup (250 mL)

3	garlic cloves	3
1/2 cup	oil	125 mL
3/4 cup	parmesan cheese	175 mL
1/4 cup	lemon juice	50 mL
1/4 cup	water	50 mL
pinch	salt and pepper	pinch
1/4 tsp	chives	1 mL
1/4 tsp	tarragon	1 mL

Mix all ingredients together in a blender 1 to 2 minutes. Thin out with milk if too thick. *TIP* If dressing gets thick as it stands, add milk to thin it to your preferred consistency.

PASTA

Pasta with some protein source such as scallops, seasoned with onions and fresh basil is delicious. Serve it with steamed vegetables for a quick and tasty lunch or supper.

KASHA

Roasted and ground buckwheat is a staple in eastern European diets. With its distinctive, nutty flavor and its versatility, buckwheat makes a good side dish or cereal and can be added to soups and stews. People who are allergic to wheat can usually eat buckwheat.

MORE ABOUT HERBS

BASIL AND OREGANO Great for tomato-based dishes. Oregano is also good with beef (i.e. hamburgers).

SAGE Commonly found in poultry seasonings. Good with pork dishes and with mushrooms.

GINGER This is a stronger spice. Great with chicken alone or on carrots.

CINNAMON This sweeter spice is most often used in cakes and cookies. It is also great on chicken or pork chops. Cinnamon is one of the key ingredients together with the meat drippings that heightens the flavor of chicken gravies.

CHILI POWDER Great as a replacement for black pepper on chicken or pork chops.

CURRY POWDER This has a similar taste to butter if used on chicken and it also gives a nice color to chicken. Fry spices in a teflon pan with a bit of oil. Or try a combination of curry powder and chili powder if your taste buds can handle something a little more spicy.

Limit the quantity of spices/herbs used. A little goes a long way in heightening the natural flavor of vegetables. Milder herbs such as thyme, oregano, chives, chervil, and parsley are suitable for vegetables.

BARBECUE SAUCES
with a Difference

KETCHUP

Dilute with water. Add chili powder, onion powder, garlic powder, and seasonings that go with your particular dish.

PEACH NECTAR

Add milder seasonings such as mint, oregano, and thyme. Add water or yogurt if too thick.

Other ideas

Pour a version of diluted cranberry juice over barbecued meat while cooking, especially chicken to keep it moist and heighten the flavor. Beer also works well.

For more tender meat, marinate in beer overnight. Pierce with fork ahead of time so that beer penetrates well.

Tenderized meat such as round steak (mechanically tenderized) is a nice change.

Use leftover soup to baste meat (can also be used as a topping for a casserole).

Use yogurt or tomato paste as a base or a neutral thickener. Add juice for flavor and spices to taste.

SNACKS

A snack that is both healthy and yummy seems to be the main question that arises in classes. Here are some suggestions that are lower in fat and taste good too.

YOGURT DIP

3/4 cup	low-fat yogurt	175 mL
1/4 cup	light mayonnaise or light miracle whip	50 mL
2 tbs	onion soup mix or other preferred seasoning	30 mL

Serve with vegetables.

PRETZELS (UNSALTED)

PUFFED WHEAT

Melt a little butter and mix with seasoning such as chili powder. Pour over and toss.

PITA CHIPS

Cut pitas in half and spread garlic butter or margarine lightly on inside. Sprinkle additional garlic powder on top for a strong garlic flavor. *Variation* Sprinkle with grated parmesan cheese.

TORTILLA SHELLS

Pop in microwave for 1 to 2 minutes until done. A great, satisfying snack. Sprinkling some seasoning before baking can add zip! Crisp, low-fat, crunchy-like chips.

Another method Place under broiler until brown.

CHOW MEIN NOODLES (UNCOOKED)

Crunchy as is and low in fat.

287

PARTY MIX
Makes 10 cups (2.5 L)

4 cups	Shreddies	1 L
2 cups	puffed wheat	500 mL
2 cups	Cheerios	500 mL
2 cups	small thin pretzels	500 mL
1/3 cup	vegetable oil	75 mL
1 tbs	Worcestershire sauce	15 mL
1 tsp	garlic salt	5 mL

Combine Shreddies, puffed wheat, Cheerios, pretzels in a large bowl. Mix together oil, Worcestershire sauce, and garlic salt. Sprinkle over cereal mixture and toss to coat lightly. Spread out in a large shallow cake pan or roaster. Toast for 1 hour in a 250°F (120°C) oven, stirring every 15 minutes.

Seasoned lentils, bulgur, or couscous dish (cold) makes a great snack!

LENTILS
BASIC COOKED LENTILS

1 cup	lentils	250 mL
2-1/2 cups	water	625 mL
2	beef bouillon cubes	2
1	bay leaf	1
1 tsp	salt	5 mL

Bring all ingredients to a boil and simmer 20 minutes.

Flavor options

CURRIED LENTILS

Heat a small amount of oil in a fry pan. Add 1 large onion, chopped and 1 clove garlic, minced. Sauté. Add 1 tsp (5 mL) salt and 1 to 2 tbs (15 to 30 mL) curry powder. Fry and stir. Add to lentils with 2 tbs (30 mL) lemon juice and chopped parsley.

288

SWEET-SOUR LENTILS

Reduce water by 1/2 cup (125 mL) in preparing Basic Cooked
Lentils. When lentils are cooked, add

1/4 cup	apple or pineapple juice	50 mL
1/4 cup	cider vinegar	50 mL
1/4 cup	brown sugar	50 mL
1 clove	garlic, crushed	1
1/8 tsp	cloves	dash
	sautéed onion (if desired)	

Heat until bubbly. Serve lentils over rice or eat as a snack by
themselves.

BREADS

As discussed earlier, quark cheese is a lower fat substitute for
cream cheese. Yet it is quite a transition in lower fat content. What
follows is a hardy snack high in carbohydrate and fiber but, at the
same time introduces you to quark cheese. Note that quark cheese
and yogurt add to the protein content, making this a more
substantial snack.

QUARK YOGURT BREAD

Makes 1 loaf or 18 rolls. Freezes well

1 tsp	sugar	5 mL
1/4 cup	warm water (115°F or 45°C)	50 mL
1 package	dry yeast	1
2 tbs	butter	25 mL
1/2 cup PLUS 2 tbs	plain yogurt	150 mL
1/2 cup	quark cheese	125 mL
1 cup	all-purpose flour	250 mL
1 cup	whole wheat flour	250 mL
1/4 tsp	baking soda	1 mL
2 tbs	sugar	25 mL
1 tsp	salt	5 mL

Dissolve sugar in warm water. Sprinkle yeast over and let stand for
8 to 10 minutes, until foamy. Stir to dissolve.

Melt butter in small saucepan. Stir in yogurt and quark cheese.
Heat to lukewarm.

In a large mixing bowl or food processor using the steel knife,
blend 2 cups (500 mL) of flour with the baking soda, sugar, and

289

salt. Add dissolved yeast. Add yogurt mixture and mix well. Knead on a well-floured board until smooth, about 5 minutes. Place in a greased bowl, cover with plastic wrap and let stand at room temperature until double in bulk, about 1 hour. Punch down.

Roll dough on a lightly floured board into a 9 in x 12 in (22 cm x 30 cm) rectangle. Roll up, sausage-style, from the shorter side. Seal ends by pressing down with the edge of your hand. Place seam side down in a greased 9 in x 5 in x 3 in (22 cm x 12 cm x 7 cm) loaf pan. (You may also place the bread on a greased cookie sheet and bake it free-form.) Cover with a towel and let rise until double, about 1 hour.

Bake at 375°F (190°C) for 25 to 30 minutes, until golden brown. There should be a hollow sound when you tap the crust lightly. Remove immediately from pan and cool on a wire rack.

To make rolls Follow above recipe and let dough rise as directed. Punch down. Divide dough into 18 equal portions. Roll each portion between your palms into a rope about 8 in (20 cm) long. Tie each piece into a knot. Place on a greased baking sheet, cover with towel and let rise until double in size. Brush with beaten egg yolk which has been blended with a few drops of water. Bake at 375°F (190°C) for 15 to 18 minutes, until golden.

COTTAGE CASSEROLE BREAD

Makes 12 slices

No kneading is required and the protein in the bread makes it suitable for a substantial snack.

1 tsp	sugar	5 mL
1/4 cup	warm water	50 mL
1 package	active dry yeast	1
1-1/4 cups	2 percent cottage cheese	300 mL
2 to 2-1/2 cups	all-purpose flour	500 to 625 mL
1 tbs	sugar	15 mL
1 tbs	poppy seeds	15 mL
1/2 tsp each of	salt and baking soda	2 mL
1	egg (well beaten)	1

Dissolve sugar in water. Sprinkle yeast over water mixture. Let stand 10 minutes, stir well. Heat cottage cheese very gently, in a saucepan just until warm. Combine 1 cup (250 mL) flour, sugar, poppy seeds, salt, and baking soda in a mixing bowl. Stir in warmed cottage cheese, egg, and yeast mixture. Beat about 3 minutes until mixture becomes elastic. Stir in remaining flour to form a stiff dough. Cover with plastic wrap. Let rise in a warm, draft-free place about 1 hour until doubled in volume. Stir down dough. Turn into a well greased 6-cup (1.5-L) casserole. Cover. Let rise in a warm place 30 to 45 minutes until light. Bake in a 350°F (180°C) oven 30 to 35 minutes until golden brown. Remove from oven. Immediately turn out of casserole. Cool. Cut into wedges.

COUNTRY GARDEN MUFFINS

Makes 12 muffins

These muffins contain protein because of the ham in the recipe. They make a more substantial snack and a nice change for breakfast! Other leftover meat can be used in place of cooked ham.

1-1/2 cups	flour	375 mL
1/2 cup	quick rolled oats (uncooked)	125 mL
2 tbs	dark brown sugar	25 mL
2 tsps	baking powder	10 mL
1/2 tsp	cinnamon	2 mL
1/4 tsp	nutmeg	1 mL
1/4 tsp	salt	1 mL
1 cup	1 percent milk	250 mL
1	egg (beaten)	1
1/4 cup	vegetable oil	50 mL
3/4 cup	lean ham (cubed, cooked)	175 mL
1/2 cup	zucchini (unpeeled, finely shredded)	125 mL
1/2 cup	carrots (finely chopped, cooked)	125 mL

Preheat oven to 425°F (210°C). Prepare a 12-cup muffin pan by putting a little oil on a paper towel to lightly coat the muffin tin cups. Combine flour, oats, brown sugar, baking powder, cinnamon, nutmeg, and salt in a large mixing bowl; set aside. Combine milk, egg, and oil in a separate mixing bowl. Stir in ham, zucchini, and carrots. Pour liquid mixture into dry ingredients and stir just until dry ingredients are moistened; do not over mix. Divide batter evenly into prepared muffin tin (about 1/4 cup or 50 mL per muffin cup). Bake at 425°F (210°C) for 20 to 25 minutes, or until golden brown. Remove immediately to cooling rack and cool thoroughly. Refrigerate until ready to serve.

LOW-FAT MUFFIN RECIPE
and Modifications

A great muffin for those chefs who have difficulty making muffins without the tunnels and peaks.

1/3 cup	margarine (at room temperature)	75 mL
1/2 cup	sugar	125 mL
2	large eggs	2
1 tsp	pure vanilla	5 mL
3 tbs	baking powder	45 mL
2-1/4 cups	all-purpose flour	550 mL
1 cup PLUS 3-1/2 tbs	plain low-fat yogurt	300 mL
1 level tsp	baking soda	5 mL

Preheat oven to 375°F (180°C). In a large mixing bowl combine the margarine, sugar, eggs, and vanilla. Beat very well with an electric mixer for about 5 minutes on high until the mixture is light in color, fluffy, and very thick.

Sift the baking powder into the flour. Place the yogurt in a measuring cup. When the creamed mixture in the bowl has been beaten enough, add the baking soda to the yogurt. Mix the yogurt until the baking soda is blended. When the yogurt foams up, add half of it to the creamed mixture, along with half the flour. Beat the mixture until it is well blended. Add the remaining flour and yogurt, and beat until well blended. The batter will be very thick. Do not add moisture.

Remove the beaters and divide the batter into a greased, oversized 12-muffin tin. For an average-sized muffin, divide the recipe to make 18 muffins. Bake for 20 to 25 minutes. Loosen the muffins from the tin 5 minutes after they are removed from the oven.

Note These muffins freeze well. Defrost in a microwave on low or defrost for 70 seconds.

Other versions

Apple Bran Substitute brown sugar for the granulated sugar. To the well-beaten creamed mixture, add 2 tbs (25 mL) pure un-sweetened cocoa and 1 cup (250 mL) all-bran cereal that has soaked in and absorbed 3/4 cup (175 mL) nonfat milk. Proceed as in the basic recipe. Before scooping the batter into the muffin tin, use a large spoon to mix in 2 medium-sized apples that have been cored and chopped into about half-inch (1 cm) chunks and sprinkled with 1 tsp (5 ml) pure cinnamon. Sprinkle the top of each muffin with cinnamon.

Banana To the creamed mixture, add 2 medium-sized very ripe bananas, well mashed. Adding raisins also gives a nice flavor.

Banana Chocolate The basic banana muffin can become banana-chocolate if you add 1/4 cup (50 mL) of pure unsweetened cocoa to the creamed mixture.

Banana Oatmeal Reduce the flour by 1/2 cup (125 mL) and add 1/2 cup (125 mL) of uncooked rolled oats to the banana muffin recipe. Raisins can also be added.

Blueberry or Cranberry After making the basic recipe, remove the beaters and fold in 1 cup (250 mL) of fresh washed and floured blueberries or cranberries. Frozen unsweetened berries can be used in the same way.

Corn Reduce the flour by 1/2 cup (125 mL) and substitute 1/2 cup (125 mL) corn flour. Substitute 1 tbs (15 mL) of Scotch whiskey for the vanilla, and fold 1 cup (250 mL) of frozen corn kernels into the completed batter. Place the batter into the muffin tins, and sprinkle each muffin with a mixture of 2 tbs (25 mL) parmesan cheese and 3 tbs (45 mL) of cornmeal.

Mocha Marble To the well-beaten creamed mixture, add 2 tbs of strong black coffee and 2 table-spoons (30 mL) of pure unsweetened cocoa. In a small cup, mix together 1/4 cup (50 mL) of unsweetened cocoa, 1 tbs (15 mL) of mocha flavoring, and a heaping 1/4 cup (50 mL) of batter. Marble the chocolate mixture through the batter just before putting it into the muffin tin.

Oatmeal Chocolate Reduce the flour by 1/2 cup (125 mL) and add 1/2 cup (125 mL) uncooked rolled oats. Add 1/4 cup (50 mL) of pure unsweetened cocoa and 1 tbs (15 mL) of Cream de Cacao or brandy to the creamed mixture.

Pineapple Bran Follow the directions for apple bran muffins. Substitute 1 can of chunk pineapple (packed in its own juice), well drained, instead of the chopped apples.

Whole Wheat Use 1/2 cup (125 mL) whole wheat flour and 1-3/4 cups (425 mL) all-purpose flour.

SANDRA'S FLAVORED YOGURT MUFFINS

Makes 12 large muffins

1 cup	rolled oats	250 mL
1 cup	flavored yogurt	250 mL
1/4 cup	vegetable oil	50 mL
1/4 cup	brown sugar	50 mL
1	egg	1
1 cup	all-purpose flour	250 mL
1 tsp	salt	5 mL
1/2 tsp	baking soda	2 mL
1 tsp	baking powder	5 mL

Soak oats in yogurt. Add oil, sugar, and egg. Mix until moistened. Sift in flour, salt, soda, baking powder. Fill muffin tins and bake at 400°F (200°C) for 20 minutes.

This is a moist flavorful muffin that uses up yogurt that has been in the fridge for a while.

BARS, SLICES, CAKES, COOKIES

Peanut butter can be incorporated into recipes to make interesting snacks instead of always settling for the old stand-by—peanut butter and bread or crackers. Here are some ideas to add to your repertoire.

Peanut Butter Bars

2-1/2 cups	bran flakes	625 mL
1/2 cup	wheat germ	125 mL
1/2 cup	raisins or dried fruit	125 mL
1/4 cup	honey	50 mL
3/4 cup	natural chunky-style peanut butter	175 mL
1/3 cup	instant nonfat dry milk	75 mL
1/3 cup	sunflower seeds	75 mL

Combine cereals, wheat germ, raisins, nuts, and seeds in a bowl. In a small saucepan heat honey. Remove from heat. Blend in peanut butter with dry milk mixing quickly and well. Pour over cereal mixture. Stir to cool. Press mixture into greased 8-in (20-cm) baking dish. Chill overnight. Cut into bars and store in airtight container.

KRISPIE PEANUT BUTTER SQUARES

Yields 25 1-1/2 inch (4-cm) squares

1/2 cup	brown sugar (firmly packed)	125 mL
1/2 cup	corn syrup	125 mL
1/2 cup	peanut butter	125 mL
3 cups	Rice Krispies	750 mL

In a large saucepan, combine sugar and corn syrup. Cook over medium heat, stirring frequently* until sugar is dissolved and mixture bubbles. Remove from heat. Stir in peanut butter, and mix well. Stir in cereal, mixing until well coated. Press evenly and firmly into lightly buttered 8-in (20-cm)-square pan. Let stand until firm. Cut into squares.

Microwave note: Microwave on high for 2 minutes, stirring every 45 seconds.

For chocolate lovers, here are a few recipes.

CHOCOLATE CHERUB CAKE

Makes 8 slices

1/4 cup	all-purpose flour	50 mL
2 tsps	baking powder	10 mL
1/3 cup	unsweetened cocoa powder	75 mL
1/3 cup	water	75 mL
1/2 tsp	vanilla extract	2 mL
	whites from 4 large eggs (at room temperature)	
	pinch of salt	
1/3 cup	sugar	75 mL
Optional	Confectioner's sugar (for dusting on top)	

Heat oven to 350°F (180°C). Have an 8-in (20-cm)-square cake pan ready. Mix flour and baking powder, set aside. Put cocoa and water in a small saucepan over low heat. Bring to a simmer, and cook about 1 minute stirring constantly until thick and smooth. Remove from heat; stir in vanilla. Beat egg whites and salt in a large bowl with electric mixer until foamy. Gradually add sugar, beating until soft peaks form when beaters are lifted. Quickly add cocoa mixture; beat just until blended. Fold in flour mixture in 2 additions just until blended. Pour into ungreased cake pan. Bake 20 to 25 minutes until the top cracks and looks dry. Place cake, still in pan, upside down on wire rack to cool 20 minutes. Run knife around edge of cake to loosen; carefully turn onto wire rack. Cool completely. Sprinkle with confectioner's sugar, if desired.

CHOCOLATE CHIP COOKIES

Makes about 24 cookies

1 cup	sifted all-purpose flour	250 mL
1	large egg	1
1/4 cup	unsifted whole wheat flour	50 mL
1	large egg white	1
1/2 tsp	baking soda	2 mL
1 tbs	almond extract	15 mL
1/4 cup	unsalted margarine	50 mL
1 square (1 oz)	semi-sweet chocolate (grated fine)	28 g
1/4 cup	granulated sugar	50 mL
1/4 cup	light brown sugar (firmly packed)	50 mL

Preheat the oven to 375°F (180°C). In a small bowl, combine the all-purpose flour, whole wheat flour, and baking soda and set aside.

In the large bowl of an electric mixer, beat the margarine, granulated sugar, and brown sugar at moderately low speed for 2 minutes or until smooth and creamy; then beat in the egg, egg white, and almond extract.

Using a wooden spoon, mix in the dry ingredients and the grated chocolate.

Drop the dough by rounded tbsfuls (15 mL) onto ungreased baking sheets, spacing the cookies about 2 in (5 cm) apart. Bake for 8 to 10 minutes or until lightly browned around the edges. Remove immediately to wire racks to cool.

> **TIP**
> When using your own recipe try substituting half the flour with whole wheat flour using the following formula:
>
> 1 cup (250 mL) = 2/3 cup (150 mL)
> all-purpose flour   whole wheat flour

CHOCOLATE CHEESECAKE

Sugar was decreased in recipe from the original recipe and cream cheese was replaced with quark cheese, a lower fat version with a similar taste. The result is a lighter cake that is loaded with a chocolate flavor.

3/4 cup	graham wafer crumbs	175 mL
1 tbs	sugar	15 mL
2 tbs	butter (melted)	25 mL
1 pkg (4-serving size) chocolate pudding and pie filling		1 pkg
1/2 cup	sugar	125 mL
1 cup	1 percent milk	250 mL
1 oz	unsweetened chocolate	28 g
26 oz	quark cheese	750 g
3	egg yolks	3
2 tsps	vanilla	10 mL
1/4 tsp	salt	1 mL
3	egg whites	3

Mix together graham cracker crumbs, 1 tbs (15 mL) sugar, and butter. Grease sides of 9-in (22.8-cm) spring-form pan to 1 in (2.5 cm) from top; coat with about 2 tbs (30 mL) crumb mixture. Press remaining crumb mixture firmly on bottom of pan.

Combine pudding mix, 1/2 cup (125 mL) sugar, and milk in saucepan. Add chocolate. Cook and stir over medium heat until chocolate is melted and mixture comes to a full bubbling boil. Remove from heat. Cover surface with wax paper and set aside to cool.

In large bowl, beat quark cheese until fluffy. Add egg yolks, beat well. Blend in vanilla, salt, and pudding. Beat egg whites until soft rounded peaks form; fold into cheese mixture.

Pour into prepared pan. Bake on lowest oven rack at 425°F (210°C) for 30 minutes, or until center is set when lightly touched and top is golden brown. Cake becomes firmer when cool. Remove outside ring of spring-foam pan only when cool.

Spread top of cheese cake with cooked rhubarb mixture or other cooked or fresh fruit. Also good by itself without any added fruit. Refrigerate until firm before serving.

COCOA BROWNIES

These brownies are moist and lower in fat than most brownies because they are made with cocoa instead of chocolate and with egg whites instead of whole eggs.

1/2 cup	soft margarine	125 mL
1 cup	granulated sugar	250 mL
1/2 cup	all-purpose flour	125 mL
1/2 cup	cocoa	125 mL
1 tsp	baking powder	5 mL
1 tsp	vanilla	5 mL
4	egg whites	4

In bowl, using electric mixer, beat margarine and sugar until light and creamy. Beat in flour, cocoa, baking powder, and vanilla. In another bowl, using hand electric mixer, beat egg whites until they are white and hold their shape. Fold beaten whites into cocoa mixture until completely blended. Transfer to greased and floured 8-in (20-cm) -square baking pan.

Bake in 325°F (160°C) oven for 20 to 25 minutes. Top should be slightly underbaked in the middle and firm to the touch near the edges. Remove from oven and allow to cool completely before cutting.

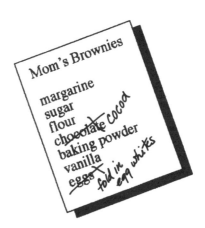

TIP

For a quick and simple dessert or to accent a cake to make it special, try using a yogurt-flavored sauce on cake or fruit instead of whipping cream. Take low-fat plain yogurt and mix in a bit of flavoring from a flavor of your choice; for example, coffee yogurt is nice.

APPLE OAT BREAD

Makes 1 loaf

1-1/2 cups	quick-cooking or old-fashioned oats (uncooked)	375 mL
1-1/2 cups	all-purpose flour	375 mL
1-1/2 tsp	baking soda	7 mL
1-1/2 tsp	cinnamon	7 mL
3/4 tsp	allspice	3 mL
1/4 cup	honey	50 mL
1/2 cup	skim milk	125 mL
3 tbs	salad oil	45 mL
3	egg whites	3
3 medium	green cooking apples (unpeeled, diced)	3

Preheat oven to 350°F (180°C). Grease 8.5 in x 4.5 inch (21.5 cm x 11.4 cm) loaf pan with oil on paper towel.

In large bowl, mix oats and next 4 ingredients. In small bowl, beat honey, milk, oil, and egg whites until blended; stir into flour mixture just until flour is moistened (batter will be lumpy). Fold in apples.

Spoon batter evenly into loaf pan. Bake 65 minutes or until a toothpick inserted into center of bread comes out clean. Cool bread in pan on wire rack 10 minutes; remove bread from pan. Cool bread completely on wire rack.

STREUSEL PLUM CAKE

1/4 cup	margarine	50 mL
1/2 cup	granulated sugar	125 mL
2	eggs (separated)	2
1-1/2 cups	all-purpose flour	375 mL
1 tsp	baking powder	5 mL
1/2 cup	1 percent milk	125 mL
2 – 14-oz cans	plums (drained)	400 g
2 cups	ripe plums (halved)	500 mL

Grease 9-inch (22.8-cm)-square cake pan, or use greased spring-form or flan pan. Cream together margarine, sugar, and egg yolks in large bowl. Beat until fluffy. Combine flour and baking powder. Beat into egg mixture alternately with milk. Beat egg whites until stiff but not dry. Fold into batter. Turn into prepared pan. Halve and pit plums and arrange over top.

Bake in preheated 350°F (180°C) oven for 35 to 45 minutes or until top is golden and toothpick inserted into cake comes out clean.

299

FRUIT PIES

Some tips on how to modify your recipes.

Crust
Roll the crust out thinner and use latticework on top or try a crumb crust for a change. Try using half the fat content as called for in your recipe for a lighter version that makes the fruit the focus rather than the crust.

For filling
Use light pie filling or if you are feeling creative, try using canned fruit in its own juice, drained (peaches or pineapple cubes work well). Another option would be to use those crabapples from your freezer. Chop in half, and leave them unpeeled for more flavor and color.

For thickener
Use flour, cornstarch, and/or oat bran. Guideline 1/4 cup (50 mL) flour or 2 tbs (25 mL) cornstarch per large 9-in (22.8-cm) fruit pie.

For flavor
Cut back on sugar content slightly depending on the type of filling (i.e. crabapples are sour and therefore, you will need more sugar); add other flavor enhancers.

For crabapples Use rum extract, cardamom, cinnamon, cloves.

For pineapple Use almond extract, slivered almonds, cinnamon, bit of juice that was drained.

Dots of butter on top are not necessary.

Make only slight modifications to your regular recipe so that you are assured of success.

The above recipes and suggestions have given you a sampling of the kind of changes you can make to eat in a healthier way. Many other recipe books are available to give you additional ideas of how to modify recipes. By following the principles of HUGS™ as outlined in the previous chapters you can start from where you are right now and proceed to where you want to be one step at a time. Break free from continually trying new recipes and learn to take what you are familiar with and make it better.

Looking ahead

If your main goal as you come into the HUGS™ program was to lose weight, but you have not yet lost any weight, perhaps the goal has to be looked at again. If you remember we said a goal of weight loss does not achieve health and permanent life-style change. Focusing on a goal of weight loss shifts the emphasis from life-style habits that are integral in stabilizing and maintaining any weight lost. Remember that fluctuations in body weight are more harmful to health than if you stabilize at a higher weight.

We all make decisions that affect the rest of our lives. We can choose to take responsibility for them and move on or continue to dwell on the past causing more stress and unhappiness which leads to more eating. In this way, the process of healthy living is no longer natural but forced. The journey is no longer enjoyable. Rather the destination becomes foremost in your mind.

It's your choice — continue the HUGS™ philosophy recognizing and accepting the internal benefits gained and striving for unconditional self-acceptance, or go back on the bandwagon that brings with it irritability, preoccupation with weight and food, and even larger body size a few years later.

DIETS DON'T WORK. The greatest chance to reach your health potential is through healthy living. Why give up that chance now that you have come so far. Life-style change doesn't happen overnight. If it did it would simply be another diet under the new banner "life-style."

HOW FAR HAVE YOU PROGRESSED?
• Have you cultivated a preference for lower fat foods?
• Have you cultivated a preference for less sweetening foods?
• Are you starting to enjoy incorporating more activity into your life-style?
• Are you dealing with why you are eating in the first place?
• Are you using confrontation to really determine if you want certain foods?

301

- Are you making small changes to build in some time for yourself?
- Are you thinking like a nondieter?

Every yes answer is a success!

When you can answer yes to all these life-style shifts, physical changes might take place. If you rush this process, you will certainly end up in the diet thinking. The more you have dieted and the older you are the longer it will take to make the new process enjoyable. But if it's fun and you have an attitude of self-discovery and experimentation, it really doesn't matter how long the new process takes. If you allow changes to take place over a 5-year period, your body will readjust to its natural weight comfortably, and will maintain it. No matter what the outcome, you are to be congratulated on taking this road. This is the way you will be healthier and happier.

Your success is renewed confidence and self-acceptance, energy, enjoyment of increased activity, feeling better about yourself, and improved eating habits.

The qualities expressed in the next chapter will guide you on what needs to be done to really begin to focus on your needs. If you are younger than 40, gather preparation ideas for moving through menopause comfortably and painlessly. If you are in your 40s or 50s, draw what you need to reassess and gain the skills to do what it takes to enjoy the process of change that is taking place; the metamorphosis to a new you, one of vitality and vigor and confidence. If you have already gone through menopause and do not possess these qualities, the characteristics alone can help you grab onto this new adulthood that can transport you to new heights. Men and women will be guided in this stage of transition, midlife, a time when many of us step back and reassess before we move on.

HUGS may be in your area.
Check the yellow pages or ask your nutritionist or dietitian for the program in your area.
Visit our web site at   http://www.hugs.com
for a current listing of HUGS facilitators worldwide.

15
Midlife — a time for empowerment

Shift the focus from meeting other's needs to meeting your own

Midlife is a time when, if we have not already done so, we should learn to take as good care of ourselves as we do of others. We can do many things to help keep our minds and bodies in smooth running order before problems arise. We need not wait until we are sick to invest energy in ourselves and our bodies. We can start by simply devoting a bit more time to being in touch with ourselves, what we need, how we are feeling. We can re-think the habits that affect our health and make decisions about changing our lifestyle. The focus of this chapter is on applying the characteristics of balance that have been presented throughout *You Count, Calories Don't* to the passage through midlife and menopause.

The word menopause means different things to different women. For some, menopause is a process that begins at midlife and lasts for the rest of their lives. Other women think of menopause as the signs, such as hot flashes and night sweats, that they experience around age 50 as their hormonal levels drop. Actually, the word menopause refers to the end of all menstrual bleeding. While most women go through menopause between the ages of 48 and 52, some women stop menstruating as young as their late 30s or early forties, while others continue to menstruate into their mid-50s.

For most women, the process that leads up to menopause happens gradually, triggered by a slowdown in the function of their ovaries. This process begins 4 to 6 years before the last menstrual period and continues for several years after. During this time, there is a decrease in the estrogen production from the ovaries, finally dropping to such low levels that the periods become irregular and finally stop entirely. For some women this change to a new hormone level is easy and uneventful. For many women, however, the change comes at a time when other events going on in their lives combined with the physical signs of menopause lead to unhealthy levels of stress.

The social and cultural factors occurring before, during, and after menopause may be quite stressful. Menopause can be a time when children leave home

304

and move away, major career changes are made, and marriage ends in divorce or starts anew. Often the caring for older parents or a disabled family member falls on the shoulders of the 45+ woman. It should be no surprise that these issues have been found to have a much bigger impact on the mental and physical health of women than the hormone changes of menopause do.

Since many of these changes are unavoidable and out of our control, the extra weight which most women naturally gain at menopause may cause women to attempt to exert control over their bodies by dieting to lose weight. We seem to forget that genetic factors play an important role in body shape, and that this weight has been shown to help protect women's bones from thinning too fast and lessens other signs of menopause such as hot flashes. We also seem to forget that dieting leads to increased levels of stress, and a return to food and weight preoccupation.

At this point in time it becomes particularly important that women understand the unrealistic pressure society puts on women to be ultra-thin. Women need to learn to appreciate and accept their body as it is and not strive for some unrealistic goal. To create healthier alternatives and counter social pressure to be thin, we can learn to celebrate our diversity and love our bodies. In doing so, we hold the power to push public consciousness. There is not a moment to lose. Our daughters are counting on us.

The transferable characteristics of balance—the qualities that sustain a nondiet life-style also facilitate the passage through menopause.

During the hectic early years of adulthood we may have completed our education, started families, raised children, and established a job or career. This can leave little time for our own needs. The changes of midlife encourage us to take stock of our lives and remind us to take care of ourselves physically and emotionally. The following application of the characteristics of balance that have been presented throughout *You Count, Calories Don't* to the passage through menopause will help you stay healthy at

305

midlife and beyond.

Balance (and the peace and harmony this state implies) is a lifelong search that evolves with changing life circumstances. What's interesting is that the personal qualities that you acquire throughout your life journey power the small action steps that will enable you to move from one goal to another. Acquiring each one of these qualities is not a goal unto itself. The naming of the quality enables you to see "what you are made "of and how that strength can create your personal action plan for change. As you recognize that you already have one or more of the qualities for balance you'll be encouraged to look for the new ones to put into your personal repertoire. Each action suggestion that arises from the identification of the personal quality is transferable to life circumstances involving the need for change. Sustaining your nondiet life-style, developing your own business, nurturing the growth of your children or encountering the realities of midlife changes are all examples of these kinds of life circumstances. As you read through the steps, claim your personal description. For example, if you are one of those remarkable people who can plan systematically, look at what you will be able to gain from applying that quality to your personal midlife issues. Put up a mirror to past behavior and discover that you do have the "right stuff" to move forward in acceptance of midlife changes.

The quality of courage . . . **helps with your acceptance of your changing body size and shape.**

KNOW WHAT YOU WANT

Dig deep, find a name for your personal desire, and be definite with that name. Many people think weight loss will bring happiness, self-esteem, self-acceptance, health, energy. Naming these items defines what they truly want — diets and weight loss aren't the route to achieve those desires.

At midlife we have the opportunity to expand our choices, to reach out for new, possibly long delayed experiences, to create lives that reflect our values and desires. The fact that there are large women who seem to truly accept their bodies challenges the conventional assumptions that one cannot possibly "accept oneself" without being slender. One woman tells about the difficulty and value of making the

306

effort to accept her body:
"I think it takes courage to go against the norm
established by society. I think the effort that goes into
dieting and self-abuse over being fat should be
converted into frank self-examination. Fat can
provide a convenient excuse not to be or do all you
want. Deciding to accept yourself as a fat woman
frees you to find out who and what else you are. It
isn't easy to reach self-acceptance. Everything in our
society is aimed at women being discontented with
their bodies. Without the help of supportive friends
and/or family and help from the size acceptance
movement, it's very difficult to be objective about our
weights. It's important to do all the things about
which you say, 'I can't do that until I lose weight.'
You'll discover that you can do many of them
without weight loss. You've got to take risks . . . not
accepting your body is the craziest form of self-denial
I can think of."[1]

And some further comments . . .
"I'm tired of being Sisyphus and rolling the weight-
loss boulder up the hill over and over. I'm accepting
my body having been the innocent victim of society's
torment. I want to love it, not hate it. I have finally
grown to love my body and respect it. What's
changed is a shift from knowing I 'should' like it to
internalizing that belief and truly believing it. Years
of affirmations, therapy, massage, dancing, moving
my body, and doing other positive things to improve
my self-esteem have helped. I gave up the false belief
that I was a victim, not fitting in anywhere. My body
is beautiful in its curves, softness, and roundness and
has the right to fit in all kinds of spaces. I used to
think I didn't have that right." [1]

*The quality of
integrity . . .
provides you with
effective coping
strategies for hot
flashes.*

NETWORK AND GROUP

> **Broadcast and stand up for your message. Express your true
> feelings publicly to your family, work or social groups, or in a
> support group. All of us benefit from an understanding of
> menopausal changes, and from being able to talk openly about
> the feelings and experiences that accompany these years.**

In folk wisdom and humor, hot flashes are the sign
most commonly associated with menopause. Surveys
report that anywhere from 47 to 85 percent of women

will experience hot flashes. Many women never experience hot flashes at all.

For most women, a hot flash or flush can be nothing more than transient sensations of warmth. For others it is "perpetual summer." Some women report their hot flashes are pleasant. Some women experience waves of heat and drenching sweats, often followed by chills; some experience chills first. Feelings such as tension, anxiety, heart palpitations, and nausea may also accompany hot flashes or may be preceded and be relieved by the hot flash.

Hot flashes can begin when menstrual cycles are still regular or when they are becoming irregular. They typically continue for less than a year after the final menstrual period; however, for some women they persist for 5, 10, or even more years. Generally, the body gradually adjusts to the lower level of estrogen and, for most women, the hot flashes stop or become infrequent.

To take care of ourselves during this period, some medical knowledge certainly helps. But the experience we have accumulated during 50 years of life is equally important. So are the experiences that other women have had and are willing to share with us. Self-help techniques for hot flashes that come from women who have shared their experiences and wisdom include:
• *Keep track* Chart your hot flashes in relationship to your menstrual periods and other events to see if you can find a pattern. The more you know about yourself, the better you'll be able to manage your hot flashes and the better you will feel.
• *Keep healthy* Some women have found that caffeine, alcohol, sugar, spicy foods, hot soups and hot drinks, and very large meals may trigger hot flashes.
• *Keep moving* Activity relieves hot flashes, stress, and depression, and helps you sleep better.
• *Keep cool* Dress in layers. Clothes made of natural fibers may be more comfortable than those made of synthetic material. When you feel a hot flash starting, take off some clothes. Go to a cooler spot, stand by an open window. Relax, take a few deep breaths. There

308

is no reason to feel embarrassed.

• *Keep talking* Break the taboos against menopause. Stay comfortable by letting people know when you are having a hot flash and reaffirm that it is nothing to be ashamed of. Use positive, not demeaning humor. Tell household members or co-workers what is happening.

Talking with others, sharing our experiences and feelings, acquiring knowledge about how our bodies are changing, and giving each other support eases our "change of life." A group of women coming together in a menopause support group or workshop to learn from one another in a respectful, informative, and supportive setting, can effectively counteract fears and uncertainties with support and information. By talking with other women we will continue to discover and exchange new self-help methods.[2]

The quality of patience . . . enables you to accept the natural growing transitions in your family.

ENJOY THE PROCESS

Measurements of time are not relevant if continual change and growth is occurring. The journey to lifelong better health is just that. There is no destination in mind, but a continual and maintained state of well-being — personal harmony.

Our bodies change continually throughout life. Our roles and relationships change too. Menopause is one of these changes. While passing through menopause might bring doubt and difficulties, it is a bridge to the second half of life — a potential "Second Adulthood" often ushered in by a flourish of new vitality. Many women report feeling more confident, empowered, involved, and energized than in their earlier years.[3]

The years that coincide with menopause are years rich with awareness gained through experience. Women arrive at their middle years wiser about the world, people, and themselves. Most now know their strengths and their vulnerabilities, and feel more confident and self-accepting. We are entering our peak years for participating in the workplace and in the community.

The quality of generosity . . .

creates a delegation system to support your short-term memory.

CREATE WIN/WIN SITUATION

Discover how to enable. Understand that you don't need to be perfect or always responsible. A situation that is a barrier to growth may not require change on your part; but an acceptance of the approach and style of the other people in the situation. Be yourself and understand that others will be themselves also!

Taking care of ourselves requires certain life-style decisions: to eat well or not, to exercise or be sedentary, to stop smoking or give up the battle, to delegate or delete routine tasks, or to strive to meet perfectionist standards. We live with many competing pressures, doing the best we can under our own circumstances. We need to have faith in ourselves to be able to live with our compromises.

A perfect tool to combat the short-term memory loss that sometimes accompanies hormonal fluctuations in the premenopausal stage is the art of enabling. Pass it on! We often carry too long a list of to-dos that can be passed on to family members, friends, committee members, or peers at work. A common objection to this passing on of "power and control" is that the delegatee is resistant. Sometimes this occurs because we fail to pass along the secrets to doing the task successfully along with the task. We transfer the task but not the confidence to do the task. When we are generous with what we have learned, others become able to take on some of our responsibilities lessening our memory load.

Another good idea for overload prevention is the one step at a time. Wait until each aspect of a delegated task is being comfortably handled by the new doer before adding new elements. Realize that you need not be all things to all people. Learn how to let go of multi tasks so that you are able to focus on the task at hand.

The quality of systematic planning . . .

offers you building blocks for the new habits to combat lack of focus and concentration.

SET GOALS IN STEPS

This is the tested and true way to meet objectives. A permanent life-style change won't be accomplished overnight. Setting too many enthusiastic expectations will overwhelm — one step at a time.

There are no magic wands or potions for good health, no fountains of youth, no products that cure all ills, no vitamins that prevent all ailments. A wellness program requires effort, planning, and persistence, but it is an investment that pays back with unbelievably high interest. When we feel good we are more likely to exercise, eat well, and take care of ourselves, all of which in turn are likely to make us feel better. Thus we create the Healthy Living Cycle (p55).

Habits are like the backbones of our lives — the firm structures upon which we can rely. It helps not to have to think about every step we take — to have comfortable routines in our lives. But as we grow older, some habits may no longer serve us well. The morning mad rush routine that helped us get ourselves and a whole family off to school and work may no longer be necessary. We may be happier and calmer with 15 minutes of quiet meditation before starting our day. Illness may require us to change from a vigorous exercise program to a more gentle one. Or we may be inspired by new information or changes in our lives to pay better attention to ourselves, to pursue renewed health and vitality by dramatically altering our pattern of health habits.

A "clean slate" approach may be your style of change, and can be very helpful when you're ready. A gradual approach may be more successful for many of us. You may want to begin with a single change. Identify the roots of the problem. Ask yourself these questions:
• When did I first establish the habit?
• What need did it serve then?
• What need does it serve now?
• Can other habits provide more satisfaction?

Become aware of your real needs — for example, when you reach for a cigarette or coffee, you may be looking for a relaxing break or sociability. Fulfill them directly and in healthier ways.

Make changes in small, manageable steps. Many habits interact, so changing one may help you change others that are harder to break. For example, if you are trying to quit smoking, drink milk, fruit or

311

vegetable juice, or herbal tea instead of coffee to break the coffee-and-cigarette association.

No matter which approach you choose, take on changing a habit when you feel strong and have no other major issues pressing on you. But watch out for procrastination. When you feel overwhelmed, call a friend, change environments, if possible, or vary your activity. Get support from others to help you in your new behavior. Form a partnership with a friend to support each other's new habits.

The quality of honest analysis . . . assists you with your hormone replacement therapy decision.

LEARN FROM SETBACKS

Today's hindsight is tomorrow's foresight. Periods of binge eating, dieting, back to the scale, etc. are to be expected when embarking on a change. If you have been doing these things for years, it's unrealistic to think habits can disappear overnight. The key is to analyze what set off the incident and try a different approach next time. Be gentle to yourself.

This may be a time in your life when you first need to make a decision whether or not to go on medication, that is, whether or not to take hormone replacement therapy. If you decide to do so, the process involved will be one of experimentation to find the right combination and amount that is right for your body. The first thing you take may not relieve your symptoms, or if it does, you need to weigh out the facts to determine if it is safe to remain on it on a long term basis. There will be pros and cons to the decision and the benefits need to outweigh the risks of the decision.

You're already acquiring the ability to tune into hunger and fullness. You can draw on this skill for this situation as you learn to tune into the signals your body is giving you about the level of medication that is working for you. Also, the decision you make may only be for a short term in the initial stages of hormonal fluctuations until you find a new balance. Your symptoms, how you feel, and the risk/benefits will be your guide. Be honest with yourself in how you feel. Be careful not to think you feel the symptoms because you know that these are the symptoms of this stage of life. Pay attention to what you really feel, not what people may tell you that you will probably feel.

Allow yourself to learn from setbacks. If your choice of medication doesn't work the first time around, be willing to persevere and try again. If your symptoms are manageable, your choice may be no medication. Determine if your symptoms relate to your hormone level or just the busy midlife stage of life you are in. Make adjustments in your life-style to accommodate some of these facets of the new you and then see if the symptoms remain or go away.

Be honest with yourself . . . part of the old you may be going away and the process of grieving during a time of loss is quite normal. Recall the universal pattern of the grieving process:
1) denial, 2) anger, 3) bargaining/negotiating, 4) depression, and 5) acceptance. Recognize which stage you are in and work through each stage on your own time schedule until you arrive at acceptance. Are you denying that you are getting older? Does it bother you or make you angry? Are you re-assessing your life situation? Are you trying to find ways to get back those younger years? Does it depress you? Or have you arrived at the point where you are ok with it; the point where you will openly find information that can help you feel better and make the best of your health and genetic predisposition to disease?

Weigh out the facts, be realistic, take off those rose colored glasses and do a frank examination of what is right for you. You already may have worked through this process in acceptance of changes in your body; now apply them to midlife and the changes you may need to make. One of your decisions is whether or not to take hormone replacement therapy. And do realize that whatever you decide is not written in stone; you can always return to doing what is most natural for you.

The quality of perseverance . . . **supports you through the unfamiliar episodes of memory lapse or fuzziness—it will pass.**

HANG IN THERE WITH AN OPEN MIND

Just the right time will emerge. Think of a growing child — they have their own internal state of readiness. A time to crawl, a time to walk, a time to read, a time to be independent in other ways. Review your own progress.

313

Realize that short-term memory loss will improve in time. Hanging in there and simplifying one's life and tasks will enable you to ride out the waves and minimize frustration. In other words, if you find that it's hard to hold everything in your head and the thought is gone as quick as you got it, then pick up a helpful habit of keeping lists and notes and relish in those check marks that indicate a job is done. Write down everything, even the little things that you used to be able to keep in your head. This new method will help you to slide through those memory lapses with ease.

Hang in there with an open mind. There are 2 ways we can respond to what we are doing: point out what's wrong and how it should be righted, or affirm what has already been accomplished and point out what else can be done and why. Why do we so reflexively choose the former? The "diet mentality" believes that we need to be hounded to change, to be hammered with rights and wrongs. In the Healthy Living Cycle (as illustrated on p55), we reward ourselves for every step, and encourage ourselves to relinquish our own whip and appreciate ourselves.

The quality of conversation. . . educates you about your osteoporosis risk.

PACE YOURSELF AND GO WITH THE FLOW

Focus or tunnel vision? Watch the road signs. When trying out a new physical activity, pace yourself to work at a level that is leaving you energized, not exhausted. Be careful of going into an activity too full force and then conking out. Relax and feel the enjoyment of the activity.

Chapter 3 discussed the benefits to our physical and emotional health that walking provides. At midlife other benefits of walking, such as an opportunity for socializing, conversation, exploration, and meditation, take on increasing importance.

With a lot of exercise, we know it's good for us so we force ourselves to go out, then can't wait to get home. But with walking, we can listen to self-improvement tapes, learn a language, sightsee with friends, including the family. Now that we know we needn't overdo to get worthwhile results, we can look forward to our walks.[4]

One way to enhance the relaxing effects of a walk is to walk mindfully. Walking can lure you into a general state of awareness — a kind of moving meditation. Mindful walking allows you to live in the moment, to notice and enjoy things, whether it's your own breathing or a hummingbird feeding at a flower. By listening to nature, we are also reconnecting with ourselves. On a mindful walk, you don't concentrate on the finish line, but on every step along the way.[5]

Weight-bearing activities such as walking, jogging, and dancing not only provide a relaxing detour from your everyday routine, they play an important role in reducing the risk of osteoporosis. Osteoporosis is an issue closely associated with menopause because of the role that estrogen appears to play in protecting bone strength in women. A slow loss of bone density is a natural part of aging in women and men. In women, however, loss of bone density speeds up during the 5 to 6 years immediately following menopause then slows again to the same rate as for men of that age.

In North America one woman in 4 over age 65 is affected by osteoporosis. The effects of osteoporosis can be painful and serious. Bones anywhere in the body can break, but the most common are the hip bones, wrist, and spine.

At this time there is no way to be sure who will develop osteoporosis, but certain factors are known to increase risk. The more risk factors that you have, the more likely you are to develop osteoporosis after menopause. Risk factors for osteoporosis include:
• *Genetic factors*   If your mother or sister has osteoporosis you have an increased risk of developing it. Caucasian women, especially those who are fair skinned, small boned, and from a northern European ancestry are also at greater risk.
• *Nutritional factors*   Our bodies use calcium for bone formation but calcium has other functions as well. When calcium levels in the blood are not high enough to carry out these functions, the body takes it from bone. An eating pattern low in calcium increases the risk for osteoporosis. In some studies, heavy intake of alcohol and caffeine has been

315

associated with decreased bone mass.

• *Low body weight* Some body fat is necessary for the production of estrogen — the predominant type of estrogen in post menopausal women — which seems to provide some protection to bone density. Estrogen starts as a hormone substance produced in the adrenal glands and is converted into estrone in the fatty tissue of our bodies.

• *Smoking* Cigarette smoking slows estrogen production and reduces the protection against osteoporosis. As well, women who smoke tend to have an earlier menopause than those who don't smoke. Studies have shown that menopause tends to occur one or 2 years earlier, on average, in women who smoke. The earlier that menopause occurs, the greater length of time a woman will spend without the protection of high estrogen levels.

• *Inactive life-style and little exercise* At all ages exercise increases bone mass. If you are physically active you will have greater bone density and muscle mass than if you remain sedentary. Exercise affects bone by straining the muscles which support the skeleton. The muscles in turn put stress on the bones. Like a see-saw, muscle pulls on bone and bone resists. This resistance strengthens the bone. Without this kind of regular exercise, osteoporosis is more likely to develop.

Estrogen therapy will prevent rapid loss of bone density at menopause. Women with many risk factors for osteoporosis may want to use estrogen therapy to help prevent osteoporosis. Remember that when you stop the estrogen you will then lose bone density quickly for a time. Compare the risks and benefits of long-term estrogen use to decide what is best for you. You may find it helpful to discuss your own risk factors with a dietitian, physician, nurse practitioner, or public health nurse.

The quality of flexibility . . . **lifts a depression with an overcoming approach to roadblocks.**

AVOID ALL OR NOTHING THINKING

Options are always available. Remember how that old diet thinking went — "either I will eat 'perfectly' and faithfully follow my diet or I will not be on it at all." Realize you're human and perfection in eating or any other life activity is not a realistic goal.

A friend and colleague was recently struggling with her decision to leave the dietetics profession and return to school to train for a new career. As the time for her course to begin grew closer, it seemed that more and more life events were occurring that threatened to overwhelm her. She was undergoing a course of radiation therapy for breast cancer that would overlap the starting of the course by 5 weeks, her mother was scheduled for surgery 6 weeks into the course, she had 2 teenage children who required her physical and psychological presence, and her husband was very busy with his work and hobby life. My friend considered delaying returning to school until the following year, but soon realized that she could, in fact, move ahead in her career aspirations this year by letting go of the idea that she had to be a "perfect" student.

She could still attend classes most days, would be able to do well enough on the assignments and tests, and would still graduate with a recognized credential even though she was not a "perfect" student. Recognizing when you need to let go of unrealistic standards in order to get to where you really want to go can be a lesson well learned in midlife.

There is a popular belief that women become prone to depression at menopause but research shows that depression and anxiety are no more common in women at menopause than in any other group.[6] A few women do describe occasional, inexplicable emotional changes at this time. It appears that a combination of hormone changes and life events may be the cause.

Some women report temporary mood swings, irritability, or a "cotton head" feeling during the premenopausal stage when hormone levels are fluctuating and readjusting. This will likely pass when cycling ends. As well, sleeping patterns often change at midlife. If your sleep is interrupted by night sweats, hot flashes, or wakefulness, make time to rest during the day.

While the middle years have the potential for growth and enhancement, statistically many significant losses, such as an illness of our own or a loved one, job loss or change, widowhood, or death of others close to us, may cluster in the years between 45 and 59.

We may find ourselves feeling resentful about some of our roles. Our anger may surprise us and those around us but it can often be a healthy recognition of a situation that needs changing for our emotional well-being. It is more helpful to recognize these issues and to talk about them than simply to blame our hormones.

The quality of regularity . . . inspires you to start the premenopausal care routine that is an investment in your future body.

CONSISTENCY

Remember who won the race between the tortoise and the hare. Focus on small, gradual changes maintaining regularity and consistency in the approach. Making too drastic changes (i.e. cottage cheese syndrome on p129) can lead to abandonment of your new life-style.

Many people concern themselves with retirement planning and act to ensure financial security in later years. Yet in our culture it is not yet habitual to plan carefully for a "savings account" of health and fitness— to act as if "investing" in one's future body.

People who are consistently, permanently inspired to care for themselves have the conviction that the body is precious and worth their investment. You don't treat precious things badly, only things you don't think are valuable. If you are deeply in touch with how precious you are, you won't want to mistreat the package you come in either. If you value yourself and the body you come in, looking after your physical, emotional, and spiritual needs is an instinctive course of action.

We live in a society that values the quick fix and the slick package. However, as with financial investing, little can be done to suddenly turn a meager investment into instant fortune. Health and fitness — like savings accounts — are built consistently, not suddenly. And it's consistent self-care, not money, that represents investment in your body.

The quality of good listening . . . offers you the potential for close friendship and support.

OPEN TO COMPLAINTS AND CRITICISMS

Don't make the mistake of assuming that you know what will be said; active listening is full of surprises.

318

No one should be without a friend. There are all sorts of opportunities at work (paid or volunteer), in educational settings, in social situations linked to work or club membership. Why, given all these opportunities, do some women still feel friendless? Part of it may be the low level of self-esteem that follows from being housebound. Some of it is sheer lack of experience in nurturing friendship. Some of it comes from a misplaced reticence about "personal matters."

Comments and perceived criticism of your size or your chosen way to better health may be received when you have a nondiet life-style. Pay attention to the detail of these kinds of remarks. Recognize that remarks about your personal appearance are actually rude and unacceptable. If a person close to you is critical, you have an opportunity to re-educate them about your new health goals.

It is difficult to become intimate with a woman who avoids self-disclosure. It is impossible to complain about one's own husband to a woman who admits no flaw in her own, to express outrage about one's children to a woman who appears to have perfect offspring, to mutter about the ceaseless demands of an aging parent to a woman who is a Florence Nightingale. Perhaps such women feel that to admit to a problem would be to lower themselves in the eyes of others. Frankly, I find such attitudes a barrier to friendship. How wonderful to have a woman friend who makes no judgement calls, who allows you to unload all the anger, disappointment, and spite, and who is never surprised to find that after all the anguish, you've forgiven and forgotten by the following day.[7]

Menopause gives us an opportunity to strengthen old friendships or to forge new ones — friendships that will stand us in good stead in the years to come when many of the men in our lives will have passed on.

The quality of assertiveness . . . combats sleeplessness and anxiety as you learn to say "yes" to you.

PRIORITIZE AND BE PREPARED TO SAY NO

Often the "no" to others is the "yes" to you. The influence of the diet industry and the cultural icon of thinness is still very strong. **You will be challenged in the art of assertiveness as you present an alternative to diet and weight loss. Your priority is health. Realize that learning to say "no" will build in the "pause" which will keep your life-style in balance.**

Sally, a HUGS participant in rural Canada, wrote in her journal:

"I am the mother of 2 boys, aged 10 and 7 years, have been married 13 years to Bob, and have been a public health nurse since 1980. I work full-time with a 45-minute commute. Bob has in the past 4 years been attempting to adapt to not farming. He began farming at 14 years when his dad was dying of cancer (quit school) but recently due to changes in agriculture has become a partsman at a farm equipment dealership. He is at times very sad and bitter. I have no physical activity due to no time — very busy with full-time job, commute, and unhappy man who still misses farming deeply. We eat meals at the table and are learning the purposes of food but the message from media and peers is strong. The kids sit in front of the TV too much —- while I try to catch up with life."

In responding to her journal, I congratulated her for taking the time to stop, look back, pay attention to her needs, and attempt to make some positive changes to make her life more enjoyable and made the following points in my response to her:

"You seem to be rushed so frequently and that may be due to your difficult and demanding schedule and your role as a mother, wife, commuter, public health nurse, and provider of meals, laundry, cleanliness of house, etc. etc. etc. No wonder you are tired many times. On top of that, living with perfectionism is very very hard. Have you ever tried to talk to your husband about women's roles in the 90s, sharing tasks at home, how hard it is to fit in all your chores, workload, and still somehow squeeze in time for yourself? If Bob is feeling sad about his transition in work from farming to working at a dealership and you are feeling sad and frustrated because there is too much to do and too little time, one way to relieve the burden of sadness is to help each other out. When a person is able to help someone in need, it makes both the receiver of the need and giver feel better . . .

320

the receiver because she/he relieves some type of pressure from the individual; the giver because they are helping someone out. How about using the assertive technique in Chapter 12? How about saying to Bob, I know you feel that I need to be preparing all meals and my time is limited with commuting and a full time job, so perhaps I could do some advance preparation the night before and you could pop it in the oven and start the vegetables at 5:30 so it's ready when I come home. It seems you are caught in the role of "people pleaser" . . . please the hubby in keeping house as perfectly clean as you can get it, having supper ready, taking care of the boys and the homework, and listening to his woes. Compromise with little changes instead of assuming all responsibility.

The quality of resourcefulness . . .
breaks down the barriers to change.

IDENTIFY OPPORTUNITY

Stretch your imagination to new heights of possibility. If your life-style situation is uncomfortable with regard to workplace, home or social life, recognize that changes can be made by you. Identify what is making you uncomfortable. Start taking small risks in the way you relate to others. If you have longed to do something, what is holding you back? You don't have to quit your present job to request information about a new career direction. And you don't have to stop being active because you are afraid to fall on the ice again while walking outside during winter.

Now is the time to experiment with new activities or revive those old activities that you used to enjoy. It's a time to prepare and strengthen your body and bones. You want to retain your independence as you get older rather than depending on someone else to do those simple tasks of everyday living. Observe others in their 40s and 50s who have been on skis for the first time in their lives or are taking up aquacise and boogeying to the music. Watch the way their bodies move and the smiles on their faces as those endorphins kick in. In some cases, they are merely transferring skills they already knew and picking up a few new ones along the way.

Many of us become so used to caring for others and helping others achieve that we lose sight of our own goals or never get around to formulating any. In the

321

second half of life, many of us have an opportunity to pay attention to ourselves and our own needs and aspirations, perhaps for the first time. The added years we gain with increased longevity can be ours to grow spiritually and intellectually. Midlife is often spoken of by women in metaphors of birth and rebirth, a time to nurture our own talents, casting off the external criteria by which we may have devalued ourselves and blossoming in new ways.

Once the menopausal transition is complete, a woman enters a new state of equilibrium. Her energy, moods, and overall sense of physical and mental well-being should be restored, but with a difference. It is a time when all the wisdom a woman has gathered from 50 years of experience in living comes together. If we think of our future years as providing an opportunity to develop our creativity, our passions, and our activism, we can look forward to our older years with confidence and enthusiasm.

Notes for Preface

1. *University of California, Berkeley Wellness Letter*, "Great bodies come in many shapes," Vol. 7, issue 5, Feb. 1991.
2. Joe McVoy, PhD, "Treatment: New directions needed for 1990s," *Obesity & Health*, Vol. 5, No. 6, Nov./Dec. 1991.
3. "Obesity: Year 2000 crisis?" *Obesity & Health*, Vol. 5, No. 5, Sept./Oct. 1991.
4. Donna Ciliska and Carla Rice, "Body Image/Body Politics," *Healthsharing*, Summer, 1989.

Notes for Introduction

1. S.C. Wooley, PhD, and O.W. Wayne Wooley, PhD, "Thinness Mania," *American Health*, October, 1986.
2. S.C. Wooley, PhD, and O.W. Wooley, PhD, "Should obesity be treated at all?" in *Eating and its disorders*, Stunkard, A.J., and Stellar, E. editors, New York, 1984.

Notes for Chapter 1

1. *International Obesity Newsletter*, Vol. 2, No. 9, Sept. 1988.
2. *Ann Intern Med.*, Dec. 1985, pp1006-1009.
3. *Mayo Clinic Nutrition Letter*, Vol. 2, No. 7, July 1989.
4. *Dairy Council Digest*, Vol. 59, No. 3, May/June, 1988.
5. *University of California, Berkeley Wellness Letter*, Vol. 4, No. 12, Sept. 1988.
6. Kevin Anderson, PhD, Framingham Study; Dr. W.B. Kannel, Boston University of Medicine.
7. Dr. George Christakis, "The Effect of Dietary Cholesterol on Serum Cholesterol: An Interpretive Review," Adjunct Professor of Nutrition, University of Miami, School of Medicine, Miami, Florida.
8. *Dairy Council Digest*, Vol. 58, No. 5, Sept./Oct. 1987.
9. *Harvard Medical School Health Letter*, Nov. 1987.
10. *Dairy Council Digest*, Jan./Feb. 1988.
11. Macdonald, CDA Conf., 1988.
12. *New England J Med* 322: 147, 1990.
13. *Nutrition & the M.D.*, Vol. 15, No. 1, Jan. 1989.
14. *University of California, Berkeley Wellness Letter*, Vol. 6, issue 1, Oct. 1989.
15. *New England J Med* 1991:324:1839-44, taken from *Obesity & Health*, "Yo-yo dieting threatens heart. Gain-lose-gain cycle may be as risky as staying obese." Vol. 5, No. 6, Nov./Dec. 1991.
16. *Int J Obesity* 14: 303, 1990
17. *Nutrition & the M.D.*, July 1990.
18. Dr. Steven L. Shumak, M.D., F.R.C.P.(C), "Deterioration of Glucose Control in NIDDM," *Canadian Diabetes*, Vol. 4, No. 2, June 1991.
19. Dr. Coopan, "Special report on Type II diabetes," *Joslin* magazine, Fall, 1986.
20. *Diabetes Education Resource Manual*, Winnipeg, MB, 1986.
21. Sandi Meredith R.P. Dt.., Lawrence A. Leiter M.D., F.R.C.P.(C), F.A.C.P., Loren D. Grossman M.D., F.R.C.P.(C), "Commercial Weight Loss Clinics in the Treatment of Obese Patients with Diabetes: Are They Safe?" *Canadian Diabetes*, Vol. 4, No. 1, March 1991.

22. *Nutrition Forum*, Jan. 1988.
23. *University of California, Berkeley Wellness Letter*, Vol. 7, No. 5, Feb. 1991.
24. *Nutrition News*, Winter 1990.

Notes for Chapter 2

1. Dr. Frank Katch, Nutrition and Life-style, Kellogg Symposium, 1988.
2. Dorice M. Czajka-Narins PhD, and Ellen Parham, PhD, R.D., "Fear of Fat: Attitudes toward Obesity–The Thinning of America," *Nutrition Today*, Jan./Feb. 1990.
3. *Nutrition & the M.D.*, Changing Body Fat Patterns," Vol. 14, No. 11, Nov. 1988.
4. Cheryl Jennings-Sauer, M.A., R.D., L.D., *"Living Lean by Choosing More,"* Taylor Publishing Co., 1989.
5. *Obesity and Health Newsletter*, Vol. 4, No. 6, June 1990.
6. *Obesity & Health*, "The world of weight loss fraud," Vol. 4, No. 9, Sept. 1990.
7. *Ann Intern Med* 99:14, 1983 taken from *Nutrition & the M.D.*, Aug. 1990.
8. S.C. Wooley, and O.W. Wooley, "Obesity and Women— I. A Closer Look at the Facts," *Women's Studies Int. Quart.*, Vol. 2, Pergamon Press Ltd., pp 69-79, 1979.
9. *Nutrition & the M.D.*, Vol. 16, No. 7, July 1990.
10. *Am J Clin Nutr* 49:1105, 1989.
11. *Am Intern Med* 103:994, 1985.
12. *New England Journal of Medicine* 1991:324:1839-44, taken from *Obesity & Health*, "Yo-yo dieting threatens heart. Gain-lose-gain cycle may be as risky as staying obese," Vol. 5, No. 6, Nov./Dec. 1991.
13. *Int J Obesity* 14:303, 1990.
14. Ibid ref. 11.
15. *New England Journal of Medicine* 1991:324:1839-44; taken from *Obesity & Health*, Vol. 5, No. 6, Nov./Dec. 1991, "Yo-yo dieting threatens heart. Gain-lose-gain cycle may be as risky as staying obese."
16. Linda J. McCargar, PhD, R.D.N., and Helen Yeung, BSc, R.D.N., "The Effects of Weight Cycling on Metabolism and Health," *J Can.Diet. Assoc.* 52:101-106, 1991.
17. *University of California, Berkeley Wellness Letter*, Vol. 7, issue 1, Oct. 1990.
18. *Dairy Council Digest*, Vol. 59, No. 3, May/June, 1988.
19. C. Brown and D. Forgay, "An Uncertain Well-Being: Weight Control and Self Control," *Healthsharing*, Winter:11-15, 1987.
20. William Bennett and Joel Gurin, *"The Dieter's Dilemma,"* Basic Books, New York, May, 1982.
21. *Harvard Medical School Health Letter*, It"s the Butter, not the Bread," Vol. 13, No. 9, July 1988.
22. *J Clin Invest* 76: 1019, 1985.
23. *J Clin Invest* 64: 1336, 1979.
24. *National Institute of Nutrition*, "Metabolic Consequences of Weight-Reduction Diets," Review No. 6, July 1988.
25. Ellen Parham, PhD., R.D., "Alternative goals render successful outcomes likely," *Obesity & Health*, Vol. 5, No. 4,

July/Aug. 1991.
26. *Dairy Council Digest*, Mar./Apr. 1985, published by National Dairy Council.
27. *Dairy Council Digest*, Vol. 62, No. 2, Mar./Apr. 1991.
28. F.W. Ashley, W.B. Kannel. Relation of weight change to changes in atherogenic traits: The Framingham Study, *J Chronic Dis* 27: 103-114, 1974.
29. Kelly Brownell, "American Health and Obesity and Weight Control: The Good And Bad of Dieting," *Nutrition Today*, May/June 1987.
30. *Obesity & Health Newsletter*, Vol. 5, No. 4, July/August 1991.

Notes for Chapter 3

1. *Nutrition & the M.D.*, Nov. 1990
2. *Sports Mecidine* 1: 446, 1984.
3. *University of California, Berkeley Wellness Letter*, Oct. 1990.
4. *National Institute of Nutrition, Rapport*, "Effective Energy Content of Fat," Vol. 2, No. 3, July 1987.
5. Kathy King Helm, R.D., "Sports Nutrition Basics," *Nutrition Forum*, Vol. 5, No. 6, July/Aug, 1988.
6. *Member's Magazine*, Participation Network, Vol. 3, No. 1, Winter, 1986.
7. Ibid. ref. No. 5.
8. J.P. Flatt, "Dietary fat, carbohydrate balance, and weight maintenance; effects," *Am J Clin Nutr* 45: 296, 1987.
9. Faulkner, International Conference on Exercise, Fitness, and Health, Toronto, 1988.
10. *Dairy Council Digest*, Vol. 60, No. 4, July/Aug. 1989. Published by National Dairy Council, 6300 North River Road, Rosemont, Il. 60018-4233.
11. Greenwood, M.R.C. (Ed), *Obesity: Contemporary Nutrition*, New York: Churchill Livingstone, 1983.
12. *University of California, Berkeley Wellness Letter*, Vol. 5, No. 7, April 1989.
13. *University of California, Berkeley Wellness Letter*, Oct. 1990.
14. Ibid. ref. No. 5.
15. *Nutrition & the M.D.*, "Exercise and Metabolic Rate, Diet Therapy/Obesity Update," Feb. 1988.
16. Health & Welfare Canada's *New Guidelines for Healthy Eating*, 1991.
17. James O. Hill, PhD; Phillip B. Sparling EdD; Toni W. Shields, MS; and Patricia A. Heller, R.D., "Effects of exercise and food restriction on body composition and metabolic rate in obese women," *Am J Clin Nutr* 46: 622-30, 1987.
18. Lindsey C. Henson, M.D., PhD; David C. Poole, PhD; Clyde P. Donahoe, PhD; and David Heber, M.D., PhD, "Effects of exercise training on resting energy expenditure during caloric restriction," *Am J Clin Nutr* 46: 893-9.
19. Ibid ref. No. 9.
20. Paffenbarger et al, of Harvard Alumni. *Diabetes Care*, Vol. 13, No. 2, Feb. 1990.
21. "Exercise & Renal Stone Formation, Diet Therapy/Obesity Update," *Nutrition & the M.D.* Feb. 1988.

22. *University of California, Berkeley Wellness Letter,* Vol. 5, No. 3, Dec. 1988.
23. *University of California, Berkeley Wellness Letter,* Vol. 6, issue 4, Jan. 1990.
24. *University of California, Berkeley Wellness Letter,* Vol. 7, issue 5, Feb. 1991.

Notes for Chapter 4
1. *Lancet* 2:614, 1964.
2. Obesity and Weight Control, Aspen, 1988.
3. Ibid.
4. Dr. Wayne Callaway, Kellogg Nutrition Symposium, Toronto, April, 1988.
5. N. Theresa Glanville, PhD, "Central Nervous System Regulation of Food Intake: the Role of Dietary Signals," *J Can. Diet. Assoc.,* Vol. 50, No. 3, Summer, 1989.
6. Barbara J. Rolls, Marion Hetherington, and Victoria J. Burley, "The Specificity of Satiety: The Influence of Foods of Different Macronutrient Content on the Development of Satiety," *Physiology & Behavior,* Vol. 43, pp 145-153, Pergamon Press, 1988.
7. *University of California, Berkeley Wellness Letter,* Nov. 1988.
8. *Am J of Clin Nutri* 45: 1323, 1987. Article taken from *Nutrition & the M.D.,* Vol.16, No. 3, March 1990.
9. *University of California, Berkeley Wellness Letter,* June 1991.
10. Ibid.
11. D.J.A. Jenkins, T.M.S. Wolever, R.H. Taylor, et al., "Glycemic Index of foods: a physiological basis for carbohydrate exchange," *Am J Clin Nutr* 34: 362-6, 1981. (Data obtained from normal individuals.)
12. F. Xavier Pi-Sunyer, M.D., "Fiber: What's in it for You?" *Diabetes Forecast,* May/June, 1983.
13. *Protect Yourself,* Nov. 1987.

Notes for Chapter 5
1. *Dairy Council Digest,* July/August 1988.
2. *University of California, Berkeley Wellness Letter,* Vol. 5, No.1, Oct. 1988.
3. *National Institute of Nutrition,* July 1988.
4. *Harvard Medical School Health Letter,* July 1988.
5. Beef Information Centre News Release, March 4, 1987.
6. *Obesity & Health,* July/Aug. 1991.
7. *International Journal of Obesity,* 17:237, 1993
8. L. Omichinski and H. Wiebe Hildebrand. *Tailoring Your Tastes.* TAMOS Books Inc., Winnipeg, Canada, 1995.
9. Ibid.
10. Ibid.

Notes for Chapter 6
1. Janet Polivy and Peter Herman, *Breaking the Diet Habit.* Basic Books, New York, 1983

Notes for Chapter 9
1. *ESHA Research,* Spring 1991.

Notes for Chapter 10
1. *University of California, Berkeley Wellness Letter*, Vol. 5, No. 3, Dec. 1988.

Notes for Chapter 11
1. *University of California, Berkeley Wellness Letter*, June 1991.
2. A.B. Natow, J. Heslin, *Geriatric Nutrition*. Boston, Mass. 1980:192.
3. *University of California Berkeley Wellness Letter*, June 1991.
4. *Am J of Clin Nutr 37*: March 1983, pp 416-420.
5. *Mayo Clinic Nutrition Letter*, Feb. 1990.
6. *National Institute of Nutrition Review*, No. 2, May 1987.

Notes for Chapter 13
1. Richard Earle, *Your Vitality Quotient*, Random House, Mississauga, Ontario, 1989.
2. *Obesity and Health Journal*, Vol. 4, No. 6, June 1990.

Notes for Chapter 15
1. Debby Burgard, "Is giving up on dieting giving up on yourself?" *Radiance*, Fall 1991.
2. Paula B. Doress-Worters and Diana Laskin Siegal. *Ourselves, Growing Older*. Simon & Shuster, New York, 1994.
3. Gail Sheehy. *Menopause The Silent Passage*. Pocket Books, New York, 1998.
4. Katherine Vaz, "Best foot forward: Walking for fitness, health and self-awareness," *Shape*, Winter 1994.
5. Marjorie Harris. *The Healing Garden. Nature's Restorative Powers*. Harper Collins Publishers Ltd., Toronto, Canada, 1996.
6. Nancy E. Avis and Sonja M. McKinlay. "The Massachusetts women's health study: An epidemiologic investigation of menopause." JAMWA, 50:45-49,63, 1995.
7. Janine O'Leary Cobb. *Understanding Menopause*. Key Porter Books Ltd., Toronto, Canada, 1993.

Further Reading

Carol Johnson, *Self-Esteem Comes in All Sizes: How to Be Happy and Healthy at Your Natural Weight*, Doubleday, September, 1996.

YOU, living with VERVE, 37 Hanna Avenue, Unit 1, Toronto, Ontario M6K 1X1. *An excellent Canadian magazine on health.*

Radiance, P.O. Box 30246, Oakland, California 94604. *A visionary publication devoted to the positive health and well-being of all sizes of large women.*

Terry Poulton, *No Fat Chicks:How Women are Brainwashed to Hate Their Bodies and Spend Their Money*, Key Porter Books, 1996.

Frances M. Berg, *Afraid to Eat:Children and Teens in Weight Crisis*, Healthy Weight Publishing Network, 1997, 402 South 14th Street, Hettinger, ND, 58639, tel 701 567 2646, fax 701 567 2602, website: www.healthyweightnetwork.com

Further Reading for Health Professionals
interested in the growing movement
for health and self-acceptance

Healthy Weight Journal. Healthy Weight Journal, Decker Periodicals, P.O. Box 620 LCD1, Hamilton, ON, Canada, L8N 3K7, Telephone 1-800-568-7281, email info@bcdecker.com. *An excellent journal containing very progressive articles and research findings.*

"After the Diet" quarterly newsletter, A Better Way Health Consulting, Inc., P.O. Box 11985, Glendale, AZ, USA, 85318-1985, email Monika at the couch@aol.com. An excellent practical newsletter resource for lifestyle professionals to learn and grow in areas of nondiet and disordered eating. Includes research, interviews, case studies, medication update, evaluation, and handout highlight.

Donna Ciliska, R.N., Ph.D., *Beyond Dieting: Psychoeducational Interventions for Chronically Obese Women: A Non-Dieting Approach,* Brunner/Mazel, Inc. 19 Union Square West, New York, New York 10003, 1990. Toll free 1-800-363-2845. *Excellent research in this area.*

Association for Health Enrichment of Large People (AHELP), P.O. Drawer C, Radford, Virginia 24143. TEL/FAX 1(540)951-3527. *Ask for AHELP brochure. Most leaders in this movement belong to this progressive organization.*

David M. Garner, Ph.D., and Susan C. Wooley, Ph.D., "Confronting the Failure of Behavioral and Dietary Treatments for Obesity," *Clinical Psychology Review,* Vol. 11, pp 729-80, 1991. *An excellent review article substantiating this approach.*

Index

Searching for more effective health promotion?

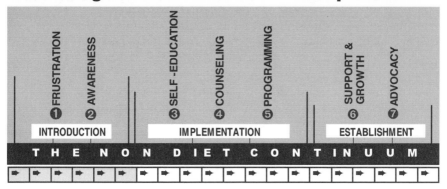

You've worked through this introductory phase on our non-diet continuum with your reading of *You Count, Calories Don't.* You may now be ready to implement new concepts into your counseling/programming.

We offer three ready-to-deliver programs for the non-diet approach (described on the next page and in detail on our website). All the programs share the following significant benefit features.

- **Save time because all the program materials are packaged for easy reference & retrieval.**
- **Save money with fully developed marketing materials that detail all aspects of program and concept promotion, includes print-ready posters, pamphlets, and advertisement ideas.**
- **Regular Updates prevent frustration and instill motivation. Share in the experiences of other program facilitators by hearing their personal and program delivery stories along with the most current news in the non-diet field.**
- **Unique and specially developed support materials for your clients will provide lasting value after the program sessions end.**
- **Evaluation tools to assess progress before and after the program use new measures of success.**

Join an international network of licensed lifestyle professionals.

From Alaska to New Zealand, east to Great Britain and west to California with 150 plus points in between, facilitators worldwide are delivering our nondiet programs and workshops (as of October/98)

HUGS.com
The website enables us to present our ever-increasing worldwide network of facilitators with contact information. As you scroll down the lists you'll understand the value in joining a network of people who've moved past the frustration of diets and weight loss goals in their own practices and diverse workplaces. You can read selected facilitator stories and feel their new successes. A closed newsgroup is available for facilitators who are regularly on-line to keep in contact with one another and grow through shared experiences.

The next step for readers wanting to stay off the diet roller coaster.

It's your choice from our array of support options

We suggest you start with....

Tailoring Your Tastes, the companion book to *You Count, Calories Don't,* was written by Linda Omichinski, RD & Heather Wiebe Hildebrand, RN, BSN and facilitator for all three HUGS programs.
We call this book a concept cookbook because it links recipe concepts, nutrition concepts, taste concepts, gradual concepts and experimental concepts in one package.
Shatter the diet myths further with this approach to cooking

CAPTURE TASTE
**A step by step process tunes your taste buds to health
Find out how to keep your family happy and still get these results in your cooking**

SALT   ∨
SUGAR ∨
FAT   ∨
FIBER   ∧

MYTH
Healthy eating means diet & sacrifice
REALITY
**Taste dictates choice
Changed tastes will mean healthier eating by choice**

Your other choices include...

Enroll in one of the HUGS programs

Already a HUGS graduate?
We've got further support for you with our quarterly print newsletter that includes all the discussion tools for support group meetings or
if you have the opportunity to be on line, we hold a hosted chat line meeting each Thursday at 9 pm est. You can get into some interactive exchange by posting to our message board.

HUGS not available in your area...
At home options are described in detail on our website. You can choose from a Journal Analysis or the complete HUGS at Home package.

We understand that sustained change requires a support system. We're continually fine-tuning our services to meet your needs.

334

You Count, Calories Don't
Break the diet cycle & rebuild self-esteem
Help clients off the diet roller coaster
& on to life long health

since 1992

- 10 sessions with detailed plans, registration materials, handout masters
- More than 300 pages of marketing experiences from other facilitators
- Support materials
  The core book, *You Count, Calories Don't* is a complete guide to the non-diet lifestyle that enjoys worldwide reputation and respect. Four issues of our support group newsletter, HUGS Club News, are included with the basic client package creating a follow-up system which helps maintain the non-diet mindset.

Teens: girls & guys 12-17

TEENS & DIETS
NO WEIGH

Teens & Diets: No Weigh
Flexible Prevention Programming Package
Confronts Teen Dieting, Body Shape Preoccupation
& Eating Disorders

since 1995

- 8 stages feature colorful laminated graphics & props
- Highly facilitative scripts & games to interest teens
- Support materials
  The Teen Journal sets up a tool for teens to develop awareness and skills around personal decisions.
  The Parent Guide provides the parents with a window into the program.
  Tailoring Your Tastes concept cookbook.

Adult

Tailoring Your Tastes
Workshop Tours
Journey to Healthier Eating
With Taste Training & Recipe Analysis

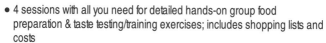

since 1997

- 4 sessions with all you need for detailed hands-on group food preparation & taste testing/training exercises; includes shopping lists and costs
- Support materials
  Journey Log Book for a permanent record of class teachings
  Tailoring Your Tastes concept cookbook

Visit our website for more information including excerpts from program materials and color photos.

Helpers from HUGS

An array of products and services that are designed to assist with continuing the healthy living process.

Make your selection and follow the instructions on the order form.

☐ ***HUGS FITNESS VIDEO**
A chance to have some fun and make an increase in physical activity a lifestyle change. The video takes you through the basics of a fitness routine that includes warm-up, cool down, mat portion and relaxation. Specifically designed for the person not previously involved in much aerobic activity. It shows you how to work at your own level and HAVE FUN getting fit. Can also serve as supplement to one's present level of activity. *Unit price* $24.95

☐ ***HUGS AFFIRMATION TAPES**
This set of three tapes include 5 — 20 to 30 minute sessions. It is recommended to accompany the book program because it moves you along faster to learning, practising, and enjoying your way to better health. This audio journey may also be used as an introduction to HUGS™ to whet your appetite prior to taking the program itself. *Complete Set of 3 Tapes* $41.95

☐ **JOURNAL ANALYSIS**
Your own personal check-up for eating habits. An individual assessment of one week of your journal will show to what extent your life-style is in balance. Suggestions provided. $60.00

☐ **HUGS CLUB NEWS**
A support network for your decision to get off the diet roller coaster. *Annual (4 issues)* Canada $20 plus GST (Can); USA $20 (US); Overseas $25 (Can)

☐ ***YOU COUNT, CALORIES DON'T**   *Each* $24.95

☐ ***TAILORING YOUR TASTES**
Our new cookbook sets out gradual steps toward healthier eating and serves as a valuable nutrition and food preparation guide.   *Each* $19.95

Please send with payment to:
HUGS International Inc.
Box 102A, RR#3, Portage la Prairie, Manitoba, Canada R1N 3A3
Call toll free (Canada and US) 1-800-565-4847 or FAX (204)428-5072
Add $5 (Cdn) per item for shipping and handling for those items marked with an *.

NAME _____

ADDRESS _____

CITY _____ PROVINCE _____ CODE _____

HOME PHONE _____ WORK PHONE _____

I would like to purchase the items marked above (total payment enclosed)

Cheque _____ VISA No._____Mastercard No. _____

If paying by credit card, please include expiry date _____

and sign below.

_____
Signature

Prices are listed in Canadian funds unless noted otherwise.
Visit our web site at: http://www.hugs.com
email: linda@hugs.com

Cost	_____
Shipping	_____
Sub-Total	_____
PST (Manitoba)	_____
GST (in Canada)	_____
TOTAL $	_____